an explorer's guide

CHRISTINA TREE

the countryman press
woodstock,
vermont 05091

For Liam Christopher Davis

Library of Congress Cataloging in Publication Data

Tree, Christina.
  Maine: an explorer's guide.

  Includes index.
    1. Maine—Description and travel—1981-   —Guide-
books. I. Title.
F17.3.T73   917.41'0443   82-2421
ISBN 0-914378-92-9 (pbk.)   AACR2

Cover design and photograph by Wladislaw Finne

Maps by Richard Widhu

Printed in the United States of America
by The Courier Printing Company

Contents

Introduction

Maine is almost as big as the other five New England states combined, but her residents add up to less than half the population of Greater Boston. So there is plenty of room for us—the out-of-staters—who have learned to swim in her icy waters and to depend on Maine's boundless beauty for our own renewal.

Personally, this out-of-stater is addicted to many Maines: to the cliff-side paths on Monhegan Island, to the peace of mighty lakes like Moosehead and Sebago, to the lines of sea captains' homes in villages like Kennebunkport and Castine, to the new shops and restaurants in Portland's old buildings and to the grandeur of the White Mountains and the Katahdin Range. My presumption to guide you Down East grows from numerous vacations, fifteen years of writing newspaper travel stories about Maine, and from a spell of intensive research in the summer of 1981.

Every guidebook reflects the interests and limitations of the author. As a mother of three young boys I am more knowledgeable about reasonably priced cottages and inns than elegant resorts and motels, about creditable ice cream stands, lobster pounds and diners than fine restaurants, about warm water swimming spots (a surprising number of which can be found right along the coast) than gift shops.

I must also admit to being fascinated by the way in which Maine bears the marks of her unique history—by the traces of pre-pilgrim settlements on Manana Island and at Pemaquid Beach, of colorful seventeenth-century heroes like Baron de St. Castin (scion of a noble French family who married a Penobscot Indian princess), and by the State's impressive seafaring history, well told in the Maine Maritime Museum at Bath (where a total of 5000 vessels have been launched over the years) and at the Penobscot Marine Museum in Searsport, a small village which once boasted ten percent of all American sea captains. And of course there is the heady saga of the lumbering era (dramatized in the Patten Lumberman's Museum), which finally insured Maine's admission to the Union in 1820, but not until Massachusetts had sold off all unsettled land, the privately owned "Unorganized Townships" which still add up to nearly half of inland Maine.

I am fascinated by the way in which long vanished trains and steamboats still determine where you stay in Maine. With the exception of Sugarloaf USA (Maine's largest ski resort), all resort villages date from the period in which visitors from Boston and New York were ferried directly to the tips of peninsulas and coastal islands or deposited at inland train depots, frequently to board boats for lakeside hotels.

Cars have altered this picture only by degree, narrowing the number of towns geared to accommodating any volume of visitors. Nineteenth-century resorts like Stonington, Castine, Pemaquid Point and Christmas Cove—all too far off Route 1 to attract much traffic—contentedly cater to yachtsmen and inn lovers. And of all the inland villages which once welcomed guests, only Bridgton, Bethel, Rangeley and the Moosehead area now serve non-cottage owners in any number.

Gilded era summer people donated the core of Acadia National Park, now a big enough lure to draw more than three-and-a-half million visitors per year all the way to Bar Harbor, the downeast terminus of a tourist route which includes Camden and Boothbay Harbor. Otherwise summer visitors cluster in the beach towns spaced like stepping stones between Kittery and Portland.

This book describes the State's most popular resort areas but also its less known and forgotten beauty spots. The basic criteria for including an area is the availability of lodging, be it in inns, guesthouses, rental cottages or campgrounds.

After much soul searching I have included prices of admission, meals and lodging. Accept them as '81-82 benchmarks in the rising tide of inflation. But also bear in mind that the lodging prices quoted are "high season" (July and August for all but ski resorts) and may be much lower other months. June, by the way, can be rainy and cold but September is dependably sparkling and frequently warm. Early October is just as spectacular as it is in New Hampshire and Vermont—where innkeepers charge top dollar for a view of colored leaves.

This book's introductory section lists major events, and a "What's Where" quick-reference directory to activities within the state. The remainder of the book is devoted to resort areas—primarily along the coast—treated one by one.

I welcome comments from readers and appreciate the unfailing support which I received in this project from Peter Bachelder of the Maine Publicity Bureau and Sharon Chase of the Maine Innkeepers Association, as well as from the many friends who have taken the time to answer questions and check copy and the tolerant innkeepers, waiters and waitresses who have patiently coped with the three small explorers in our family. I am also extremely grateful to Gordon Pine and Christopher Lloyd of The Countryman Press, both of whom ran themselves ragged helping research this book and, last but not least, to my husband, *Boston Globe* Travel Editor William Davis, who sacrificed his summer vacation to the cause, frequently providing valuable chauffeur, babysitting and note-taking services.

Christina Tree

What's Where in Maine

AGRICULTURAL FAIRS The season opens, second week of July, with the Ossipee Valley Fair in South Hiram which boasts "Maine's largest night parade," includes horse- and ox-pulling and a string band contest. It culminates, first week in October, with the peerless Fryeburg Fair (see Fryeburg). Among the best: the Union Fair (late August), Blue Hill (Labor Day weekend) and "Common Ground" (late September at the Windsor Fairgrounds in Windsor), the one event that brings Maine's back-to-earth and organic gardeners from all corners of the state. For a full list of agricultural events, write the Maine Department of Agriculture, Augusta.

AIRPORTS The following have scheduled passenger service: Auburn-Lewiston, Augusta State, Bangor International, Bar Harbor, Portland International, Presque Isle, Rockland, Waterville.

AIRFIELDS These have no scheduled service: Belfast, Blue Hill, Livermore Falls, Norridgewock, Dover-Foxcroft, Bethel, Old Town, Fryeburg, Eastport, Bingham, Greenville, Islesboro, Lincoln, Lubec, Machias, Harrison, Millinocket, Oxford, Rangeley, Phillips, Sanford, Dexter, Moose River, Stonington, The Carrabassett Valley (near Sugarloaf/USA), Turner, Brownville and Wiscasset, and Biddeford.

AIRLINES Delta Airlines (check local phonebook) serves Bangor and Portland through New York City and Boston. Bar Harbor Airlines (1-800-732-3770 for New England area; local listings in Boston, New York City and Maine; check local 800 listings elsewhere in the country or contact Eastern Airlines, handling their reservation services at this writing) links Albany, Hartford, Boston, Worcester, Manchester (New Hampshire), and La Guardia in New York City with Augusta, Bangor, Bar Harbor, Lewiston, Portland, Presque Isle, Rockland, and Waterville.

AIR SERVICES Greenville-based, Folsom's Air Service offers year-round charter flights anywhere in the North Woods, will transport canoes or rent them to you, along with boats, tents, and camps, also acts as a communications link between a number of backwoods lodging places and the world (695-2821).

Moosehead Flying Service, Inc., operated by "Maine's only Lady Bush Pilot" (Ramona Morrell), specializes in fly-in canoe, fishing, and backpacking packages (695-2950).

Millinocket Lake Flying Service, air taxi "to all remote areas of Maine," transports and rents canoes, furnishes supplies and camps (723-9990, 723-8733 summer). Other current flying services include Central Maine Flying Service, Old Town (827-5911), Jack's Air Service in Greenville (695-3020), Del's Recreation Center in Sinclair (543-6600), Porter Flying Service at Shin Pond (528-2528), Portage Lake Flying Service at Portage (435-6747), Robbin's Air Taxi in Hudson (942-0959), Scotty's Flying Service at Shin Pond (528-2626), Young's Flying Service at West Forks (668-3383), Daigle Flying Service at Fort Kent (834-5830), Taiga Outfitters in Ashland (435-6851), Pryor Flying Service at Portage, Steve's Air Service in Rangeley (864-3349), and Maine Air Taxi in South Windham. Note that most flying services will supply canoes.

AMUSEMENT PARKS Animal Forest Park & Amusement at York Beach, Mariners Playland in Wells, and Funland in Caribou are all small areas offering kiddy rides and arcades. The big boardwalk and scary rides are at Old Orchard Beach, ME 9, daily Memorial Day-Labor Day, Sundays in spring and fall. We should also mention Funtown USA in Saco, good for kiddy rides and arcades.

ANTIQUARIAN BOOKSELLERS A listing of thirty-five dealers who buy and sell used, rare, and out-of-print books is available from H. O. Dendurent, 79 Central Street, Bangor 04401. Most specialize in books about Maine. The Owl and the Turtle in Camden also specializes in searching out-of-print titles.

ANTIQUES A listing of more than 100 dealers, produced by the Maine Antiques Dealers' Association, Inc., is available from the Maine Publicity Bureau, 97 Winthrop Street, Hallowell 04347 (send a business-size, self-addressed, stamped envelope). Both Searsport and Old Hallowell claim to be antiques capital of Maine and publish their own listings of some twenty dealers each, available from their respective chambers of commerce (Searsport is 04974, Old Hallowell is 04347). The Chamber of Commerce in Bridgton (04009) publishes a list of twenty-two dealers. Other concentrations can be found in Wiscasset and Kennebunkport.

APPLES A list of producers who permit "picking your own" comes from the Maine Department of Agriculture, Augusta. It includes a number of orchards near the town's southern borders, three in the town of Alfred.

AQUARIUMS There are just three major aquariums in Maine: the Gulf of Maine Aquarium (see Portland), the Maine Department of Marine Resources Aquarium (see Boothbay), and the Mount Desert Oceanarium in Southwest Harbor (see Mt. Desert).

ART MUSEUMS AND GALLERIES Portland Museum of Art (775-6148), 111 High Street, has just doubled its physical size, the better to display its fine collection. Galleries also abound in the Old Port Exchange area (see Portland). The Farnsworth Museum (see Rockland) also has an outstanding collection, including work by three generations of Wyeths. Among seasonal galleries, the Ogunquit Museum and Barn Gallery (see Ogunquit) stand out, as do the Maine Art Gallery in Wiscasset (open weekends year-round), the Maine Coast Artists Gallery in Rockport, and the gallery on Monhegan Island, itself a true artists' colony. The Bowdoin College Museum of Art displays some fine nineteenth-Century American works (see Brunswick), and the Joan Whitney Payson Gallery of Art at Westbrook College (see Portland) is also noteworthy.

BALLOONING A Hot Air Balloon Center at the Natural High Camping Area in Lebanon offers passenger rides (tethered: $3.50, free flight: $55 per person) and pilot training; the balloons are sixty feet in diameter, stand eight stories tall, and carry up to four people in gondolas (339-9630). Tom Handcock (772-4401), 15 Beacon Street in Portland, also offers balloon rides.

BEACHES Just 2% of the Maine coast is public, and not all of that is beach. Given the summer temperature of the water (from 59 in Ogunquit to 54 degrees at Bar Harbor), swimming isn't the primary reason you come to Maine. But Maine beaches can be splendid walking, sunning, and kite-flying places (see York, Ogunquit, Wells, the Kennebunks, Portland, Reid State Park, and Popham). At Ogunquit and in Reid State Park there are also warmer backwater areas in which small children can paddle, but families tend to take advantage of the reasonably priced cottages available on lakes, many of them just a few miles from the seashore. (See Lakes, Coastal). Other outstanding ocean beaches, not otherwise described in this book, include: Old Orchard Beach, said to be seven miles long, Higgins and Pine Point Beaches in Scarborough, and Fortunes Rock Beach in Biddeford Pool. The big state-maintained freshwater beaches are on Lakes Damariscotta, St. George, Sebec, Rangeley, Sebago, and Moosehead, also on Pleasant Pond in Richmond. All state beach facilities include changing facilities, rest rooms, and showers; many have snackbars. The State Park day use fee in '81: $1.50. The town of Bridgton, it should be noted, has several fine little beaches.

BICYCLING Biking is big on Mount Desert, which offers more than fifty miles of car-free roads; routes are outlined in local handouts, and guided tours, with rentals, are offered by Maine Bicycle Touring Company, 48 Cottage Street (288-5483). A few Maine islands are best toured by bike: see Casco Bay Islands, Vinalhaven, Islesboro, and Swans. And there are places that you can reach by bus and negotiate better by bike than car: namely Ogunquit, Kennebunkport, and Camden. Bike rentals are available in all three places, also at York Corner, Wells, Biddeford, Saco, Old Orchard Beach, Portland, Bath, Boothbay Harbor, Naples and West Bridgton. A list of bike and moped rental sources is available from the Maine Publicity Bureau (see

Gordon Pine

Antique Shop in Spruce Head

Information). Unfortunately, the only American Youth Hostels are in Blanchard and Lincoln, handy to nowhere, including each other.

BIRDING The Maine Audubon Society (781-2330), based at Gisland Farm in Falmouth, maintains a number of birding sites and sponsors nature programs and field trips. Gisland Farm itself (open year round) has seventy acres with nature trails through woodlands, meadows, and along marshes. At Scarborough Marsh Nature Center (see Portland) classes are offered in marsh life. The Mast Landing Sanctuary in South Freeport consists of 150 acres of varied habitat. Maine Audubon's field trips include cruises to Matinicus Rock and to Eagle Island. For details about the National Audubon Ecology Camp on Hog Island, see East Penobscot Area. The most popular coastal birding spots are the Rachel Carson National Wildlife Sanctuaries spotted between Kittery and Cape Elizabeth (see Wells and the Kennebunks). Biddeford Pool, Scarborough Marsh, Merrymeeting Bay, and Mount Desert are the other top birding sites. Monhegan is the island to visit. We recommend *A Birder's Guide to the Coast of Maine* by Elizabeth Cary Pierson and Jan Erik Pierson (Down East Books).

BLUEBERRYING An average crop of twenty million pounds of wild (lowbush) blueberries are harvested annually in Maine from an estimated 25,000 acres (half the actual acreage reserved for growing wild blueberries in the State). Because of pruning practices only half the acreage produces berries in a given year. And there are absolutely no man-planted wild blueberry fields. Lowbush blueberry plants spread naturally in the present commercial fields after clearing the forests or by natural establishment in abandoned pastures. Unfortunately, very few berries are sold fresh (most are quick frozen) and few growers allow U-pick, at least not until the commercial harvest is over. Then the public is invited to go "stumping," for leftovers. On the other hand berrying along roads, hiking paths, under power lines and on hilltops is a rite of summer for all who happen to be in Southern Maine in late July and farther Downeast in early August. For a look at the Blueberry Barrens—thousands of blueberry-covered acres—you must drive up to Cherryfield, Deblois, Beddington, Centerville and Columbia in Washington County. For more about Maine's most famous fruit write: Wild

Blueberry Association of North America, 142 Kelley Road, Orono, ME 04473. Also check the blueberry festivals listed in the Calendar of Events.

BOAT EXCURSIONS You don't need to own your own yacht to enjoy the salt spray and views, and you really won't know what Maine is about until you stand off at sea a ways to appreciate the beauty of its cliffs and island-dotted bays. For the greatest concentrations of boat excursions see Boothbay Harbor, Rockland and Mount Desert, but there are also excursions from Ogunquit, Kennebunkport, Camden, and Stonington. Also see Ferries and Sailing. See Bridgton for the excursion boat traversing the Songo River from Naples. For cruises on the new 400-passenger *Cushnoc* from Augusta contact Kennebec Cruise Lines (622-5562).

BOAT LAUNCH SITES Sites within state parks are listed on the Maine Department of Transportation map; a town-by-town list is available from the Waterways Section, Bureau of Parks and Recreation, Maine Department of Conservation, Augusta 04333. Public launch sites on paper company land are indicated on the sportsmen's maps available from the Paper Industry Information Office, 133 State Street, Augusta (622-3166). Other New England boat licenses are honored in Maine waters, with the exception of New Hampshire's.

BOAT RENTALS For power boats try Great Pond Marina in Belgrade Lakes, Sebago Lake Camps in North Sebago, White's Marina in Norway, Town and Lake Motel in Rangeley, Smith Hardware in Hackman, North Country Outfitters in Rockwood, and Snow Harbor Corporation in Thomaston. Also see Canoes and Sailing.

BOOKS Among the current guidebooks to Maine, the following have proven helpful to us: *The Coast of Maine—An Informal History*, by Louise Dickinson Rich (Thomas Y. Crowell Company); *The Maine Coast—A Nature Lover's Guide* by Dorcas Miller (The East Woods Press); *The Maine Atlas and Gazetteer*, published by David DeLorme and Company, PO Box 298, Freeport, Me.; and *Fifty Hikes in Maine* by John Gibson (Backcountry Publications). Down East Books (available from PO Box 679, Camden, Me. 04843) offers: *A Birder's Guide to the Coast of Maine* by Elizabeth Cary Pierson and Jan Erik

Pierson, *Walking the Maine Coast* by John Gibson and *Islands in Time: A Natural and Human History of the Islands of Maine* by Philip W. Conkling. Serious hikers should secure the AMC *Maine Mountain Guide* and all lovers of the Maine woods should take a look at *The Wildest Country—A Guide to Thoreau's Maine* by J. Parker Huber; both books are available from the AMC Books Division, Dept. B, 5 Joy Street, Boston, Mass. 02108. We also enjoy the books by Portland Press Herald columnist Bill Caldwell: *Enjoying Maine, Maine Magic* and *Islands of Maine*, all published by Guy Gannett Publishing Company of Portland.

BUSES Greyhound links New York and Boston with Portland via York, Ogunquit, Wells, Kennebunk, Biddeford, Saco, and Old Orchard Beach. It is the only line linking Portland with Bangor, stopping in Yarmouth, Freeport, Brunswick, Bath, Wiscasset, Damariscotta, Thomaston, Rockland, Camden, Lincolnville Beach, Belfast, Searsport, Lewiston, Augusta, and Waterville, among others. From Bangor there is service to Ellsworth and Bar Harbor. Trailways offers much the same Boston-to-Portland service as Greyhound. Local transport services: Citibus in Bangor (947-0536), Biddeford and Saco Bus Lines (282-9591), Hudson Bus Lines serving Lewiston/Auburn (738-2033), the Greater Portland Transit District (774-9351), and newest—and most useful to tourists —Downeast Transportation (667-5796) with weekday service linking Ellsworth with Blue Hill and Stonington in one direction, and the Schoodic peninsula in the other (see Blue Hill and Bar Harbor). Oxford Hills Transit in Norway (743-9081) also serves its rural area. Seasonal trolleys on wheels circle Ogunquit and Kennebunkport.

CAMPS, FOR CHILDREN More than 200 summer camps are listed in the exceptional booklet published annually by the Maine Camp Directors Association (Box 42, Gardiner 04345) and the Maine Publicity Bureau (289-2423), 97 Winthrop Street, Hallowell 04347; available from both.

CAMPS, FOR ADULTS The Appalachian Mountain Club maintains a number of summer lodges and campsites for adults and families seeking a hiking and/or canoeing vacation. Intended primarily for members, they are technically open to all who reserve space, available only after April 1. The full service camps in Maine (offering three daily meals, organized hikes, evening programs) are at Echo Lake (see Mount Desert) and Cold River Camp in Evans Notch (near the New Hampshire border within the White Mountain National Forest). For details about all facilities and membership write the AMC, 5 Joy Street, Boston, MA 02108 (617-523-0636).

CAMPS, RENTAL In Maine a "camp" is the word for a second home or cottage. Since we assume that many of our readers don't know this, we have listed that information under Cottage Rentals.

CAMPING Almost half of Maine lies within "unorganized townships:" wooded, privately owned lands (see North Woods), most of which are open to the public on condition that basic rules be observed. These rules vary with the owners. A consortium of fourteen companies which control more than two-and-a-half million acres maintains more than 2000 miles of roads and several hundred campsites; visitors are required to register and pay fees at the access points to this area, and campsites within it may be reserved (there is an additional camping fee). For details and a map of this area, send $1 to: North Maine Woods, PO Box 382, Ashland 04732. Another basic leaflet, "Maine Forest Campsites," available from the Maine Forest Service, Department of Conservation, State House Station #22, Augusta 04333 (289-2791), describes the ninety free, widely scattered sites on land owned by other companies—several of which publish their own "sportsmen's maps." To get a complete picture of the private roads and public boat launches as well as campsites, you should also write to the Paper Industry Information Office (133 State Street, Augusta 04330, 622-3166), requesting "sportsmen's maps" published by Great Northern, Scott (which owns most of the land around Moosehead Lake), and Georgia Pacific (covering the eastern corner of the state). Camping beyond designated sites in these areas is generally permitted, but on condition that a fire permit be obtained.

For camping within Acadia National Park see Mount Desert. For the same within the White Mountain National Forest see Bethel.

For private campgrounds, the booklet "Maine Guide to Camping," lists most camping and tenting areas in the state, and is available from the Maine Publicity Bureau, 97 Winthrop Street, Hallowell 04347.

Thirteen of Maine's state parks offer camping, a fact which you can deduce from the state highway map or a brochure available from the Maine State Development Office, State House, Augusta 04333. Since their location is about all you can learn from these easy sources, we have attempted to describe the state parks in detail wherever they appear in this book (see Camden, Damariscotta, Mount Desert, Greenville, Rangeley, and Sebago). Note that no reservations are accepted for campsites, with the exception of those in Baxter State Park (see North Woods), and while most campsites can accommodate average-size campers and trailers, there are no trailer hookups. Primitive campsites along the Allagash Wilderness Waterway are also maintained by the state; a detailed leaflet about the trip is available from the Bureau of Parks and Recreation Commission, Augusta 04330. Note that Warren Island is the one state-maintained site offering off-shore camping (see Camden). Outstanding state-maintained campsites not otherwise mentioned in the book: Cobscook Bay State Park (726-4412), 220 miles east of Portland—868 waterside acres, 125 campsites, most for tents. Peaks-Kenny State Park near Dover-Foxcroft (564-2003)—56 sites and a beach, also fishing and hiking.

CANOEING, BOOKS ON   Maine offers the best choice of canoeing spots and services in the East—everything from a guided trip down a placid stream for a first-timer to a ten-day, fly-in expedition through wilderness. A leaflet brochure, available from the Maine Publicity Bureau (see Information) lists most other sources of information (AMC *River Guide I/Maine* covers the state's eight watersheds, with maps for each; query AMC Books Division, Department 40, 5 Joy Street, Boston, MA 02108). There are also three books by Thomas Eben: *Hot Blood and Wet Paddles*—"an illustrated guide to canoe racing on fourteen Maine and New Hampshire rivers," *No Horns Blowing* –" Canoeing ten great rivers in Maine," and *The Weekender*–" a guide to family canoeing, ten more great rivers in Maine," all published by Hallowell Printing. *The Maine Atlas and Gazetteer*, DeLorme Publishing Company, Freeport, also describes dozens of canoe trips and supplies the maps to go with them. Further good reading on the subject: John McPhee's *The Survival of the Bark Canoe* (Farrar, Straus, Giroux),

and *The Woods and Lakes of Maine–*" a trip from Moosehead Lake to New Brunswick in a birch-bark canoe, to which are added some Indian placenames and their meanings," by Lucius Lee Hubbar, first published in 1883 and reprinted by the New Hampshire Publishing Company.

CANOEING, GUIDED TRIPS   In Western Maine several groups are geared to putting beginners onto the Saco River: Saco River Canoe & Kayak (935-2369), Box 111, Fryeburg 04037, offers one-day guided tours during summer months (in '81 the price was $11 per person including canoe, lunch, transport); a similar service is offered by Saco Bound, just over the New Hampshire line (Box 113, Center Conway, NH 03813; 603-447-2177). A number of "outfitters," specializing in Allagash Waterway and other wilderness trips are listed on a sheet available from North Maine Woods, PO Box 382, Ashland 04732. Write to Maine Guide Wilderness Adventure, Yarmouth 04096 and you will also receive brochures of the major outfitters serving the Moosehead, Allagash, and Baxter State Park areas. Also see Canoeing the Allagash section in North Woods. A list of twenty commercial operators who "will provide transportation and guide service in the Allagash Wilderness Waterway" is also available by request from the Maine Publicity Bureau.

CANOEING THE ALLAGASH   The ultimate canoe trip in Maine—and on the entire East Coast for that matter—is the seven- to ten-day expedition up the Allagash Wilderness Waterway—a ninety-two-mile ribbon of lakes, ponds, rivers, and streams through the heart of northern Maine's vast commercial forests. Since 1966 the land flanking the waterway has been owned (500 feet back from the waterway on either side) by the state of Maine. A map pinpointing the sixty-five authorized campsites within the zone, also supplying other crucial information, is available free from the Bureau of Parks and Recreation, Maine Department of Conservation, State House Station 19, Augusta 04333. A more detailed map, backed with historical and a variety of other handy information, is DeLorme's "Map and Guide to the Allagash and St. John." Anybody contemplating the trip should also be aware of black flies in June and the no-seeums when warm weather finally comes. For further information check Camping, Guide Services, see North Woods, also read below.

CANOE RENTALS According to a "Canoe Rentals 1981" leaflet available from the Maine Publicity Bureau, canoes can be rented in Allagash (Maine Canoe Adventures), Augusta (Kennebec-Augusta Canoe Rental), Bar Mills (Saco River Canoe & Sail), Belgrade Lakes (Great Pond Marina), Bethel (Intervale Outfitters, Sunday River Inn, Denison's, and Ordway Brook Campground), in Bridgton (Mainestream Canoe), Brownfield (Woodland Acres), Cape Elizabeth (Peter A. Brawn), Damariscotta (Lake Pemaquid Camping), Fort Kent (Greg P. Jalbert), Franklin (Maynard G. Connors), Fryeburg (Canal Bridge Canoes), Greenville (Allagash Wilderness Outfitters, Folsom's Air Service, and Jack's Air Service), in Houlton (Houlton Rental Center), Island Falls (Birch Point Log Lodge), Jackman (Guay's Camps, Smith Hardware, and Cozy Cove Cabins), in Millinocket (Katahdin Canoe Outfitters), Mount Desert (Maine Wilderness Paddlers), North Bridgton (North Country Outfitters), North Jay (Moose Horn Trading Post), North Sebago (Sebago Lake Cottages), Norway (White's Boats), Orono (Villa Vaughn Campground), Rangeley (Quimby Pond Camps, Davis Marine, Mooselookmeguntic House, Town & Lake Motel), Rockwood (North Country Outfitters, Moose River Country Store, and Ronald Douglas), St. Francis (Edwin Pelletier), Sangerville (Hall's Trading Post), Searsmont (Aldus Shores Lakeside Camping), Springfield (Maine Wilderness Canoe Basin), Weld (Dummer's Beach Campground), and West Forks (Webb's Wilderness Outfitters). For details request the leaflet from the Maine Publicity Bureau.

CHILDREN, ESPECIALLY FOR Andre the Seal (see Rockport), Aqualand (see Bar Harbor), Animal Forest Park (see York Beach), Aquaboggan Water slide (older children only; Saco), Children's Museum (see Portland), The Seashore Trolley Museum (see Kennebunkport), Boothbay Railway Village (see Boothbay), Craig Brook National Fish Hatchery (see Bucksport), and the rocks at Pemaquid Light (outstanding climbing and tidal pools, see Pemaquid), Rumford Zoo (see Bethel), Fort Knox (a treat for boys of all ages), Monorail ride at Mount Abram (see Bethel), Scarborough Marsh Nature Center in Scarborough (883-5100), Portland Observatory on Munjoy Hill (see Portland), Desert of Maine (see Freeport), Owl's Head Transportation Museum (see Rockland), King's Mountain Giant Slide in South Lebanon, the Game Farm in Dry Mills (657-4977), Histori-cal Indian Village at Norridgewock (seasonal: replica fort, Indian relics, next to Oosoola Park), the Sandy River RR (see Phillips), also see Aquariums.

CLAMMING Maine State law permits the harvesting of shell fish for personal use only. Individuals can take up to a half bushel of shellfish, or three bushels of hen or surf clams (the big ones out in the flats) in one day without a license, unless municipal ordinances further limit "the taking of shellfish." Be sure to check before you dig. Some towns do prohibit clamming, and in certain places there is a temporary stay on harvesting while the beds are being seeded.

CHRISTMAS TREES A twenty-two-page list of Maine Christmas tree growers is available by request from the State of Maine Department of Conservation, Bureau of Forestry, Augusta 04333.

COTTAGE RENTALS Cottage rentals are the only reasonably priced way to go for families who wish to stay in one Maine spot for more than one week. If you have no special preference about where you want to be, request the booklet, "Maine, Guide to Camp & Cottage Rentals" from the Maine Publicity Bureau (see Information). The '81 booklet's rates for coastal cottages began at $125 a week, and we can attest to the quality of the cottage in Boothbay which was going for that price. Each spring we browse through this book when it comes out and then shoot off postcards to a half dozen places. We always receive pleasant letters back, and if cottages are already filled for the time we request their owners frequently refer us to others. If you have your heart set on one particular area and cannot get satisfaction through the booklet, we recommend obtaining a printout of the realtors just for that county, then sending notes off to agents in the precise area in which you are interested. The printouts are available for $2.50 by writing to the Maine Department of Business Regulation, Central Licensing Division, State House Station #35, Augusta 04333 (289-2217).

COVERED BRIDGES Of the 120 covered bridges which once spanned Maine rivers, just ten survive. A booklet guide to these is periodically available from the Department of Commerce, State House, Augusta 04330. The most famous, and certainly as picturesque as a covered bridge can be, is "Artist's Bridge" over the Sunday River (see Bethel). The others are: Porter Bridge over the Ossipee River (1876), one-half mile south of Porter; Babb's Bridge, recently rebuilt, over the Presumpscot River between Gorham and Windham; Herlock Bridge (1857), three miles northwest of East Fryeburg; Lovejoy Bridge in South Andover (1868); Bennett Bridge over the Magalloway River, one-and-one-half miles south of the Wilson's Mills Post Office; Low's Bridge over the Piscataquis between Sangerville and Guildford; Robyville Bridge in the town of Corinth; the Watson Settlement Bridge between Woodstock and Littleton; and Morse Bridge, in Coe Park, Bangor.

CRAFTS "Directions," a leaflet guide "to the professional craftspeople of Maine," is available from Box 122, Stonington 04681. A thirty-two-page "Directory" of United Maine Craftsmen, the statewide craft society which stages an annual fair in early August at the Cumberland Fairgrounds (just north of Portland), should be available through the Maine Publicity Bureau. *Handcraft Centers of New England* ($7.95, Yankee books) details a number of Maine crafts events, shops, co-ops, and the like.

CRAFTS CENTERS Haystack Mountain School of Crafts, Deer Isle 04627 (348-2816) is a nationally respected summer school in a variety of crafts, offering three-week courses beginning mid-June and continuing through September 14. Applicants must be more than eighteen years old; enrollment is limited to sixty-five. Work by students is displayed in the visitors center which also serves as a forum for frequent evening presentations. The surrounding area (see Blue Hill to Stonington) is known for the quality of its potters; and many other craftsmen have opened summer studios and shops.

DIVE SHOPS Aqua Sports and Congress Hardware in Portland, Skin Diver's Paradise in Auburn, The Dive Shop in West Southport, Northeast Divers in Brewer, Salt Water Sports and Service in Rockland, Downeast Scuba in Grove, and Atlantic Diving Company in East Boothbay.

FARMERS MARKETS Farmers markets are held June through fall in Farmington (Saturday morning), Blue Hill (Saturday morning), Ellsworth (Thursday afternoon), Camden (Saturday morning), Damariscotta (Saturday morning), Waldoboro (Monday, mid-day), Bath (Saturday morning), and Saco (Saturday morning), among other places. Detailed information is in "Farmer to Consumer," a booklet available from the Bureau of Agricultural Marketing, Department of Agriculture, Station 28, Augusta 04333 (289-3491).

FACTORY OUTLETS Shoes. Quoddy Moccasin outlets can be found in Auburn, South Portland, Wells, Bridgton, and Brunswick. Bass outlets: Bangor, Belfast, Ellsworth, Falmouth, Kittery, Wells, Wilton, and Wiscasset. Dexter outlets: Auburn, Bangor, Brewer, Brunswick, Calais, Dexter, Ellsworth, Madawaska, North Windham, Portland, Presque Isle, Rockport, Saco, Sanford, South Portland, Waterville, Wells, Wilton, Wiscasset, and York. Dunham, in Wells. For children's shoes we also favor Eastland Shoe in Freeport and Northland Shoe Factory Outlet in Fryeburg (open summer only).

Hathaway Shirts, a Maine product since 1837, has US 1 outlets in Ellsworth and Wells. In Kittery's Mini-Mall, Seventh Avenue is an outlet for discounted quality clothing, and next door is a Dansk Cookware outlet. Bates Mill Stores in Lewiston and Wells are good for bedclothes. Emple Knitting Mills in Brewer sells primarily sweaters, but also carries a variety of women's clothing. In Rockland the Van Baalen Pacific Corporation outlet (US 1) carries men's bathrobes and swimwear, ladies lounge wear. In Guilford the Guilford Mill Store is a genuine source of bargain fabrics (including upholstery and drapery), as is the Oxford Mill End Store in Oxford (539-4451). Cascade Woolen Mill Factory in Oakland specializes in wool and wool blends.

While L. L. Bean's in Freeport is better known for quality than bargains, there are always items to be found in the store itself which fall way below its catalog prices. Last but not least, there is the Maine State Prison showroom (see Thomaston), good for sturdy maple furniture, wooden lamps, cutting boards, and souvenirs at unbeatable prices.

FACTORY TOURS Quoddy Moccasins in Auburn (year-round: 784-3555), Caratunk Snowshoes (672-3906), A. L. Stewart & Sons Blueberry Processors Growers in Cherryfield (just August and September: 546-2612). Lobster trap makers: Tucker Traps in Eliot (439-4040), and Anderson Sons in Cumberland Center (829-3374). Boat builders: Goudy Stevens in East Boothbay, Handy Boat Service in Falmouth Foreside (781-5110); Shaw Tenney in Orono makes oars, paddles, and nautical accessories (866-4867), and Old Town Canoe in Old Town is one of the nation's oldest, most prestigious producers of wood and canvas canoes (827-5513). Furniture manufacturers who welcome visitors are the Moosehead Manufacturing Company in Monson and Dover, and Thomas Moser in New Gloucester (926-4446). G. H. Bass Company in Wilton, shoes (645-3131); R. V. Peacock Canning Company in Lubec, sardines and herrings (733-5556), Penobscot Frozen Foods in Belfast, potato processing; and Port Clyde Foods in Eastport, sardines (853-2932) also stage tours, as do most of the paper mills—contact the Paper Industry Information Office, 133 State Street, Augusta 04330 (622-3166). Scott Paper offers tours of its woodland operations during summer months—phone 672-5512 in Bingham, 695-2241 in Greenville, 668-2041 in Jackman, and 872-2751 in Winslow.

FALL FOLIAGE "A Downeast Experience, Maine Fall Foliage" is a booklet available from the Maine Publicity Bureau (see Information) which outlines eleven circle tours ranging from the White Mountains through the western and central lakes to the shore. Autumn is extremely pleasant along the coast; days tend to be clear and the changing leaves against the blue sea can be spectacular. Many inns remain open through foliage season, and the resort towns of Ogunquit, Kennebunkport, Boothbay Harbor, and Camden all offer excellent dining, shopping, and lodging through Columbus Day weekend. Off season prices prevail, in contrast with the rest of New England at this time of year.

FERRIES, TO CANADA Portland to Yarmouth, Nova Scotia: Prince of Fundy Cruises offers nightly (departing 9:30 PM) sailings, late April through the Columbus Day weekend. The ferry itself is a car-carrying cruise ship with gambling, restaurants, and cabins aboard. (800-482-0955 in Maine; 800-341-7540 in the eastern U.S.).

The Canadian National Marine line also offers overnight car and passenger service aboard the *Marine Evangeline* between Portland and Yarmouth year-round (800-492-0622 in Maine and 800-341-0222 for the mid- and northeastern

U.S.). C. N. Marine also operates *The Bluenose* auto-ferry between Bar Harbor and Yarmouth spring, summer, and fall; a casino, cabins, and cafeteria make the ten-hour trip go quickly (800-341-7981 in the northeastern U.S.; 800-432-7344 in Maine). At this writing plans have been announced for a new Bar Harbor service to replace the Portland run in 1983.

FERRIES, IN MAINE Maine State Ferry Service, Rockland 04841 (594-5543) operates year-round service from Rockland to Vinalhaven and North Haven, from Lincolnville to Islesboro, from Bass Harbor to Swan's Island and Long Island, and from Northeast Harbor to the Cranberry Isles. For private ferry services to Monhegan see Port Clyde and Boothbay Harbor, for the Casco Bay Islands see Portland, for Matinicus see Rockland, and for Isle au Haut see Stonington.

FIRE PERMITS Maine law dictates that no person shall kindle or use outdoor fires without a permit, except at authorized campsites or picnic grounds. Fire permits in the organized towns are obtained from the local town warden; in the unorganized towns from the nearest forest ranger. Portable stoves fueled by propane gas, gasoline, or sterno are exempt from the rule.

FISHING "Maine Guide to Fishing," published by the Maine Publicity Bureau (see Information) is a handy overview of rules, license fees, and other matters of interest to fishermen, ranging from deep-sea fishing charter and party boats (see The Yorks, Ogunquit, Kennebunkport, Portland, Bailey Island, Boothbay Harbor, Stonington, and Mount Desert). There are also the *Mary C* out of Biddeford Pool, the *San R Marie* out of Scarborough, *Chief* out of Jonesport, and *Quoddy Dam* based in Eastport. A detailed listing of all deep-sea fishing boats is available from The Maine Publicity Bureau.

FLYING SCHOOLS Central Maine Flying School in Old Town, Maine Aviation at Portland International Jetport, Folsom's Air Service in Greenville, Maine Instrument Flight School at Augusta Airport, and Air Tech Corporation at Northern Maine Regional Airport in Presque Isle.

FORTS I am married to a fort freak and so realize that there are people in this world who will detour fifty miles to see an eighteenth-century earthworks. Maine's forts are actually a fascinating lot, monuments to the state's own unique and largely forgotten history. A leaflet guide to "Maine Historic Memorials" available from the Maine Publicity Bureau (see Information) describes Fort William Henry at Pemaquid, Fort Edgcomb in Wiscasset, Fort George in Castine, Fort Halifax near Winslow, Fort Kent, Fort Knox near Bucksport, Fort McClary in Kittery, Fort O'Brien near Machias, Fort Popham (see Bath), and Fort Pownall at Stockton Springs.

GOLF   Golf courses which welcome visitors are listed right on the Maine State Highway Map; for those that are genuinely geared to visitors see: Bar Harbor, the Kennebunks, Bethel, Boothbay, Rangeley, and Camden-Rockport. The major resort inns catering to golfers are the Samoset in Rockland, the Bethel Inn in Bethel, Sebasco Estates, the Country Club Inn in Rangeley, and the Cliff House in Ogunquit.

GUIDE SERVICES   There are more than 1000 registered Maine Guides, men and women who have passed the test to qualify. Finding the guide to suit your needs—be it fishing, hunting, or canoeing the Allagash Waterway, can be a confusing business. A list of guides is available from the Maine Professional Guides Association, Box 265, Medway 04460. See Canoeing, Guided Trips for referral services, also Fishing. Flying services and camps also furnish their own guides, and a list of guide services is available from North Maine Woods, PO Box 382, Ashland 04732.

GUESTHOUSES   Guesthouses always seem to clump in certain towns. In Maine these are Bar Harbor, Boothbay Harbor, Ogunquit, and the Yorks. See our own listings and check with local chambers of commerce.

HIKING   For organized trips contact the Maine chapter of the Appalachian Mountain Club—the Boston office, 5 Joy Street, Boston, MA (617-523-0636) will furnish the names of current offices. In addition to the AMC *Maine Mountain Guide* and the AMC map guide to trails on Mount Desert, we recommend investing in *Fifty Hikes in Maine* by John Gibson (Backcountry Publications), which offers clear, inviting treks up hills of every size throughout the state. The *Maine Atlas and Gazetteer*

(DeLorme Publishing Company) also outlines a number of rewarding hikes.

HISTORIC HOUSES   The Maine Publicity Bureau's outstanding booklet, *Maine Guide to Museums and Historic Houses* may—and then may not—be reprinted in the future. It's worth requesting, accurate as of 1981 (see Information). A booklet guide to its properties throughout New England is available from the Society for the Preservation of New England Antiquities, 141 Cambridge Street, Boston, MA; the SPNEA sites are: the Nickels-Sortwell House, Wiscasset; the Parson Smith Homestead, South Windham; Marrett House, Standish; the Jewett Memorial and Hamilton Houses in South Berwick; the Jonathan Sayward House in York Harbor; and the Lady Pepperrell House at Kittery Point. Within this book dozens of historic houses open to the public are listed by town.

HORSEBACK RIDING   Trail riding is available by reservation at: Sargent's Riding Stable in East Corinth (884-7290), Long Horn Stables at Evergreen Valley in East Stoneham (928-3300), Triple K. Equestrian Center in Fort Fairfield (473-7600), Horsefeathers in Gorham (892-3652), Judy Ann Stables in Old Orchard Beach (934-5173), Wildwood Riding Stables at Seal Cove in Acadia National Park (276-5091), Ridgecrest Stables in Springvale (324-4681), Shores Riding Stable in Waterville (873-4748), and North Village Stable in York (646-8054).

Sleigh rides are available at Long Horn Stables and Horsefeathers. Wildwood offers bone-jolting carriage rides. A list of all riding academies and stables is available from the Maine Publicity Bureau.

HORSE RACING   Harness racing at Scarborough Downs: US 1, or Exit 6 off the Maine Turnpike, May through mid-September, closed Tuesdays, daily double, Terrace Dining Room (883-2020), Downs Club. The leaflet guide to Maine Agricultural Events also lists harness racing dates at all agricultural fairs of the current season (available from the Maine Department of Agriculture, Augusta).

HUNTING   Hunters should obtain a summary of Maine hunting and trapping laws from the Maine Fish and Wildlife Department, 284 State Street, Augusta 04333. Current hunting license fees are: $65 for big game, $87 for a combination fishing and hunting license, $35 for small game, $15 for junior small game; there are also licenses for archery and trapping. For leads on registered Maine guides who specialize in organized expeditions (complete with meals and lodging), contact the sources we list under Fishing, Guide Services, Canoeing, and Camping. You might also try the Moosehead Region Chamber of Commerce, Box 581, Greenville 04441. A handy "Maine Guide to Hunting" booklet (published annually by the Maine Publicity Bureau) is filled with information and ads for hunting lodges, guides, and the like.

INFORMATION The Maine Publicity Bureau (97 Winthrop Street, Hallowell 04347) publishes fine booklet (not leaflet) guides to Auto Touring, Fishing, Hunting, Camping, Camp and Cottage Rentals, and "Winter," a quarterly calendar of events and mimeographed sheets on a variety of specialized subjects. Write or phone (289-2423) the bureau's office if you have a special query, or stop by its superb year-round information center on I-95 in Kittery (439-1319), open daily except Christmas and Thanksgiving, 9 AM to 5 PM; from Memorial Day to Labor Day, 8 AM to 8 PM. Seasonal information booths are maintained in Augusta (Augusta Plaza, Western Avenue), Bangor (Bass Park, 519 Main Street), Bethel (Route 2), Calais (Route 1), Fryeburg (Route 302), Houlton (Route 1), and Orono (Stillwater Avenue). A small walk-in office is also open year-round, weekdays, in the basement of the Greater Portland Chamber of Commerce Building, 142 Free Street.

In New York City the New England Vacation Center carries most free Maine publications. Another essential is the "Innkeepers Association Lodging and Food Guide," available from Maine Innkeepers Association, 142 Free Street, Portland 04101 (773-7670).

INNS In this book we have made an attempt to list every pleasant inn that we could find. Of the current inn guides on the market we feel that *One Hundred Country Inns in Maine* by Mimi Steadman (Down East Books) does the best job but was already slightly outdated in 1981. *The Guide to The Recommended Country Inns of New England* by Elizabeth Squier and Suzy Chapin (The Globe Pequot Press) is also useful. Also see the "Innkeepers Association Lodging and Food Guide" above.

LAKES There are more than 5,000 lakes in Maine and every natural body of water over ten acres—which accounts for most of them—is, theoretically at least, available to the public for "fishing and fowling." Access is, of course, limited by the property owners around the lakes. Because so much acreage in Maine is owned by paper companies and other land management concerns which permit public use (provided the public obeys their rules: see Camping), there is ample opportunity to canoe or fish in unpeopled waters. Power boat owners should note that most states have reciprocal license privileges with Maine; the big exception is New Hampshire. For more about the most popular resort lakes in the state see Bridgton, Rangeley, and Greenville. The state parks on lakes are Aroostook (camping, fishing, and swimming; ME 1 south of Presque Isle), Damariscotta Lake State Park (see Damariscotta), Lake St. George State Park (swimming, picnicking, fishing; ME 3 in Liberty), Lily Bay State Park (see Greenville), Peacock Beach State Park (swimming and picnicking in Richmond), Peaks-Kenny State Park on Sebec Lake in Dover-Foxcroft, Rangeley Lake State Park (see Rangeley), Range Ponds State Park in Poland, Sebago Lake State Park (see Bridgton). Families with small children should be aware of the many coastal lakes surrounded by reasonably priced cottages; see Cottages, Rental.

LIGHTHOUSES The most popular to visit are Portland Head Light (completed in 1790) on Cape Elizabeth, Cape Neddick Light (see Yorks), marshall Point Light at Port Clyde, Fort Point Light at Stockton Springs, Pemaquid Point (see Pemaquid; the lighthouse keeper's house is now a museum and the rocks below are peerless for scrambling), Owl's Head (built 1826), Bass Harbor Head Light at Bass Harbor, and West Quoddy Head. On Monhegan Island the lighthouse keeper's house is a seasonal museum, and at Grindel Point on Islesboro there is also an adjacent seasonal museum.

LITTER Littering in Maine is punishable by a $100 fine; this applies to dumping from boats as well as other vehicles. Most cans and bottles are redeemable at stores.

LOBSTER POUNDS A lobster pound is usually a no-frills seaside restaurant which specializes in serving lobsters and clams steamed in seawater. The most basic and reasonably priced pounds are frequently fishermen's co-ops such as that in New Harbor (see Pemaquid). Expect good value but no china plates and salads at Chauncy Creek Lobster Pound in Kittery, Harraseeket (see Freeport), at the Cod End in Tenants Harbor, Beal's Lobster Pound in Southwest Harbor, and The Fisherman's Landing in Bar Harbor. The Ogunquit Lobster Pound (see Ogunquit) is more of a formal restaurant, but still good value and outstanding; other lobster-eating landmarks include Nunan's Lobster Hut in Cape Porpoise (see Kennebunks), Eaton's on Deer Isle (see Blue Hill), Robinson's Wharf at Townsend Gut (see Boothbays), and the Lobster Shack on Cape Elizabeth.

LOBSTERS TO GO
The following firms will pack and/or ship lobsters and other seafood: Saltwater Farm in York Harbor (363-3182) will ship lobster, packaged in a container which merely needs to be plunged into boiling water, anywhere in the world. The firm, which has pioneered this service over the past thirty-plus years, will deliver an entire clambake, and a wide range of other fish dishes as well. Write for their mail order catalog. Other firms include: Morrison's, and Crawford Lobster Company—both on Badger's Island in Kittery, Port Lobster Company in Kennebunkport, Pine Point Fishermen's Co-op at the town landing in Pine Point, New Meadows Lobster Pound in Portland, Allen's Seafood in Harpswell Center, Ocean Way Lobster in Brunswick, Plant's Seafood in Bath, Inland Lobster in Sebago, Atwood Brothers in Tenants Harbor, City Boat Landing in Belfast, Jeff's Lobster Pool on Verona Island in Bucksport, Stonington Lobster Co-op in Stonington, Gateway Lobster Pound in Trenton, Beal's Lobster Pier in Southwest Harbor, Smith's Cove Lobster Pound in Millbridge, and McLaughlin's Seafood in Bangor.

MAPLE SUGARING
A list of some fifty maple producers who welcome visitors to their sugar shacks during sugaring season is available from Chester Basford, Benton Station 04910. Maine produces roughly 8,000 gallons of syrup a year.

MOOSE
These creatures have made a comeback from their near-extinct status in the 1930s, and now number more than 15,000 again. Baxter State Park publishes pointers on where to see moose within its bounds. Your chances are also good around Moosehead Lake. The shallows of lakes and ponds are likely spots for moose-watching.

MUSEUMS
Maine Guide to Museums and Historic Homes, available from the Maine Publicity Bureau, is an exceptional free guide to the state's museums big and small—historical, art, whatever. Our own favorites are the Perry-Macmillan Arctic Museum at Bowdoin College (see Brunswick), the Seashore Trolley Museum in Kennebunkport, the Maine State Museum in Augusta (open daily, year-round, free), the Owl's Head Transportation Museum (see Rockland), the Robert Abbe Museum in Acadia National Park, which is outstanding for its regional Indian artifacts (see Mount Desert), as is the Wilson Museum in Castine (see East Penobscot Bay); the Patten Lumberman's Museum surprises you with the extent and quality of its exhibits, and the "Colonial Pemaquid" museum presents fascinating archeological finds from the adjacent, early-seventeenth-century settlement. The Maine Maritime Museum in Bath stands in a class by itself and should not be missed. There is also the Maine State Museum in Augusta (open daily) with exhibits on the varied Maine landscape and historical exhibits ranging from traces of the area's earliest people to rifles used by State of Mainers in Korea; you can also see exhibits on fishing, agriculture, lumbering, quarrying and shipbuilding. Also see "Art Museums."

MUSEUM VILLAGES
To our minds there are very different museum villages in Maine. There is Willowbrook at Newfield, a nineteenth-century village center consisting of twenty-seven buildings which have been restored by one man, open seasonally as a commercial attraction (see Bridgton). There is the old village center of Searsport, restored as a fine maritime museum (see Searsport). There is the Sabbath Day Lake Shaker Museum, still a functioning religious community, and there is York Village with its Old Gaol, school, tavern, church, and scattering of historic houses open to the public, adding up to a picture of late-eighteenth-century life in coastal Maine.

Then there is Norlands which belongs in a category of its own and, for lack of a better name, calls itself a "Living History Center." A former estate, Norlands is a self-contained village complete with neo-Gothic library (open in

July and August) which invites you to come and live for a weekend or longer as you would have had you been alive in this particular place (Livermore) in the mid-nineteenth-century. You eat, sleep, learn, work, worship, and dance as you would have in this rural backwater in 1870. Norlands is a non-profit foundation staffed by dedicated scholars and local people; for details: 897-2236.

MUSIC Among the most famous summer concert series are: the Bar Harbor Festival (288-5744) and the Mount Desert Festival of Chamber Music (276-5039), the Sebago Long Lake Region Chamber Music Festival in North Bridgton (627-4939), the Bay Chamber Concerts presented in the Rockport Opera House (236-4731), the Kneisel Hall concerts and Blue Hill Chamber Concerts (alternating between Blue Hill and Bangor off season; Box 140, Blue Hill 04614), concerts presented by the Downeast Chamber Music Center (see Castine: 326-4642), and the Bowdoin College Summer Concerts in Brunswick (725-8731, extension 321).

The summer music schools are: Amherst Summer Music Center in Raymond (246-5776 and 655-4560 after June 24), Bowdoin College Summer School (see above), the Downeast Chamber Music Center in Castine (see above), Kneisel Hall in Blue Hill (see above but only after June 24; prior inquiries should be addressed to Kneisel Hall, Blue Hill 04614), and the Pierre Monteux Memorial Domaine School in Hancock (442-6251). There is, of course, also the Portland Symphony Orchestra (773-8191), and the Bangor Symphony Orchestra (945-6408).

NATURE PRESERVES, COASTAL Rachel Carson National Wildlife Refuge, a total of nine separate preserves salted between Kittery and Cape Elizabeth along the Atlantic Flyway. Request a leaflet guide from the Parker River National Wildlife Refuge, Newbury, MA 01950. The 750-acre section in Wells is described in *A Birder's Guide to the Coast of Maine* (Down East Books, 1981), which also describes 3000-acre Scarborough Marsh. The Maine Audubon Society maintains a nature center at Scarborough Marsh and offers canoe tours, bird walks, and a variety of other summer programs (883-5100). There are nature trails to follow at the Audubon Society headquarters at Gilsland Farm in Falmouth. The society also maintains self-guiding nature trails (cross-country ski trails in winter) and facilities for picnicking and tenting at the 150-acre Mast Landing Sanctuary in Freeport.

Birdsacre, a forty-acre preserve in Ellsworth harbors 109 species of birds in and around a network of nature trails, and a museum which honors pioneer ornithologist Cordelia Stanwood, open June 15-October 15, and other times by appointment (667-8683). Acadia National Park, with its miles of hiking trails and extensive naturalist-led programs, is the state's single busiest preserve (see Mount Desert). Some thirty miles east of Ellsworth is Petit Manan National Wildlife Refuge (1,999 acres), a peninsula offering limited hiking trails. At the extreme eastern end of Maine the Moosehorn National Wildlife Refuge in Calais (454-3521) consists of two units, roughly twenty miles apart. The bigger (16,065 acres) is partially bounded by the St. Croix River, and the 6,600-acre Edmunds Unit overlooks Cobscook Bay; a visitors center is open May-September and there are hiking trails.

NATURE PRESERVES, INLAND Steve Powell Wildlife Management Area, described in a booklet available from the Maine Department of Inland Fisheries and Wildlife, 284 State Street, Augusta 04333 (289-3651), consists of two islands and several hundred acres of intervening tidal flats at the head of Merrymeeting Bay. There is Swan Island (four miles long) and Little Swan; on Swan Island there is a campground and a gravel road which meanders by natural and historical sites. Visitors are welcome to come by private boat (there is a state boat launch ramp just across the Kennebec in Richmond) or arrange a ride over through the Wildlife Division (see above). Southeast of Fryeburg there are the Brownfield Bog Wildlife Management Areas (5,454 acres)—a mix of marshland, floodplain and upland which invites exploration by canoe; a campsite at Walker's Falls is maintained by the Appalachian Mountain Club (see Hiking). In the Bridgton area there is the Hiram Nature Study Area maintained by the Central Maine Power Company (647-3391)—some sixty acres of woodland in Baldwin with a trail along the Saco River and picnic facilities. Vaughan Woods, a 250-acre state park offers a few fine miles of wooded hiking trails along the Salmon Falls River, good for cross-country skiing and birding as well as hiking and picnicking (from Kittery take ME 236 north more than nine miles, then west on ME 91, left at the T.). Free. The greatest inland preserve is Baxter State Park (see Maine Woods). Also see Camping, Fishing, Hiking and Hunting.

PARKS, STATE   The Bureau of Parks and Recreation, State House, Augusta 04333 (289-3821) publishes a leaflet listing of its twenty-eight state parks which we have treated in this section under the appropriate categories: Aroostook (Swimming, also Trout Fishing,) Bradbury Mountain (hiking), Camden Hills (Camping), Cobscook Bay (Camping), Crescent Beach (Beaches), Damariscotta Lake (Beaches), Grafton Notch (Hiking), Holbrook Island (Nature Preserve), Lake St. George (Beaches), Lily Bay (Camping), Mount Blue State Park (Camping), Peacock Beach (Beaches), Peaks-Kenny (Camping), Popham Beach (Beaches), Quoddy Head (Lighthouses), Rangeley Lake (Camping), Range Ponds (Lakes), Reid (Beaches), Scarborough (Beach), Sebago Lake (Camping), Wold Neck (Nature Preserve) and Baxter State Park (Hiking, Camping). Parks not otherwise covered: Fort Point State Park at Stockton Springs, a good picnic and sighting spot on Penobscot Bay (see Bucksport), Moose Point State Park, off ME 1 between Jonesboro and Machias, another good picnicking spot which also offers fresh water swimming, complete with changing rooms.

PARKS AND FORESTS, NATIONAL
Acadia National Park, which occupies roughly half of Mount Desert, also scattered areas on Isle au Haut, Little Cranberry Island, Baker Island, Little Moose Island, and Schoodic Point, adds up to a 44,000 acre preserve offering hiking, camping, rock climbing, snowshoeing, ski touring, swimming, horseback riding, canoeing, and a variety of guided nature tours and programs, as well as a scenic fifty-six-mile driving tour. The park itself is open year-round but, due to recent Federal cutbacks, the visitors center at Hull Cove is now open only May-October. Park headquarters at Eagle Lake are open weekdays 8-4:30 in winter (288-3338). For a more detailed park description see Mount Desert. The White Mountain National Forest encompasses 41,943 acres in Maine, including five campgrounds under the jurisdiction of the Evans Notch Ranger District, Bridge Street, Bethel 04217 (824-2134). For details see Bethel.

RAILROAD RIDES AND MUSEUMS
Boothbay Railway Village delights small children (see Boothbay) and offers railroad exhibits in its depot. For railfans there are two other sites to see: the Steam-Car Railroadiana Museum in Gilead (see Bethel) and the Sandy River Railroad in Philips, with a reconstructed narrow-gauge engine and authentic old coaches from the old Sandy River and Rangeley Lakes Railroad. It operates entirely with volunteer help on the first and third Sundays of summer months, and by appointment (353-8382).

ROCK-HOUNDING   Perham's Maine Mineral Store at Trap Corner in West Paris claims to attract an annual 90,000 visitors, and displays Maine minerals and offers access (for a small fee) to its five quarries. The store also offers information about other quarries, and sells its own guidebook to gem hunting in Oxford County ("Maine's Treasure Chest"). Open year-round daily (just 1-5 on Sundays, closed Thanksgiving and Christmas). Other rock-hounding meccas: Winthrop Mineral Shop, ME 202, East Winthrop; and Rock-N-Stop, ME 27, Dresden. All three stores sell gold panning equipment. Thanks to the high price of gold, prospectors are back panning Maine stream beds; a list of likely spots is available from the Maine Geological Survey, Department of Conservation, State House Station 22, Augusta 04333 (289-2801).

SAILING   Windjammers and yacht brokers aside, there are a limited number of places which will rent small sailing craft, fewer who will offer lessons to adults and children alike. Those of which we are aware are: The Chance-Along Inn (see Belfast), Captain's Quarter (see Yorks), Deer Isle Sailing Center in Mountainville (see Blue Hill-Stonington) and the Mansell Boat Company in Southwest Harbor (see Mount Desert, The Moorings Inn). For sailboat rentals only, see Bridgton. *La Nef des Fous,* based in Lubec (773-5515), takes you on half: ($24) and full-day ($48) excursions to the islands of Campobello and Grand Manan (write to Captain Charles Legris, 154 Lower Water Street, Lubec 04652). Also see "Windjammers."

SKIING   Sugarloaf USA, Carrabassett Valley 04947 (237-2000 and 237-2681), is Maine's largest ski area, the only one with a gondola; it also has five double chairlifts, five T-bars, forty-three trails and slopes and extensive snowmaking, plus a wide choice of places to stay and eat. Saddleback Mountain, Rangeley 04970 (864-5500), has two double chairlifts and three T-bars serving ten acres of open slopes and twenty-six trails, extensive snowmaking. Squaw Mountain in Greenville (695-2272) offers a double chairlift, a poma lift, and two T-bars serving twenty miles of trails, some snowmaking, and adjacent lodging. All of the above are fairly remote from population centers. Sunday River in Bethel (824-2410), which has just added another new chairlift, now has two, plus a poma lift, two T-bars serving twenty trails and snowmaking capacity from top to bottom. Sunday River and Pleasant Mountain in Bridgton (647-8444; three double chairlifts serving twenty trails, partial snowmaking) are far handier to Boston. There is also Evergreen Valley in East Stoneham (928-3000), a self-contained resort near the New Hampshire border with three chairlifts serving six miles of trails, Lost Valley in Auburn (784-1561) with two double chairlifts and a T-bar serving nine trails and twenty-five acres of open slopes, Mount Abram in Locke Mills (485-2601) just west of Bethel with a double chairlift and three T-bars serving twelve miles of trails and 100 acres of slopes, also Mount Hermon Ski Area, Hermon, with two T-bars and a rope tow serving seven trails and seventeen acres of open slopes. Camden Snow Bowl (594-2511) offers eight miles of terrain, one chair, two T-bars, twenty percent snowmaking coverage. It is managed this year by the Samoset Resort in Rockport.

SKIING, CROSS-COUNTRY

In addition to the downhill areas listed above, ski touring is a specialty at Acadia National Park (see Mount Desert), Baxter State Park (see North Woods), in the White Mountain National Forest (see Bethel) and in the following commercial centers: Akers Ski Center in Andover (six miles, 392-4582); Benloch Farm Ski Touring Center, Dixmont (257-4671); Bethel Inn Ski Touring Center (824-2175); Big Rock Touring Center, Mars Hill (three-and-one-half miles, 425-6711); The Birches in Rockwood (twenty-five miles and guided tours, 534-7305); Black Mountain of Maine in Rumford (more than four miles, 364-8977); Carrabassett Valley Touring Center (seventy-five miles, 237-2205); Edelweiss Touring Center, Rangeley (thirty miles, 864-3891); Katahdin Lake Wilderness Camps, Millinocket (base for a fifty-mile network plus access to Baxter State Park, write to Alfred J. Cooper III, Box 398, Millinocket 04462); Little Lyford Pond Camps in Brownville (forty miles of wilderness skiing, guided tours, lodging, write Joel and Luci Frantzman, Box 688, Brownville 04414); Livermore Falls Nordic Ski Association (ten-mile network, 897-3191); and Teddy Bear Touring Trails, North Turner (ten miles of marked trails, 224-8275). Portland Bicycle Exchange in Portland (772-4137) offers information about touring trails in the greater Portland area. DeLorme Publishing Co., Freeport, has published "Maine Ski Touring Map & Guide," listing and locating sixty-six touring areas in the state.

SNOWMOBILING

Maine has reciprocal agreements with many states and provinces; for licensing and rules write to the Fish and Game Department. The Maine Snowmobile Association represents 268 clubs and maintains six thousand miles of an ever-expanding cross-state trail network; for details write the MSA Office, Box 77, Augusta 04330 (622-6983). For maps and further information write to the Snowmobile Division, Bureau of Parks and Recreation, Station 19, Augusta 04333.

SUMMER STUDY

Maine Photographic Workshops (see Rockport). Hurricane Island Outward Bound School, Box 429, Rockland 04841 (594-5548), offers varied length sessions stressing fitness and self-reliance, also specialized courses such as "Women over Thirty," and "Creative Leadership." Camping, sailing, rock climbing, and navigation are part of each course. College of the Atlantic, 105 Eden Street in Bar Harbor (288-5015) offers courses ranging from folk music to history cruises. The Maine Maritime Academy (see Castine) offers a variety of noncredit courses. Other schools with summer programs include Saint Joseph's College in North Windham, Westbrook College, Colby College (Waterville 04901), the University of Maine in Orono (04469), Presque Isle (04769), Fort Kent (04743), Farmington (04938), Augusta (04330), and Machias (04654). There are summer sessions at the University of Southern Maine campuses in Portland (04103) and Gorham (04038). Also see Music and Crafts. In addition, there is the prestigious Skowhegan School of Painting and Sculpture in Skowhegan 04976 (474-9345).

TENT RENTALS

Tents can be rented from Bunganut Lake Camping in Alfred, Lake Pemaquid Camping in Damariscotta, Patten Pond KOA in Ellsworth, Don's Camper in Holden, Ossipee River Campground in Kezar Falls, 3-K Kamper in Lewiston, Sebago Basin Camping in North Windham, Kokatosi Campground in South Waterford, and Dixon's Campground in York. Trailers are available from many of the above sources and are listed on a sheet available from Maine Publicity.

TENNIS COURTS   Indoor courts: Capitol Tennis in Augusta, Tennis of Maine in Falmouth, Indoor tennis in Hampden, The Meadows Racquet and Recreation Center in Kennebunk, Central Maine Tennis Center in Lewiston, The Tennis Racquet in Portland, Samoset Resort in Rockport, Tidewater Restaurant near Bar Harbor in Trenton. Outdoor public courts are available at Atlantic Oaks in Bar Harbor, at the Bridgton Highlands Country Club, at the Snow Bowl in Camden, at Lake Pemaquid Camping in Damariscotta, at Memorial Park in Old Orchard Beach, at the Wells Recreation Area, Mariners Playland, and Congdons (all in Wells), and at Little River Tennis Courts in York.

THEATER, YEAR-ROUND   Acadia Repertory Theater in summer is at Somesville, Mount Desert Island 04660 (244-7260), and in winter at 183 Main Street, Bangor 04401 (942-3333). Portland Stage Company is at 15 Temple Street, Portland 04112 (774-0465). Also, the Portland Players (799-7337) present a winter season of productions.

THEATER, SUMMER   Lakewood Theater in Skowhegan (474-0080) and the Ogunquit Playhouse (646-5511) are among the oldest and most prestigious summer theaters in the country. The Theater at Monmouth, housed in the fine old Custom Hall (933-2952), the Brunswick Music Theater on the Bowdoin Campus (725-8769) are also well established. There is the Camden Shakespeare Company, which stages its performances in the town's outdoor amphitheater (236-8011), the Hackmatack Playhouse in Berwick (698-1807), and Acadia Repertory Theater (see above). Also the Touring Maine Summer Theater which stages productions throughout the state all season, not to be confused with the Maine Touring Program which sponsors a variety of performing artists (for details contact Maine State Commission of the Arts and the Humanities, State House Station 25, Augusta 04333; 289-2724). A list of community theaters is available from the same source. Other seasonal theaters include Carousel Music Theater (see Boothbay), Deertrees Performing Arts Festival in Harrison (583-2263), and the Thomas Playhouse in South Casco (655-7510).

WATERFALLS   The following are all easily accessible to families with small children: Smalls Falls on the Sandy River, off Route 4 between Rangeley and Philips—a picnic spot with a trail beside the falls. Step Falls on Wight Brook in Newry off Route 26 and—just a ways farther up the road in Grafton Notch State Park—Screw Auger Falls with its natural gorge. Another Screw Auger Falls can be approached via the Appalachian Trail: take the Katahdin Iron Works Road off ME 11 north of Brownville Junction. Kezar Falls on the Kezar River, is best reached via Lovell Road from ME 35 at North Waterford. An extensive list of "scenic waterfalls" is detailed in *The Maine Atlas and Gazeteer* (DeLorme Publishing Company). Check out ninety-foot Moxie Falls at The Forks.

WINDJAMMERS   Since 1935 a number of former fishing and cargo schooners have been sailing from Camden, carrying tourists up and down the Maine coast, in and around the islands of Penobscot Bay. At present just seven schooners and a ketch still are based in Camden, but from June to mid-September of 1981 a total of fifteen vessels were offering six-day cruises. A dozen of these boats belong to the Maine Windjammer Association which provides a handle for securing information: write to the Association, Box 317T, Rockport 04867 (236-4867) for brochures on each. These include Schooner *Adventure* (built 1926 in Essex, Massachusetts, a true Gloucester schooner carrying thirty-seven passengers); Schooner *Angelique* (new, steel-hulled, thirty-one passengers, captain and cook are husband and wife team); Schooner *Isaac H. Evans* (built in 1886, a clammer in Delaware Bay, husband and wife are captain and cook team, wife is also a licensed captain, twenty-two passengers); Schooner *Roseway* (another genuine Gloucester Fisherman, deep red sails, thirty-seven passengers, husband and wife captain and cook team, most famous cook in the fleet); Schooner *Mary Day* (built 1962, designed by her captain, Havilah S. Hawkins, twenty-eight passengers).

Schooner *Mattie* (twenty-eight passengers); and Schooner *Mercantile* (twenty-five passengers) are both veterans of thirty-five years carrying tourists out of Camden and, along with *Mistress* (just six guests), are now owned by Captain Les Bex and form "Windjammer Cruises" (PO Box 617, Camden 04843). All other windjammers are individually owned. They include Schooner *Lewis R. French* (built 1871, twenty-two guests);

Rafting on the Kennebec

Schooner *Stephen Taber* (built 1811, oldest documented sailing vessel in continuous use in the United States, twenty-two passengers); Schooner *Timberwind* (a former Portland pilot vessel, twenty passengers); and the *Sylina W. Beal* (built in 1911 in East Boothbay to transport herring to canneries, sails out of Belfast with eighteen passengers). There is also the *Victory Chimes* (596-6060), three-masted and the largest of all the schooners, which sails out of Rockland (PO Box 368) and is the newest Camden-based boat; and *The Joseph H. Hawkins* (built in 1922, twenty-four passengers, is Rockland-based). Schooner *Harvey Gamage* frequently has sailings with lecturers aboard (for information write: Schooner *Harvey Gamage*, 39 Waterside Land, Clinton CT; 203-669-7068).

Commercial windjammers have crews of from four to seven men and charge between $300 and $400 for a cruise which usually begins Monday morning and returns Saturday noon. Passengers usually lunch on deck, can count on a lobster bake on an island once during the week, and are encouraged to help sail the boat. Vessels anchor at night and passengers can row into shore to explore coastal towns. Electricity and hot water tend to be in short supply, but there is traditionally unlimited good food. Excessive drinking is discouraged, but guests are invited to bring their musical instruments. Children under fourteen are usually not permitted.

WHITE WATER RAFTING   White water rafting has grown so quickly in the past few years that it is difficult to keep track of all the groups offering day trips and longer expeditions down Maine's foaming rivers. Northern Whitewater Expeditions (PO Box 100, The Forks 04985; 663-2271) has been in business just seven seasons (as of 1982), and now serves some 6000 rafters a season; in Maine its rafts are on the Dead River in mid-May, the Kennebec June through September, and the Penobscot all summer. Kennebec Dories (PO Box 1, West Forks 04985; 663-2251 in summer; PO Box 800, Norwich VT the rest of the year) offers trips on

the Kennebec weekdays, the Dead River and Penobscot Rivers on weekends. Downeast Rafting Company, with its office at Northern Pines Cottages and Restaurant at the Forks (663-2277) and mailing address at Saco Bound, Box 113, Route 302, Center Conway NH 03813 (603-447-2177), offers trips weekdays on the Kennebec, weekends on the Penobscot. Eastern River Expeditions based in Greenville during the summer (Box 1173, Greenville 04441, 695-2411; rest of the year: 824 Petem Road, Kingsville MD 21087, 301-879-8555) runs trips on the Kennebec River, weekend trips on the Penobscot. There is also Unicorn Rafting Expeditions (Box 50, West Forks 04985 in summer; 31 Bracket Street, Milton MA 02186 rest of the year) with trips on the Kennebec and Penobscot. Wilderness Rafting Expeditions (PO Box 147-B, Rockwood 04478; 534-7328) offers trips on the Kennebec and Penobscot, as does Maine Whitewater, Inc. (Suite 454, Bingham 04920; 672-4814 in summer, 622-4814 the remainder of the year).

WHITE WATER CANOEING   See Canoeing

WHALE WATCHING   Beal & Bunker (244-3575 or 244-7457) in Northeast Harbor offer excursions July through August from the Sea Street Pier in Northeast Harbor. The boat leaves at 8:30 AM in search of whales, seals, and oceanic birds, returning at 4:30 PM Tuesday through Saturday; advance reservation necessary; $16 per adult, $12 per child under twelve. West Quoddy Marine Research Station (733-8895) in Lubec also offers periodic cruises, as does Maine Audubon (781-2330) which sponsors naturalist-led field trips to Jeffreys Ledge out of Portsmouth, New Hampshire—also a regular departure point for the whale watching trips with Viking Cruises (603-431-5500) that are organized by Allied Whale, College of the Atlantic, Bar Harbor, Maine. The former *Viking Queen*, now the *M/V Mount Katahdin*, offers spring and September whale watching trips from Rockland. Contact Penobscot Bay Line (PO Box 1112, Rockland, ME 04841).

A Calendar of Events

JANUARY High season for Portland cultural events: performances by the Portland Stage Company, the Portland Lyric Theater, the Portland Symphony Orchestra, and the Portland String Quartet. High season also for sports events in Cumberland County Civic Arena (Portland), and in Augusta's Civic Center. All the state's ski areas and ski touring centers are, of course, open, and at Sugarloaf/USA the last weekend and week of the month is White, White World Week, featuring theme parties and contests such as the national body sliding championships, open to all.

FEBRUARY Early in the month watch for the Southern Maine Dog Sledding Championship Races (locale changes each year), also for the Caribou Winter Carnival and Annual Snowroller Day in Monson. In mid-February Bethel's Winter Carnival Week includes stage shows, public suppers, and an ice fishing derby, as well as ski events at Sunday River. In late February the Carnival is at Rangeley, with the focus on skiing Saddleback Mountain.

MARCH Cultural and sports events continue in Portland and Augusta. At Sugarloaf/USA the month begins with a "Canoeski" (canoes race a slalom course down a slope), and the big event is the mid-month Heavyweight Ski Championships (participants must weight more than 250 pounds to enter). Major sled dog races are staged mid-month at Rangeley, and the last weekend marks the end of ski season in Bethel with a Pole, Paddle and Paw race at the Sunday River Ski Touring center (competitors use skis, canoes, and snow shoes).

APRIL Early April is sugaring season, but there is still spring skiing at Sugarloaf/USA and at Squaw Mountain at Moosehead Lake—an area where ski touring is still possible. Early in the month also watch for the Fisherman's Festival in Boothbay Harbor: events include a tug of war between Boothbay and Monhegan fishermen, a shrimp princess pageant, trap hauling, contests, and gaming. Also watch for white water canoe races.

MAY Early in May white water canoe championships are held in Rumford. Mid-month is the Sheep, Wool, and Craft Festival at the Cumberland Fairgrounds. The Maine Coast Marathon (limited to 1000 entrants) is run from Kennebunk to Biddeford Pool on the Sunday before Memorial Day, and on the Memorial Day weekend a fly-in is staged at the Owl's Head Transportation Museum.

JUNE The Miss Maine Pageant is mid-month in Brewer. Late in the month watch for the Acadian Festival in Madawaska, the Orono Festival, the North Atlantic Festival of Story Telling at the Rockport Opera House, and the Old Port Festival—a celebration of Portland's waterfront shopping and dining area which includes a parade, live concerts, performances, and games. Also watch for Schooner Days in Camden: visitors can tour the fleet of commercial windjammers; other related events include a chicken barbecue.

JULY Maine packs more events into July than the rest of the year combined. Independence Day is celebrated with exceptional enthusiasm in Bridgton, Bowdoinham, Rangeley, Bar Harbor, Gardiner, Grand Lake Stream, and in Bath (where festivities last all week). Other events usually scheduled for the July 4th weekend include: the Great Kennebec River Whatever Floats Race (beginning in Augusta), the World's Fastest Lobster Boat Races in Beals-Jonesport, the Northern Maine Lumberjack Roundup in Ashland, and the Folk Festival in Rockport. The Penobscot Indian Pageant at Indian Island (Old Town) may or may not come off, but later in the week you can count on the Miss Dumpy Pageant and Giant Trash Parade, and the following

M. D. C. I.

Skowhegan Fair

weekend is always Windjammer Days in Boothbay Harbor (events include a parade of schooners and countless smaller sailing craft, also a colorful parade, street dances, and public feeds).

Mid-month events include the Damariscotta Oyster Festival, Southwest Harbor Days, the Belfast Bay Festival (including a mammoth chicken barbecue), the Maine Potato Blossom Festival in Fort Fairfield, the annual Open House and Garden Day in Camden, the Yarmouth Clam Festival (Maine's biggest clam bake), the Maine Quilt Show and Sale in Augusta, Mollyockett Days in Bethel, "A Wild Mountain Time" in Rangeley, the Aroostook River Raft Race in Caribou, the Acadian Scottish Festival in Trenton (near Bar Harbor), and Casco Days in Casco.

Nearing the month's end watch for Friendship Sloop Days in Friendship, a major arts and crafts sale in Bridgton, the annual Fiddlers Contest in East Benton, the Bean Hole Festival in Oxford (Maine's biggest bean bake, but be sure to come by early afternoon while the supply lasts), the Central Maine Egg Festival in Pittsfield, Homecoming Weekend in Machiasport, and the Canadian-American Friendship Festival and Great Beach Race in Old Orchard Beach.

The very last weekend in July, frequently spilling into the first days of August, is the Maine Seafoods Festival in Rockland, without question the world's biggest lobster feed, also a weekend of pageantry, contests, and children's amusements.

AUGUST   The first weekend is dominated by the Maine Festival of the Arts, a celebration of things sung, danced, written, filmed, and otherwise created in Maine, staged for three days from morning to night on the Bowdoin College Campus in Brunswick. Also early in the month watch for the United Maine Craftsmen Fair at the Cumberland Fairgrounds, for Old Home Days in Andover, for the Winter Harbor Lobster Festival, the Young Fool Renaissance Fair in Blue Hill, the Annual Transportation Rally at Owls Head, the Indian Festival at Pleasant Point in Eastport, and the Central Maine Fair in Lewiston.

Mid-month there is the Island Arts Association Summer Fair in Bar Harbor, the Maine Coast Artists Auction in Rockport, the Skowhegan State Fair, the Seacoast Crafts Fair in York Harbor.

Mid-to-late-August is prime time for blueberries, offered at countless public suppers, and at

festivals held in Machias, Winslow, Rangeley, and Union—where the event is soon followed by the old-style Union Fair.

In late August also watch for the Skowhegan Logging Days, for the Downeast Jazz Festival in Camden, and a canoe race in Windsor.

SEPTEMBER   Special Labor Day celebrations occur in Buckfield, and in Blue Hill—where the old-fashioned Hancock County Agricultural Fair is held. Early in September you can also count on "Loggin Days" in Bangor, and the Springfield Fair. The Topsham Fair and Franco-American Festival in Old Town are mid-month. The Common Ground Country Fair (rallying point for the state's organic farmers) is a colorful event at the Windsor Fairgrounds in late September, also the time for the Cumberland Fair and for Fall Foliage Days in Rangeley.

OCTOBER   The big event is the Fryeburg Fair, usually a week-long happening which includes the Columbus Day weekend and coincides with peak foliage in the White Mountains, also the time for the Owls Head Fall Flying Day Finale, and for Boothbay Harbor's Fall Foliage Festival. Mid-month is the Bass Harbor Lobster Festival, and the Sugarloaf Annual Arts Auction. If you happen to be in Caribou in late October, check out the Fall Arts and Crafts Festival, and in Greenville don't miss the Octoberfest at Squaw Mountain.

NOVEMBER   This is hunting season, and there are a number of hunters' breakfasts and suppers. You can always count on the Old Town Rotary Club Hunters Breakfast served from 4 to 8 AM on the first day of deer season. In late November Boothbay Harbor fends off the coastal chill with a Coastal Country Weekend.

DECEMBER   A major Christmas Fair is put on in Portland mid-December by the United Maine Craftsmen. With its cultural offerings (see January), and its abundance of shops and restaurants, Portland is well worth visiting in December, the month during which its ski areas and ski touring centers also get under way. The official First Day of Winter is celebrated in Farmington with Chester Greenwood Day, a major celebration in the birthplace of the boy who (aged 15) invented earmuffs in 1873. At Sugarloaf/USA it is Yellow Nose Vole Day, cause for a snowdance, bonfire, and torchlight parade.

SOUTHERN COAST

The Yorks

York, Maine's southernmost coastal resort, is divided into so many villages that Mark Twain once observed, "it is difficult to throw a brick . . . in any one direction without danger of disabling a postmaster." Not counting Scotland and York Corners, it still includes York Village, York Harbor, York Beach, and Cape Neddick—all such different villages that locals can't bring themselves to talk of them as one town, referring instead to "The Yorks."

Sam Clemens (the real Mark Twain) was one among a group of wealthy nineteenth-century summer people who bought up the splendid colonial buildings in York Village. They appreciated the fact that the old jail, school, church, burying ground and abundance of 1740s homes add up to the oldest surviving village in Maine. Novelist William Dean Howells is credited with the idea of turning the "old gaol" (built 1720) into a museum in 1900, a time when you could count the country's historic house museums on your fingers.

In the Old Gaol today you learn about the village's bizarre history, about its origins as an Indian settlement called Agamenticus, one of many wiped out by a 1616 plague. Settled by colonists in 1631, in 1642 it became Georgiana, America's first chartered city, only to be demoted to the town of York, part of Massachusetts, in 1670. Fierce Indian raids followed, but by the mid-eighteenth century the present colonial village was established, a crucial way station between Portsmouth and points East. York diminished in importance again as the State of Maine evolved.

It was in the late nineteenth century that wealthy summer residents built their shingled cottages in York Harbor and the less privileged began arriving by electric street car to stay in summer hotels and walk the York Beach boardwalk. The sand at York Beach is darker and coarser than that at Ogunquit Beach, a few miles north. But here the parking is either free (along Long Sands), or just the price of the meter (at Short Sands). York Beach continues to catch the crowds, permitting York Village to cater to history buffs and York Harbor to drowse genteely.

GUIDANCE **York Chamber of Commerce** maintains an information booth on US 1 at the I-95 exit for the Yorks, open weekends in June and September, daily in July and August (363-4422). Off-season write: York Chamber of Commerce, Box 374, York Beach, Maine 03910. Request the leaflet guide to historic sites, walking and driving tours of "Old York," also the booklet guide to "Old York By The Sea," which includes lodging, dining and sightseeing information. *New England Miniature*, subtitled "A History of York, Maine," by George Ernst is an outstanding book, worth perusing in local inns or in the research room at the Emerson Wilcox House.

GETTING THERE   Greyhound stops at York Village and York Beach, Trailways at York Corners. Limo service from Portland and Boston airports available from George Munroe, year-round (646-9067).

YORK VILLAGE HISTORIC DISTRICT   The Old Gaol (363-3872). Open mid-June to mid-October, 10:30-5 daily except Sunday 1:30-5. Fee. Built in 1702, this hip-roofed combination jailer's house and jail was used until 1860, when York ceased to be the county seat. The jail itself incorporates timbers from its 1653 predecessor. This is one of the most fascinating historical houses in New England.

Emerson Wilcox House. Same hours and fees as the Old Gaol. This handsome house has been a tavern, a post office and a home. It reflects a variety of eras between the 1740s and 1830s.

First Parish Church. An outstanding mid-eighteenth-century church with a fine old cemetery full of stones with death's heads and old English spelling, even a "Witch's Grave."

Jefferds Tavern (363-4703). Open Memorial Day through mid-October, daily 10:30-5, Sunday 1:30-5. Fee. A restored eighteenth-century tavern.

Old School House. Same hours as Tavern. Free. Next to the tavern, across from the cemetery, peopled with manikins.

OTHER HISTORIC SITES   The Elizabeth Perkins House. Open late June through Labor Day, daily 10:30-5, Sunday 1:30-5. Fee. Just down Lindsay Road and across Sewall's Bridge (a replica of the first pile bridge in America, built on this spot in 1761), this 1730 house is furnished the way it was as a Victorian-era summer cottage. It is the only house in town which tells the story of the Perkins family, nineteenth-century preservationists and literati.

John Hancock Warehouse. Open same hours as the Perkins House. Small fee. Owned at one time by John Hancock, this is an old commercial building near Sewall's Bridge containing displays of antique tools and ship's models.

Sayward House. Open June 1-October 15, Tuesday, Thursday, and Sundays, 1-5. Fee. On ME 103. A fine 1730s home in York Harbor, next to the original town marketplace. $2.

BEACHES   Long Sands. An extensive stretch of coarse, grey sand stretching from York Harbor to the Nubble, backed by Route 1A and summer cottages.

Short Sands. A shorter stretch of coarse, grey sand with a parking lot (meters), toilets, and the Victorian-era resort village of York Beach just behind it.

York Harbor Beach. Small, pebbly, but pleasant. Limited parking.

Cape Neddick Beach. Smallest of all, at the river's mouth, sheltered, good for children, nearby picnicking.

WALKS   **Shore Path.** For more than a mile you can pick your way along the town's pleasantest piece of shorefront. Begin at Sewall's Bridge and walk east until you reach the Wiggly Bridge (a mini-suspension bridge) and continue across ME 103, by Sayward House, across the Saltwater Farm's entrance, down across the beach, and on along the top of the rocks to East Point.

Nubble (also known as Cape Neddick) **Light.** From Shore Road take Broadway out to this 1879 lighthouse. There is limited parking and a small park, splendid views, and rocks to climb.

Mount Agamenticus. The highest hill on the Atlantic seaboard between Florida and Mount Desert. A defunct ski area, it is accessible by its access road from Cat Mountain road off Route 1 in Cape Neddick.

DEEP SEA FISHING   **Rambler II** (363-3127) departs from Sewall's Bridge for half-day trips on weekdays, full days on weekends. Rental tackle available. Contact Richard LaBonte.

Porpoise III (363-4299) leaves York Harbor on half-day trips weekdays, all day on weekends, also evening cruises. Tackle and bait available. Contact Captain Wayne Perkins.

"E-Z" (363-5634), also out of York Harbor, is available for day-long fishing charters. Contact Lawrence Grant.

OTHER ACTIVITIES   **Golf.**   York Golf and Tennis Club (363-2683). 18 holes, par 70 course, rental carts. **Tennis.**   Little River Tennis Courts (363-5557). **Horseback Riding.**   North Village Stables Trail Rides (646-8054). **Theater.**   Hackmatack Playhouse in Berwick (698-1807) presents summer stock performances most evenings, Thursday matinees. Also check York County Summer Theater (327-2667) in Sanford, and Theatre by the Sea in Portsmouth, New Hampshire (603-431-6660). **Bike Rentals.** "Big Bob" Berger and Son, Route 1 at York Corners. **Commercial Attractions.**   In York Beach, Animal Forest Park (Route 1 and village entrances). Open daily June through Labor Day weekend. Weekends in May and through Columbus Day. Animals include goats doing tricks, paddleboats. There are also smaller, adjacent boardwalk attractions.

RESTAURANTS   **Dockside Dining Room** (363-4800). Open late May through Columbus Day, closed Mondays, otherwise open for lunch and dinner. Glass-walled, overlooking York Harbor, seafood and duckling specialties.

Bill Foster's Downeast Lobster and Clambake (363-3255; 3720). ME 12 in York Harbor. Open late June-Labor Day, through October on weekends. There is an ordinary restaurant, the Lobster Kettle. Then there is the adjacent, weather proofed pavilion on which (by reservation only) you can enjoy folk music and full-fledged lobster bakes complete with clams, hot dogs, lobster cooked in seaweed, and watermelon. The clambakes can also be reserved for groups on off-nights.

The York Harbor Inn (363-5119), route 1A in York Harbor, serves lunch and dinner year-round, and offers a Friday evening buffet and Sunday brunch in attractive old public rooms.

Nubble Light Dining Room (363-4053). Open late May to early September. Spectacular location, zero atmosphere, moderately expensive prices, moderate food.

The Goldenrod (363-2621) in York Beach. Open Memorial to Labor Day. In business since 1896, one of the best family restaurants in New England; same menu all day from 8 AM to 11 PM, served up in a polished, wooden dining room with an old-style soda fountain. Famous saltwater taffy kisses cooked and pulled in the windows. Homemade ice cream, good sandwiches, generous hot plates, reasonable prices.

El's Fried Clams (363-2101). Open March through December, US 1 in Cape Neddick. Over the past four decades this landmark has evolved from a clamshack into a restaurant seating 100, with picnic tables outside. Quality is consistent, prices reasonable, open 6:30 AM-11 PM.

Brown's Old Fashion Ice Cream. Open summer season 10:30-10:30, Nubble Road, a quarter mile beyond the Light House, all ice cream made on premises, exotic flavors.

The Lobster Barn (363-4721). Route 1, open daily, lunch and dinner, three miles north of the York exit. A good local reputation and all the steamers you can eat in the bar.

HOTELS AND INNS   **Dockside Guest Quarters** (363-2868). Open Memorial Day to Columbus Day. Harris Island in York Harbor. Innkeepers Harriette and David Lusty imbue this fine little island hideaway with a warmth which few inns possess. The centerpiece here is a gracious nineteenth-century house with five guest rooms, three with private baths, all with water views. There are also sixteen modern glass-faced units scattered along the shore, five with kitchens. A nominally priced muffins-and-juice breakfast is laid out on the dining room table, a morning gathering place for guests who check the blackboard weather forecast and plan their days. Since David Lusty also operates the neighboring marina it is easy to take sailing lessons or to arrange a run upriver or out to Boon Island. There are also lawn games and good books.

Stage Neck Inn (363-3850). Open April through November, an attractive modern complex of 56 rooms built in 1973 on the site of a nineteenth-century inn. Sited on its own peninsula, it offers water views (request the water), a formal dining room and cruise-ship luxury. It is adjacent to York Harbor Beach and has two clay tennis courts. Ideal for groups and conferences. $70-90 per couple plus tax. Much lower off-season and group rates.

The Ocean House (363-3951). Open all year. A rambling white Victorian hotel which has been renovated in recent years and offers 60 rooms between its main building and motel. $27-53 double.

The York Harbor Inn (363-5119). A dozen guest rooms, five with ocean views. Open year-round.

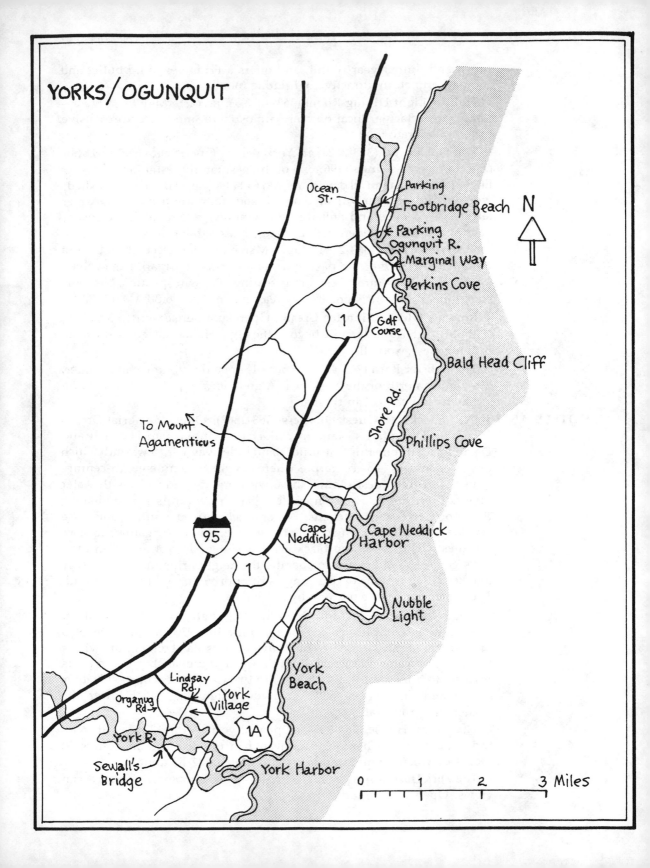

YORKS/OGUNQUIT

Ocean St.

Parking

Footbridge Beach

N

Parking

Ogunquit R.

Marginal Way

Perkins Cove

1

Golf
Course

Bald Head Cliff

Shore Rd.

Phillips Cove

To Mount
Agamenticus

95

Cape
Neddick

Cape Neddick
Harbor

1

Nubble
Light

Lindsay
Rd.

York
Beach

Organug
Rd.

York
Village

1A

York R.

Sewall's
Bridge

York Harbor

0   1   2   3 Miles

The Cliff House. Nearer to York Beach, this fine old resort bills its home as Ogunquit so we have, too (see Ogunquit).

GUESTHOUSES   **The Moorelowe** (363-2526) in York Harbor is a fine old home run by Hazel and Kenneth Day "for guests of distinction."

In York Beach **The Tides Inn** (363-4087) at 44 Freeman Street, **Nirvana By-the-Sea** (363-2628), and **The Emerald Sea Guest House** (363-4826), are all open just for the summer season.

COTTAGES   York Beach is chock-a-block with rental cottages; listings are available from the Chamber of Commerce (see Guidance), and from Ellis Insurance Agency, York Beach.

SPECIAL STORES   **Saltwater Farm** in York Harbor (363-3182) will mail Maine lobster, ready to cook in its own container, up to 1800 miles away. Request the catalog listing a variety of seafood specialties which this store will also ship.

Williams Dry Goods Store, York Village, opposite Fire Station. An exceptionally good small town shop for the basics you forgot to bring: socks, children's clothes, sweaters, and the like.

BERWICK AND KITTERY   York is well situated for exploring Portsmouth, New Hampshire (just twelve miles south) as well as the following sites in Berwick and Kittery.

Sarah Orne Jewett Birthplace, on Rte. 236 in South Berwick. A 1774 house preserved by the Society for the Preservation of New England Antiquities (SPNEA) just as the Maine author left it. Open June through October 15, Tuesday, Thursday, and Sunday, 1-5. $1.50.

Hamilton House, South Berwick, Vaughan's Lane (turn left off Route 236 opposite junction of Route 91). A magnificent Georgian mansion set in landscaped grounds overlooking the river, setting of *The Tory Lover* by Sarah Orne Jewett. Also owned by SPNEA, same hours as above. $2.

Lady Pepperell House, Kittery Point on Route 103. A fine eighteenth-century home, beautifully furnished on a fine site, built for the widow of the conquerer of Fort Louisbourg. Open June-October 15, Tuesday, Thursday, Saturday, and Sunday, 1-5. $1.50.

Fort McClary. A hexagonal fort built but never finished for the War of 1812. Further additions were built for the Civil War, but the fort was never finished. A state-owned site on Route 103 at Kittery Point, great spot for a picnic.

Kittery Historical and Naval Museum (439-3080). Open year-round and by appointment. Rogers Road off Route 1. Photos and exhibits, including several ships models. Free.

Kittery Navy Yard. No longer open to the public but still a very visible presence, responsible for building half the submarines (75) in the American service during World War II.

Fort Foster Park (439-3800). East of Fort McClary on Route 103, turn off to Gerrish Island. A ninety-two acre park with picnicking, a beach and fish pier, open June through October, 9-5. Good for cross-country skiing.

FACTORY OUTLETS   **Dansk Factory Outlet** (439-0484). Sunday-Saturday, 9-6. US 1, Kittery Mall. Dansk cookware and gift items.
Seventh Avenue (439-4258). Sunday-Saturday, 10-5:30. Next door to Dansk. Clothing for men and women: shirts, sportswear, ties, robes.
SPECIAL EVENTS   **Mid-August:** York Annual Antique Show and Firemen's Field Day. **Late August:** Annual Seacoast Crafts Fair.

Fredrik D. Bodin

Ogunquit

The Abenakis long ago picked this strip of firm beach and white dune as their "Ogunquit," or "beautiful place by the sea." The Indians' enthusiasm for the spot has been shared in more recent summertimes by generations of Americans who winter inland.

Hotels began to appear around 1888, when a bridge was built across the river dividing beach from town. Those first guests from faraway New York and Philadelphia arrived by the Boston & Maine. Residents of nearer cities began arriving by the Atlantic Shore Line trolleys in 1907. Today the village is still well served by bus lines and—thanks to the old-style trackless trolleys which connect all parts of town during summer months—it remains one of New England's best bets for a carless vacation.

The townspeople—most of whom seem to be named Perkins, Maxwell or Littlefield—have remained receptive to the needs of summer visitors and to the maintenance of the sites which attract them. Since the Twenties the town's three-mile tongue of beach and dune has been public, and since the Fifties the mile-long Marginal Way, an exceptional ocean side path, has been maintained by a town group.

Although Ogunquit is actually Maine's newest town (formally founded in 1980), it seceded spiritually from neighboring Wells many moons ago, establishing itself as a summer magnet for top artists and actors.

Still, the beach is the big lure. For our money it is the most beautiful in Maine. There are surf and soft sand, space for kite flying, and a sheltered strip along the mouth of the Ogunquit River for toddlers.

In Perkins Cove, a picturesquely cluttered inlet traversed by a much-painted draw-footbridge, more than forty restaurants, galleries and shops are housed in shingled old fish shacks and artists' studios. On weekends, daytripping Bostonians eddy through the Cove and spread over the beach, but they recede on Sunday evenings as predictably as the tide. Ogunquit is relatively peaceful midweek.

The Chamber of Commerce lists a dozen hotels and inns (many of which have spawned modern motel units), thirty-two guesthouses (most of which would be called inns anywhere else), and thirty-eight motels and cottage colonies—a number vastly augmented by the US 1 cottages and motels, where families tend to congregate. Young singles meet in clean and comfortable inns and guesthouses, which contrast in plumbing and price with the finer inns. We should mention that, since a few guesthouses are now patronized by gays, it's wise to ask before booking.

GUIDANCE **Chamber of Commerce,** Box 2289, Ogunquit, Maine 03907 (646-5533) is open Memorial Day-Columbus Day, weekdays 9-5. The Chamber maintains a walk-in information cottage at the southern end of the village on US 1, and keeps track of current vacancies. It is also a place to read menus and check excursions and events. For off-season information, write the Chamber of Commerce or phone 646-2939, 9-12.

GETTING THERE **Trailways** and **Greyhound** both offer frequent service. **Munroe's Taxis** serve the Portland and Boston airports. (646-9067).

GETTING AROUND Trolleys, sponsored by the Chamber of Commerce, circle the village at frequent intervals, late June through late September, 25c a ride. There are also moped and bike rentals (Alexandre's Gulf Station and Move'n'on).

PARKING We know of five public lots: (1) Between US 1 and River Road (convenient to village and beach but $3 in high season); (2) Foot of Beach Street at the head of Ogunquit Beach, $4 on summer weekends; (3) Limited free parking at Israel's Head; (4) Adequate parking at Footbridge Beach (half hour free, then $3); (5) Perkins Cove, free but limited.

SIGHTS TO SEE **Museum of Art of Ogunquit** (646-8827). Open late June-Labor Day, daily 10:30-5, Sunday 1:30-5, Shore Road, free. Built superbly of local stone and wood with enough glass to let in the beauty of the cove it faces, this museum displays works by such locals as Henry Strater and Reginald Marsh. There is also a sculpture garden.

Perkins Cove. A manmade anchorage with a draw-footbridge traversing its mouth, and a clutch of weathered cottages alongside. The cottages are now filled with seasonal shops and restaurants, and excursion boats are based beside the bridge. Forget trying to land one of the few parking places here in summer. Come by trolley or on foot via the Marginal Way.

Marginal Way. In 1923 this walkway along the rocky shore—from Shore Road in the middle of the Village to Perkins Cove—was given by local philanthropist Josiah Chase. It has evolved from a sandy path to a concrete one with stone benches. I liked its rustic version better, but my children love playing along the smooth rocks here as much as I did as a child. There is limited parking at the mini-lighthouse midway.

BEACHES Three-mile-long **Ogunquit Beach** can be approached three ways: (1) The most expensive ($4) and popular way is from the foot of Beach Street. There are boardwalk snacks here, changing facilities, and toilets, and it is here that the beach forms a tongue between the ocean and Ogunquit River. (2) The Footbridge Beach access (take Ocean Street off US 1 north of the village) offers restrooms, is less crowded, and is the same price as (3) the Moody Beach entrance (turn off US 1 at Eldridge Street). The question of whether Ogunquit or Wells should be getting the $3 fee for the Moody Beach entrance is being hotly debated; as of '81 it was still Ogunquit.

THEATER   **Ogunquit Playhouse** (646-5511), on Route 1 just south of the village. Billing itself as "America's Foremost Summer Theater," this grand old theater (now air-conditioned) opened for its first season in 1933, and continues to feature top stars in productions staged every evening during the season except Sunday. Matinees are Wednesday and Friday.

GALLERIES   **Barn Gallery** (646-5370). Shore Road at Bourne's Lane. Free. Mid-June to mid-September. In addition to quality exhibits there is a full summer calendar of concerts, films, lectures, and demonstrations.

Ogunquit Art Center, Hoyt's Lane (646-2453). June 21-Labor Day. Free. Changing exhibits.

BOAT EXCURSIONS   *Finestkind* from Barnacle Billy's (646-5227). Summer season. On fifty-minute trips offered frequently every day, passengers watch lobster traps being hauled. In '81 the fee was $3.70 per adult, $2 per child, more for the breakfast run. There are also cruises to Nubble Lighthouse twice daily, and 4:30 cocktail cruises.

Sea Hawk (646-7222), a party fishing boat. Contact Captain Jack Miller.

Ugly Ann '76 (646-7202). Six-hour-long deep sea fishing charters.

Go Go Girl (646-3524), a twenty-foot sloop, is available for charter for up to six people. Sailing lessons are also available.

OTHER ACTIVITIES.   **Horseback riding.** North Village Stables, Berwick Road (646-8054). Lessons, trail rides, pony rides, and hay rides.

Golf. Cliff Country Club, a nine-hole course two miles south of the village center.

Tennis. Public courts and recreation area. Agamenticus Road.

Walks. Old Trolley Trail, an interesting nature walk and cross-country ski trail, begins on Pine Hill Road North. There is also Mount Agamenticus, a defunct ski area, the highest hill on the Atlantic between Florida and Bar Harbor. Take the Big A access road off Agamenticus Road.

ACCOMMODATIONS   Note that in general the rates quoted are '81, high season.

Cliff House (646-5124). Open May to October. Atop ninety-foot-high Bald Head Cliff, Shore Road. A landmark since 1872, under the management of its founding family. Seventy-three glass-faced motel units (five with kitchens) overlooking the ocean. The main dining room, lounge, reading, and game rooms are in a handsome old building which serves as a centerpiece for the complex. Golf, pool, tennis, and a shuttle into the village. $36-$76 daily, $500-$410 per week, three-day minimum on holiday weekends, cheaper off season.

Dune Lawn (646-2403). Open Memorial Day-Labor Day. A 1921 stucco mansion on River Road just across the bridge from the beach. Rooms are huge, gracious. There is jazz Sunday nights in the Drum Room Lounge. $50-100, depending on whether bath is shared.

The Lemon Tree (646-7070). Open June 19-Labor Day. Across from the entrance to the Marginal Way on Shore Road, handy to village shops. Six attractive guestrooms $30-45, fifteen efficiency units $55-70, a pool, pleasant public rooms.

The Dunes (646-2612). Open late May to mid-October. US 1 just north of the village, fronting on the Ogunquit River which offers swimming at high tide; otherwise you can row across to the main beach. One- and two-bedroom cottages with fireplaces and motel units are offered.

The Old Village Inn (646-7088). Open year-round. US 1. Five rooms, two with private baths, two suites, nice but nothing special. $50-55, $30-35 off season. One of the few places open year-round.

The Governor William F. King (646-5534). Open May 1-Thanksgiving. The former Chapman House, an 1867 twenty-five room hotel with pleasant public rooms, halfway between the village shops and Perkins Cove. The place actors at the Ogunquit Playhouse have long stayed.

Norseman Motor Inn (646-7024). Open early April through October. Unbeatable location right on the beach, ninety-five units, five-day minimum during high season. $54-65 double, cheaper off season.

Sparhawk (646-5562). Open late June to Labor Day. Shore Road, splendid view, descended from a shingled old resort hotel by the same name but completely rebuilt as a luxury motel. Tennis. $59-70. Four-day minimum on holiday weekends.

Perkins Cove Inn (646-2232). Open May through Columbus Day. Beautifully sited on Woodbury Lane overlooking Perkins Cove. Fourteen rooms in a rambling old summer inn, very clean, pleasant, private baths, coffee served. $30-45, cheaper off season.

Yardarm Village (646-7006). Open May through mid-October. A delightful complex of main house and cottages within walking distance of Perkins Cove. Nine rooms in the house, thirteen cottages, breakfast served. $25-30, cheaper off season.

Ye Olde Perkins Place (646-2249). Open late June to mid-September. Overlooking the ocean beyond Perkins Cove on Shore Road, a 1717 homestead with five second-floor rooms, three in an annex, coffee served, within walking distance of a pebble beach. Not for children. $20-$25 double.

The Hayes Guest House (646-2277). Mid-May to Columbus Day. Handy to both village shops and Perkins Cove, five rooms in the Federal-era house, plus two apartments. Guestrooms are $25-38 double, a studio is $40, and a two-bedroom apartment with dining room and sun porch is $60 per night. Elinor Hayes is a fine hostess with a loyal following.

Captain Lorenz Perkins Lodging (646-7825). Open year-round. US 1, northern edge of the village, eight guest rooms with shared baths and efficiency apartments. $30-40 double in high season.

Marimor Motor Inn (646-7397). Open mid-June to early September. Attractive central guestrooms, efficiency units, two apartments, $20-28 double, $290-385 weekly for apartments.

Blue Shutters (646-2163). Open year-round. Centrally located, includes continental breakfast served in room. Five rooms in the house, efficiencies. $40-55 in season.

RESTAURANTS   The Whistling Oyster (646-9521). Open year-round for lunch, dinner, Sunday brunch, closed Tuesdays in winter. A fine old restaurant —the original burned in '76 but has been nicely rebuilt—with an elegant dark wood-paneled dining room and hearth, located in Perkins Cove. Bostonians drive here for dinner, and it is a first rate, moderately-expensive-but-well-worth-it place.

Tavern at Clay Hill Farm (646-2272), on Agamenticus Road. Open year-round, closed Monday and Tuesday in winter. Dinners and Sunday brunch. An old farm, with a gracious setting, expensive, but strong local following.

Ogunquit Lobster Pound (646-2516), on US 1 north of the village. Open Memorial Day to Labor Day; lunch, dinner. Approaching its fortieth year under the same family, this is an exceptional restaurant. You order and watch your lobster cook in the big stone pits, eat either in the rustic log building or outside on swinging, wood-canopied tables. Beer and wine are available along with cheeseburgers and steak, but lobster and clams are what the place is about. Try the lobster stew and deep dish blueberry pie.

Barbara Dean's (646-2241), in the village. A summer season landmark specializing in splendid breakfasts, but also a pleasant lunch and dinner spot.

Barnacle Billy's (646-5575). Open May through mid-October. No longer the bargain family dining spot it once was, this continues to be a popular place to eat lobster, clams and other basics either on outdoor dining decks overlooking Perkins Cove, or in the attractive dining room with cheerful fireplaces. A blackboard lists daily specials.

The Old Village Inn (646-7088), in the village. Open year-round, closed Monday and Tuesday in deep winter. Open for lunch and dinner. Attractive dining rooms, one glassed-in as a greenhouse, an English pub-style bar, lunch from $5 and dinner from $10.

Valerie's (646-2476). Mid-May through mid-October, cocktails and dinner. An old-shoe landmark on US 1 just south of the village.

Gypsy Sweethearts (646-7021) in the village. Late May through October 12. Breakfast and dinner, cocktails. Moderately priced, atmosphere, imaginative menu.

SPECIAL EVENTS   Sidewalk Art Show, in mid-July and mid-August. **Antique Shows** at the Dunaway Community Center. **Photo Contest,** sponsored by the Chamber of Commerce, begins October of one year, and is judged September 30 of the following year.

Wells

There is far more to Wells than the lineup of motels, cottage colonies, shops and restaurants which meet the eye along US 1. Named for the English cathedral town, Wells is actually very old, incorporated in 1653. Because of its seven miles of oceanfront, it has been a resort since the late 19th century. Here, however, the Webhannet River and extensive marshland divide the beach from US 1. Wells Beach itself is now backed with summer cottages, most of them private or rented only by the month or season. Motor courts began opening along US 1 in the 1920s; many of the best of them are still in business.

Because of the spread-out nature of the place, you need a car here to get around. And there is a lot to see, especially if you are a birder or a person who can appreciate the beauty of the town's beach, harbor and marshland.

GUIDANCE **Wells Chamber of Commerce,** PO Box 356, Wells, Maine 04090 (646-2451). Open daily June through August, weekends in September, housed in an old red schoolhouse just off US 1 on Eldredge Road. Request their booklet guide.

GETTING THERE Exit 2 off the Maine Turnpike takes you right into Wells Corner. **Trailways** and **Greyhound** also offer frequent service.

BEACHES Reasonably priced parking permits for visitors staying in Wells are available from the Municipal Building.

Wells Beach. Limited free parking right in the middle of the village of Wells Beach. Wooden casino and boardwalk, clamshacks, clean public toilets, a cluster of motels, and concrete benches—a gathering point for older people who sit enjoying the view of the wide beach.

Moody Beach. From the village drive south more than a mile along the beach on Webhannet Drive (a road lined with summer cottages), or take Eldredge Road from US 1, and you come to Moody Point. The parking area here charges $3 in season.

Wells Harbor. From the village drive north along Atlantic Avenue to the parking lot of Wells Harbor, which charges $2 at this writing.

Drakes Island. There are three parking areas on this land spit (take Drakes Island Road off US 1) with varying fees.

OTHER SIGHTS TO SEE **Wells Harbor.** A pleasant place to walk along a granite jetty, and a good fishing spot.

Rachel Carson National Wildlife Refuge is off ME 9, subtly marked.

There are 1600 acres here, but the nature trail is just one mile long, a loop through a white pine forest and along the Little River through a salt marsh area. Maps and guides are available from the resident manager's office. This is primarily a birding spot, one of a number of preserves along the Atlantic Flyway.

Wells Auto Museum (646-9064). Open mid-June to Labor Day daily, 10-9; from Memorial Day and into mid-September on weekends, 10-6. More than sixty antique cars, including a 1908 Baker Electric once owned by John D. Rockefeller, also assorted memorabilia: nickelodeons, picture machines, toys. In '81: $2 adult, $1 child, free under six.

Museum at Historic First Church. Opposite Wells Plaza, basic memorabilia, check with Chamber of Commerce for current hours.

OTHER ACTIVITIES **Golf.** Mini-golf at Wells Beach Resort Campground, otherwise see Ogunquit and the Kennebunks. **Tennis.** Wells Recreation Area, ME 9A and Ocean View Tennis Court, Landing Road. **Fishing.** Tackle and bait can be rented at Wells Harbor; the obvious fishing spots are the municipal dock and harbor jetties, surf casting near the mouth of the Mousam River. Sailboat and motorboat rentals are available from Wells Harbor Marina (646-7087). **Sailing.** *The Song Bird,* a thirty-four foot Tartan sloop, is available for charter, complete with captain. Phone the Seagull (646-9087).

FACTORY OUTLETS Wells calls itself the "Outlet Capitol of Maine," with good reason. Within a mile or so along US 1 you can shop for shoes at Bass, Dexter, Dunham, and Quoddy Moccasin outlets, also pick up children's bargains at the Carter Factory Outlet, sportswear at Jaymar Ruby, sleepwear at Formfit Rogers, and shirts and quality clothing at Hathaway; also bedding and towels at Bates Mill Store and the Cannon Outlet, both on Rte. 1.

ACCOMMODATIONS Some five dozen lodging places are listed in the current Chamber of Commerce guide. These include motels, apartments, cottage colonies and guesthouses in Wells Beach (within walking distance of the beach), and a long lineup of "motor courts" along US 1. A number of the motor courts are outstanding—a special breed of Maine coastal cottage with knotty pine interior and screen porches, spanking clean and comfortable. Most of those on the ocean side of US 1 have property extending into the marshes. For an additional listing of privately owned beach cottages ($200-750 per week) check with Garnsey Bros. Real Estate (646-8301), RFD 1, Box 598, Moody Point, Wells. Most of these rentals are booked by phone in the spring.

Grey Gull Inn (646-7501), 321 Webhannet Drive, Wells Beach. Open year-round. Built in 1902, this classic beach hotel offers twelve rooms, pleasant, bright, and all but two with sea views. A good place to visit in winter as well as in August. Charlotte Much is a fine hostess and housekeeper, while her husband Dennis is a locally respected chef. The attractive dining room is open to the public for breakfast (included in the guest rates) and dinner in warmer months, and for Sunday breakfast

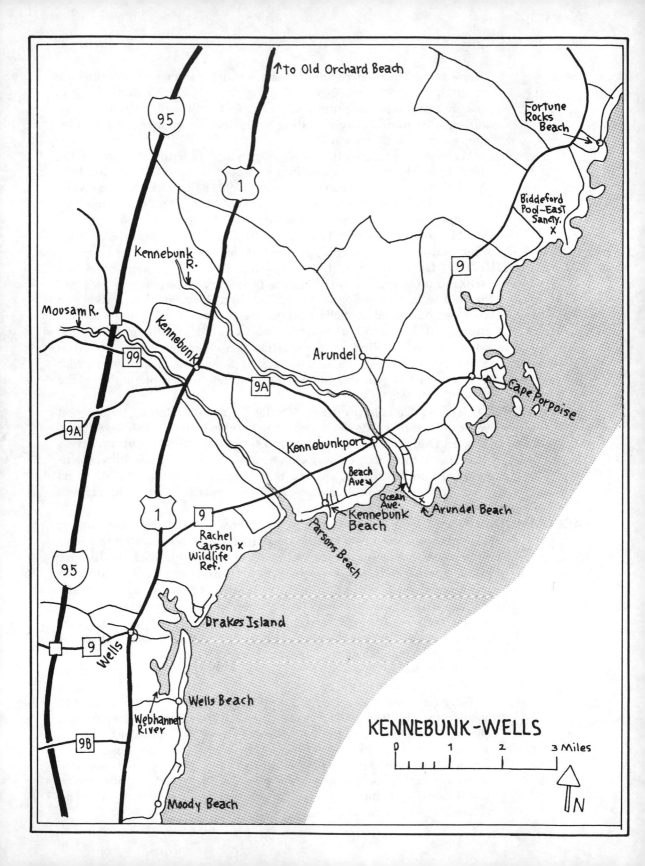

↑to Old Orchard Beach

95

1

Fortune
Rocks
Beach

Kennebunk
R.

Biddeford
Pool-East
Sandy.
×

9

Mousam R.

99

Kennebunk

Arundel

Cape Porpoise

9A

9A

Kennebunkport

Beach
Ave.

Ocean
Ave.

× Arundel Beach

Kennebunk
Beach

1

9

Parsons Beach

Rachel
Carson ×
Wildlife
Ref.

95

Drakes Island

9   Wells

Webhannet
River

Wells Beach

KENNEBUNK-WELLS

0   1   2   3 Miles

9B

Moody Beach

N

year-round. Thanksgiving and Easter meals are also served to guests. $24-33 in season. No pets.

Wonderview Motor Village Motel and Housekeeping Cottages (646-2304), US 1. Open May 1-October 12. Thirty units scattered on four acres; one and two-bedroom cottages, well stocked, screen porches, lawn games, tv, $26-40 per night, $210-266 per week, cheaper off season.

Seagull Motor Inn (646-7082), US 1. Open late June-Labor Day. Twenty-four motel units, twenty-four cottages, a pool, playground, lawn games. Having spent four summer vacations here as a child (thirty years ago), I am happy to report that the place is still essentially the same solid value, with a loyal following. $33-45 per day (double) for non-housekeeping units, $220-350 per week for the cottages (which are by the week only), cheaper in off season.

Sleepytown (646-5545), US 1. Open May-November. "A family resort": eighty units composed of forty-two motel rooms with color tv and refrigerators, thirty housekeeping cottages and some "bedroom cottages," strung out along twelve acres. Pool, children's boating pond, picnic facilities, playground, dining rooms on premises. High season motel rates are $42-48 per night, cottages are $250-395 per week, bedroom cottages $32-38.

Somerset Motor Court (646-2782). Open May to mid-October, US 1. We find the interiors of these cottages less charming than those of the two above, and they lack screen porches, but they are perfectly adequate: thirty cottages and ten mobile homes set in twenty acres overlooking the marsh, $36-46 daily; $275-305 weekly in high season, less if off season.

RESTAURANTS **Lord's Harborside Restaurant** (646-2651). Open April-November. *The* lobster pound in town. Wells Harbor.

The Grey Gull Inn. See above.

Howard Johnson's Restaurant (646-8361). Late April-mid-October. Exceptionally good, about the best family restaurant in town.

Lord's Inc. Seafare Restaurant (646-5959). Housed in an outsized old barn, cafeteria-style and a good buy if you want a "plate" of something. Nothing below $2 for children, and we frankly found the atmosphere too plastic, but a very busy place with a strong local following.

The Kennebunks

The Kennebunks have been around under one name or another since the 1620s. They began as a fishing stage near Cape Porpoise. It was repeatedly destroyed by Indian raids, but in 1719 the present "Port" was incorporated as Arundel, a name which stuck through its peak ship-building and seafaring years until 1821, when it became Kennebunkport. Later, when *Arundel,* the novel by Kenneth Roberts (born in Kennebunk), had run through thirty-two editions, residents attempted to reclaim the old name and succeeded in doing so in 1957, at least for North Kennebunkport.

Geographically, the Kennebunks are extremely confusing. Kennebunk is a busy commercial center which straddles the strip of US 1 between the Mousam and Kennebunk Rivers. A ten-minute ride downriver brings you to Kennebunkport. Then there is Kennebunk Beach (west of the river mouth), and Cape Porpoise (several miles east of the river), and to get from Kennebunkport to Kennebunk Beach you have to go through Kennebunk Lower Village. Luckily, free detailed maps are readily available, and all most visitors care about is finding Dock Square in Kennebunkport and getting from there to some sand.

Dock Square, described in Booth Tarkington's 1930 novel *Mirthful Haven* as "Cargo Square," is one of the liveliest summer spots on the New England coast. Clustered around the classic monument "to our soldiers and sailors," the weathered, waterside buildings house an assortment of shops and restaurants. It's a place to spend hours sipping, munching, and browsing—eventually strolling down Ocean Avenue along the river, here lined with inns. You pass the picturesquely sagging dock at which Tarkington used to summer, writing on his schooner. The River Club across the way is very private, a gathering point for the families who have been summering here in roomy "cottages" for generations. Chances are that you have already passed the place you are staying. An assortment of excursion boats plus the chamber-sponsored trolleys which circulate regularly, and the availability of rental bikes make this one of the few Maine summer resorts in which you can survive comfortably without a car. On sunny days you can always get to the beach, and on rainy days there are plenty of art galleries and antique shops.

GUIDANCE **The Kennebunk-Kennebunkport Chamber of Commerce,** 43 Main Street, Kennebunk, is open year-round, weekdays, summer 9-5, winter 9-3 (985-3608), and publishes a fat informative booklet as well as detailed maps.

GETTING THERE **Greyhound** and **Trailways** both stop in town. **Munroe's Limousine Service** (646-9067) serves Boston and Portland airports. You can fly your own plane into Sanford Airport, or drive up the Maine Turnpike to Exit 3.

GETTING AROUND A **trolley on wheels,** circulates between Dock Square and Kennebunk Beach every forty-five minutes, daily, late June to Labor Day. 50c.

PARKING A free municipal parking lot is hidden just off Dock Square, behind the stores, near the fine old Congregational Church.

SIGHTS TO SEE **The Brick Store Museum** (985-4802). Open year-round, Tuesday-Saturday, 10-4:30. Main Street, Kennebunk. $1. A block of nineteenth-century commercial buildings, including William Lord's brick store (1825), exhibiting fine and decorative arts, historical and marine collections.

Taylor-Barry House, 24 Summer Street, Kennebunk. Open June 1-October 15, Tuesday, Thursday, 1-4, or by appointment. $1 adult, 50c child. An 1803 sea captain's mansion, hip-roofed, with a fireplace in every room.

Seashore Trolley Museum, Kennebunkport (967-2712). Open mid-April to mid-November; on a varying schedule until late June and after mid-September, when the only rolling stock is on weekends: a 1:30 PM ride lasting one-and-three-quarters hours. During high season rides are offered daily 10-5:30. Well worth the trouble of finding (it's a way out Log Cabin Road from Dock Square, also marked from that road's junction with US 1), this non-profit museum displays 145 vehicles from the world over. In a depot-style visitors' center, learn about how the Atlantic Shore Railway shaped the local resort scene in the days when you could come by trolley right from Boston to Dock Square. The two-mile circuit which visitors ride includes the old electric railroad right-of-way. $3.25 adult, $1.75 child.

Kennebunkport Historical Society, North Street (967-2751 or 985-4878). Open during summer months: Tuesday, Wednesday, Thursday 1-4, Saturday 10-12, and by appointment. Housed in an 1899 school, local exhibits tell of shipbuilding in the early nineteenth century, and of the summer colony which mushroomed in the 1880s.

St. Anthony Monastery and Shrine (967-2011). A tudor-style estate on Beach Road in Kennebunk, now maintained by Lithuanian Franciscans as a shrine and retreat center. Visitors are welcome to stroll the extensive grounds.

Wedding Cake House, Summer Street, Kennebunk, on Route 35. Definitely not open to the public, but probably the most famous land-

Brick Store Museum, Kennebunk

mark around: an 1826 house laced up and down with white wooden latticework. The story goes that a local sea captain had to rush off to sea before a proper wedding cake could be baked, but he more than made up for it later.

Louis T. Graves Memorial Public Library, open Monday, Wednesday, Friday 1:30-5, 7-9; Saturday 1:30-5. Kennebunkport. Built in 1813 as a bank, which went bust, it later served as a customs house, and was subsequently donated to the library association by artist Abbott Graves whose pictures alone make it worth a visit. You can also still see the bank vault and the sign from the customs collector's office.

BEACHES   Kennebunk avoids the glut of weekend daytrippers by requiring a permit to park at its major beaches. Permits cost $2 (available at Town Hall, Police Dept., or from lodging places).

Kennebunk and **Gooch's Beaches** are both long, wide strips of firm sand backed by Beach Avenue, and divided by Oak's Neck.

Goose Rocks Beach, a few miles north of Kennebunkport Village on Route 9, is another wide, smooth stretch of sand backed by the road.

Arundel Beach, off Ocean Avenue at the mouth of the Kennebunk River, offers permit parking, and limited sand too, but nice rocks for climbing.

Parson's Beach, south of Kennebunk Beach on Route 9 (near the Rachel Carson National Wildlife Refuge), is so beautiful and little known that we hesitate—but can't resist—mentioning it. The approach is down a grand avenue of trees, and the area is undeveloped. A splendid place for an evening walk.

BOAT EXCURSIONS   Cap'n Pete (985-3893). *Sonnie W.,* a thirty-two foot passenger party boat, departs daily from Reid's Boat Yard offering deep sea fishing June 15-Labor Day, pole and tackle included in the $18 fee; beer and sandwiches available. On Saturdays a longer trip is offered. Also off season charters.

Indian (967-5912), based at the landing by the Dock Square bridge (or write Box 746, Kennebunk 04043) is another party boat, departing daily June 19-Labor Day 8:30-2:30, $15 per person plus $2 for bait and tackle. Also evening cruises at 5 PM, $3 adult, $2 child under 12.

Captain Al Voorhis (646-8129). Deep sea fishing aboard the *Captain Al,* which departs from the Landing Restaurant, Ocean Avenue, May 30-October 30. $17, equipment included.

Captain Ben Emery (985-2286 or write Box 142, Kennebunk) offers party boat trips aboard his *Deep Water,* departing Reid's Boat Yard May-September, 8:30-3, $18 per person. Charters off season. Also scenic cruises in July and August at 6 PM, $3 adult, $2 child.

SPORTS   Canoes can be rented from **Cape Porpoise Canoe Rental** (967-3861), which also dispenses information about where to paddle in the local tidal rivers.

Cape Arundel Golf Club (967-3494) in Kennebunkport and the

Webhannet Golf Club in Kennebunk Beach (967-2061) are both eighteen-hole courses. The Dutch Elm Golf Course in Arundel (284-8831) is eighteen holes. All welcome guests for a fee.

The Kennebunk Fish and Game Club, Campbell Road, Kennebunk, offers free boat launching on the Mousam River.

The Meadows Swim and Racquet Center, US 1 north of Kennebunk, offers four indoor tennis courts and a swimming pool (985-2986).

CHILDREN'S PROGRAMS   The Kennebunk Beach Improvement Association, founded 1910, offers sailing and swimming, and an arts and crafts program for ages 3-19, on a weekly basis. $50 membership fee plus weekly charges.

WALKS   Henry Parsons Park on Ocean Avenue is a path along the rocks leading to Spouting Rock and Blowing Cave, both sights to see at mid-tide. Birders can't say enough for the Biddeford Pool-East Sanctuary (follow Route 9 north from Kennebunkport) as a place to observe shorebirds.

The Boardwalk at Old Orchard Beach. The Pier, an old-style arcade with shops and restaurants, and Palace Playland, an amusement park with a restored 1906 carousel, are a dozen miles up US 1.

SHOPPING   The 1790 House, a 1790 mansion set above Dock Square, open mid-May to mid-September, is crammed with candy and chocolates. Much of it is made on the premises by Naomi Turner, a lady from North Augusta known as "Old Yummy," who keeps her hands in chocolate and nuts year-round, moving the business to Hollywood, Florida when she closes up in Kennebunkport.

The Book Port, open year-round in the oldest commercial building in the Port (1775), is one of the most pleasant bookstores in New England. Located up an outside staircase in Dock Square, you will find it an inviting place to browse and read, as well as buy.

LODGING   The Kennebunks retain a greater number of Victorian-era summer hotels than any other New England coastal resort. Proudest of the survivors is the Nonantum, and the neighboring Breakwater (a conglomerate of the remnants of the two old inns) is very pleasant. Small inns have also proliferated in recent years. There are few bargains in high season. Families are better off checking the housekeeping cottages near Goose Rocks Beach. There are also a few local, private campgrounds. Our listings are, however, largely limited to the type of lodging most representative of the Kennebunks. This area has one of the largest concentrations of fine lodging places in all of Maine.

Captain Lord Mansion (967-3141). Open year-round at the corner of Pleasant and Green Streets in Kennebunkport. A splendid, 1812 foursquare mansion with an octagonal cupola. One of the most romantic inns around: sixteen rooms, each with its own name and antique furnishings, all with private baths, eleven with working fireplaces. Much of the furniture and even some paintings have always been here. Innkeepers Bev Davis and Rick Litchfield enjoy the house's beauty. Hot muffins in the kitchen are included in the $54-74 double tariff.

The Breakwater. (967-3118), mid-May to mid-October. Parts of two nineteenth-century hotels merge to form this deftly restored Kennebunkport inn with its sixteen attractive guest rooms and popular riverside dining room. Muffins and coffee are included in the $30-45 double rate, cheaper off season.

The White Barn. (967-2321). Open all year except January and February. Beach Street. The barn is now the dining room (open to the public), and is adjacent to the old inn, built in 1865 as the Forest Hills Hotel. The cheapest five units—three with kitchenettes—are $30-38, depending on bath. Fifteen rooms are in the inn itself, $30-39 double, efficiencies in the motel are $40-44, and six three-room suites in "May's Annex" are $68 per night, $420 per week. Off season cheaper. We like everything about the place.

The Green Heron. (967-3315). Early June to mid-October. Ocean Avenue, within walking distance of the village and shore. This old house has just nine guestrooms, and innkeeper Wallace Reid (dean of Port hoteliers) claims that it is his retirement hobby. Still, it's the busiest spot in town every morning, especially Sundays, when customers begin lining up at 8 AM for Virginia Reid's famous breakfasts (see food), included for guests in the moderate prices which vary with each room. Our family of five paid $48 in June '81 for a riverside suite of two rooms with connecting bath, five four-course breakfasts included.

The Nonantum (967-3338). Mid-June to early September. Ocean Avenue. Just seventeen rooms are open beyond the high season—when there are seventy, sixty-five with private baths. Nearing its century season, this is still a fine old landmark, with spacious sitting rooms filled with wicker rockers, and bentwood chairs in the vast diningroom. There is also a pool, and attractive grounds sloping down to the river. $92 (single) to $120 (double—two adjoining rooms) with two meals a day included, $25 less per person per day without meals, much cheaper off season.

Village Cove Inn (967-3993). Year-round. Not an inn, a motel with a central dining room, modern, with an indoor pool. $45 double high season, but much less off, specializing in week-long art workshops.

English Meadows Inn (967-5766). May to November 1. A Victorian farmhouse within easy walking distance of Dock Square. Twelve rooms ($40-50 high season), and an efficiency apartment for two ($275 per week); a full breakfast is included, cheaper off season.

Chetwynd House (967-2235). Open all year, central. An 1840s house with four guest rooms and an efficiency, full breakfasts included in $36-55 double.

Tides Inn By-the-Sea (967-3757). Mid-May to early October. At Goose Rocks, away from Kennebunkport, but across from the beach, twenty-two plain but bright rooms, six with private baths, geared to singles and young couples, attractive dining room open to the public. Expensive for what you get.

The Sundial Inn (967-3850). Mid-May through September. Across from beach, accommodates seventy-five guests in thirty-two rooms, old furniture as opposed to antiques, homey, simple food, $28-38 double.

The Kennebunk Inn, Kennebunk (985-3358). Open year-round. A stage stop since 1799, a flophouse when Arthur and Angela Le Blanc bought it in 1978, now an inn with charm and a center-of-town feel. Twenty-eight guestrooms, ten with baths, and a pleasant dining room, bar. $26-45 double.

Seacrest Inn and Motel (967-2125). April through October. Out on Shore Drive in Kennebunkport overlooking the Atlantic between Spouting Rock and Blowing Cave. There are eight rooms in the inn, six motel rooms, and some efficiencies. We find the Victorian parlor a shade stiff. Three meals are served daily, open to the public. $30-33 double for guestrooms, less off season.

Olde Garrison House in Cape Porpoise (967-3522). Summer months. A 1730 fussy guesthouse, ideal for older people, reasonably priced, kitchen privileges, shared baths, nice location.

Goose Rocks Beach Motor Inn (967-3421). Mid-April to mid-October. Handy to Goose Rocks Beach and salt water marsh, good for birding, pleasant efficiency units, ideal for families, $40-44.

RESTAURANTS   **Olde Grist Mill** (967-4781). Open late April through October. A genuine mid-eighteenth-century tidal gristmill, operating until 1937, when the Lombard family turned it into one of Maine's favorite coastal restaurants. Soup and salad lunch is $4.50, and suppers are around $10. Predictable but dependable food.

Nunan's Lobster Hut, Cape Porpoise (967-4362). Memorial Day to Labor Day. A low, shed-like landmark which packs them in and charges, too ($8.95 for a lobster dinner in '81), but no one complains. The menu is limited to lobster, clams, and home-baked pastries. Opens at 5 PM for dinner, beer and wine, sinks with paper towels to daub off the melted butter.

Spicer's Gallery, Cape Porpoise (967-2745). Year-round for dinner only. Small, children's menu, reasonably priced.

The Ole Spudger Lobster Pound at Cape Porpoise (967-2410). Lobster live and cooked, chowder, stew, grilled cheese, outdoor eating only with a splendid view. Marigolds growing out of plastic sandpails in the middle of the tables. Seasonal only, moderately priced.

Ciao (967-2746). The spot for a $2 quiche, upstairs next to the Book Port in Dock Square, a cafe specializing in imaginative soups, salads, and teas, served out on a flower-filled deck.

White Barn Inn (967-2321). Seasonal, lunch and dinner served in an attractively renovated barn (see Lodging).

The Breakwater Restaurant and Inn (967-3118). Ocean Avenue. Dinner open to the public in a riverside dining room, moderately priced for the atmosphere and food, reservations suggested. (See Lodging).

The Port House (967-3358). Ocean Avenue. Seasonal. Lunch and dinner in a glassed-terraced dining room in a fine old mansion with expensive guestrooms upstairs. More of an eating than a lodging place.

SUMMER EVENTS   Church and public suppers occur all summer, check with Chamber of Commerce. **The Miss Dumpy Contest** is the big event of the summer, complete with a "Dump Parade" in early July. **Antiques Show,** early August. **Merchants Seacoast Festival,** early August.

Maine Development Office

Portland Headlight

CASCO BAY

Portland

Portland is a peninsula city where seagulls perch atop downtown sky-scrapers and there is a pervasive sense of the sea.

The most sophisticated and important city in northern New England ever since the 1820s, it is blessed with distinguished buildings from every era. Maine's largest city, it is a showcase for her painters, musicians, actors, and craftsmen. The wonder is that Portland remains so compact, walkable, and friendly.

In one five-block wide section, hundreds of shops and dozens of galleries and restaurants are packed into ornate little Victorian buildings, all with a view of the harbor. Known as "The Old Port Exchange" this delightful area was a canker at the city's heart just a decade ago, a skid row condemned for urban renewal.

Portland's motto "Resurgam" ("I shall rise again") couldn't be more appropriate. First settled in 1632, it was wiped out twice by Indians, then once by the British. It wasn't until after the Revolution that the community really began to prosper—as you can see from Federal-era mansions and commercial buildings like the granite and glass-faced Mariner's Church, built in 1820 to be the largest building in the capital of a brand new state.

This is the port that a small boy named Henry Wadsworth Longfellow loved, later writing:

> I remember the black wharves and the ships
> And the sea-tides tossing free
> And the Spanish sailors with bearded lips
> And the beauty and mystery of the ships
> And the magic of the sea.

Portland continued to thrive as a lumbering port and a railroad terminus through the Civil War, right up until the Independence Day which was to celebrate that war's end. Then it happened again. On July 4, 1866, a firecracker flamed up in a Commercial Street boatyard and quickly destroyed most of downtown Portland. When the city rebuilt this time, it did so with sturdy brick buildings which are replete with the kind of flourishes you would expect of the Gilded Era, years in which these blocks were the core of northern New England's shipping, rail and manufacturing center.

These were the very buildings that were later "going for peanuts," in the words of a realtor who began buying them up in the late 1960s. The city's prominence as a port had been eclipsed by the opening of the Saint Lawrence Seaway in 1959, and its handsome Grand Trunk Station had been torn down in 1966. Decent folk did their shopping in the department and chain stores up on Congress Street, itself threatened by the Maine Mall which was burgeoning out by the Interstate highway.

Down by the harbor artists and craftsmen were renting shopfronts for $50 a month. Soon they formed an Old Port Association, hoping to entice people to stroll through the no man's land which divided the shops up on Congress Street from the few famous fish restaurants and the Ferry dock down on Commercial. That first winter they strung lights through upper floors at night to convey a sense of security, and shoveled their own streets, a service which the city had long ceased to provide to that area. At the end of the winter they celebrated their survival by holding the first Old Port Festival, an exuberant street fair which continues to be staged on the final weekend in June.

Today the Old Port Exchange—unchecked by twentieth-century highways or buildings—is spreading like wildfire along Commercial Street and through neighboring blocks to the east and west of the core Old Port streets (Middle and Exchange). As yet unspoiled by success, the area has become a genuine windowcase for the best in northern New England craftsmenship, sculpture, painting and—increasingly—for music and the performing arts.

Custom House Wharf remains a saggy, funky holdout from the "new" waterfront. Until the advent of the Old Port Exchange it housed the harbor's only tourist attractions: Boone's Restaurant and the Casco Bay Lines. Both enterprises are still very much in business and no first-time visit to Portland is complete without a Casco Bay Line "cruise" to the Calendar Islands. There is a state beach on Long Island and a fine inn on Chebeague. From Portland's waterfront you can also take a deep sea fishing boat, a sailboat ride, or sail off to Yarmouth, Nova Scotia.

Portland is, however, increasingly a destination rather than a departure point or waystop. In addition to shops, restaurants, and galleries there are an abundance of historic sites to see, and there are even fine beaches and inns—not right in town (where there are, instead, plenty of adequate, quality chain motels), but just fifteen minutes north and to the south, the reason we have described Portland in the context of its framing shore.

GUIDANCE   **Chamber of Commerce of the Greater Portland Region** (772-2811), 142 Free Street, publishes *Greater Portland,* a glossy magazine with current listings of restaurants, sights, and galleries.

The Maine Publicity Bureau maintains a basement office in the same building, good for walk-in inquiries, well-stocked with area leaflets. Both offices are open year-round 8:30-4:30. For details about guided walking tours of the city, contact **Greater Portland Landmarks** (774-5561), 165 State Street. Be sure to request their leaflet guides (also available from the Chamber) which outline walking tours of Congress Street and the Old Port Exchange.

GETTING THERE   Plane. Portland International Jetport (779-7301) is served by Delta and Bar Harbor Airlines, connecting it with Boston, New York, and Quebec, as well as all regional centers. City buses connect airport and city, as does Independent Taxi (774-5081).

Bus. Both Greyhound (772-6587), with a terminal at 950 Congress Street, and Trailways (773-5400), with a terminal at 169 High Street, offer extensive service out of Portland. Vermont Transit, based in the Greyhound terminal, connects Portland with Burlington and Montreal.

Boat. Lion Ferry (775-5616 or a seasonal toll-free number) offers overnight cruises mid-May through October aboard its car-carrying cruise ship *Scotia Prince* to Yarmouth, Nova Scotia. Prices vary, depending on the season, cabin, or a variety of special packages. Restaurants, shops, and a casino are available aboard. Departure time at this writing is 9 PM, arriving Yarmouth at 10 AM. The luxury cruise vessel accommodates 1500 passengers, 800 in cabins, also 250 cars.

The Canadian National Marine line (775-6581, 800-492-0622 in Maine, 800-341-7540 in the eastern United States) also offers year-round car and

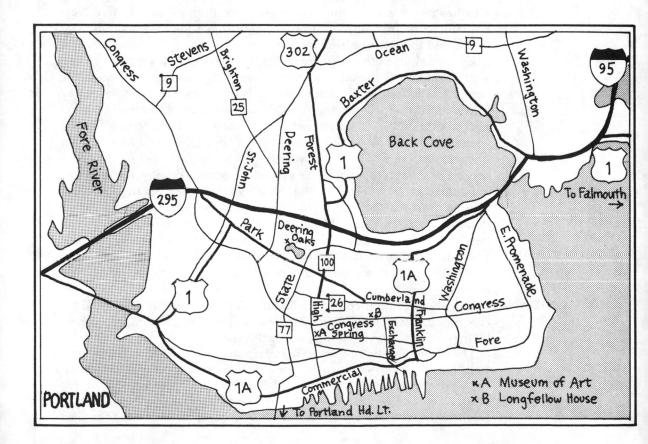

passenger service from Portland to Yarmouth, aboard the *Marine Evangeline;* slightly less expensive than Lion, without all the cruiseship frills, but with cabins and a restaurant.

Car. Via I-95, Portland is just two hours from Boston. We generally take Exit 6A onto ME 295, then downtown exit 4.

GETTING AROUND   The **Metro** serves Greater Portland (774-0351). The basic fare is 50c (no zones), 25c for senior citizens. Major rental car firms are represented at the Jetport or in town. Bikes may be rented at the **Portland Bicycle Exchange** (772-4137), which also rents cross-country skis. With a little help from bus and bike, Portland is a city you can truly enjoy sans car, especially since you can hop into a maxi-van provided by the **Great Atlantic Tour Company** (775-7700), and get a first rate tour of the town (9-2, $9.75 per person), as well as daytripping to Boothbay Harbor (with a stop enroute at L.L. Bean) or down the coast of Ogunquit.

SIGHTS TO SEE   **Portland Museum of Art** (775-6148), 11 High Street. Open year-round Tuesday-Saturday 10-5, Sunday 2-5. Free, but $1 adult, 50c child if you want to tour the adjoining McLellan Sweat House. With the completion of its major new wing designed by the firm of I.M. Pei & Partners, the museum can finally display its extensive collection of American artists—particularly Maine-based masters like Winslow Homer, Edward Hopper, and Andrew Wyeth. The adjoining museum buildings include the splendid Federal style McLellan-Sweat mansion built for Portland's biggest shipowner in 1800. The museum itself was founded in 1882.

Wadsworth-Longfellow House, maintained by the Maine Historical Society Museum (774-1822), offers its own exhibits and an extensive research library at the rear of Portland's first brick House (487 Congress Street, open June-September, Monday-Friday 9:30-4:30, closed July 4 and Labor Day, $2 adults, $1 children under 16). Built by the poet's grandfather, this is a homey, fascinating house, in which Henry Wadsworth Longfellow spent his boyhood. Most furnishings are original. Allow for a set, 45-minute tour.

First Parish Church, 425 Congress Street, June-August, Tuesday noon-3, free. If you happen to be walking down Congress Street on a summer Tuesday between noon and 3, don't fail to step into this vintage 1826 meeting house in which the pews are tipped forward—so that dozing parishioners would fall onto the floor.

Portland Observatory (773-5779 or 774-0637), 138 Congress Street. Open Memorial to Labor Day, daily 10-7, 50c adults, 25c children. This is the last surviving nineteenth-century signal tower on the Atlantic—an octagonal, shingled landmark which you can climb to find a surprisingly rewarding view at the top, as well as a sense of what it must have been like to scan the horizon for your returning ship in the 1800s.

Gulf of Maine Aquarium. Open spring and fall, 12-5; late June to Columbus Day daily 10-5; $1 adults, 50c children. Housed in a barge moored at Long Wharf. Tanks display local marine life; also slide shows, tidal pools, special programs.

Neal Dow Memorial (773-7773). Open year-round, Monday-Saturday, 11-4, 714 Congress Street. A handsome Greek Revival house, built in 1829 by the man responsible for an 1851 law which made Maine the first state to prohibit the manufacture and sale of alcoholic beverages. Current headquarters for the Maine Women's Christian Temperance Union, the mansion is a memorial to Neal Dow.

Portland Fire Museum. Open June to September, Saturday 2-5, Monday 7-9. Free. 157 Spring Street. Given Portland's unusual fire fighting history, this collection of artifacts and photos is something to see. Housed in a granite Greek Revival firehouse.

George Tate House (774-9781). Open July 1-September 15, Tuesday-Saturday 11-5, Sunday 1:30-5, $1.50 adults, 50c children, 1270 Westbrook Street. (Follow Congress Street west across the Fore River to Westbrook.) George Tate, mast agent for the Royal Navy, built this house in 1755 to reflect his important position. Both outside and in it is unusual, noted for its windows, its gambrel roof, the fine paneling within, and elegant furniture.

The Children's Museum of Maine (797-3353) 746 Stevens Avenue. Open year-round, Tuesday-Friday 10-5, Saturday and Sunday 12-4, closed Mondays, $1 person, maximum family charge of $5. Off the beaten downtown track—take Forest Avenue from Congress Street, left on Stevens Avenue. A hands-on collection of exhibits, special programs.

Payson Gallery of Art (797-9546). Open Tuesday-Friday 10-4, weekends 1-5, 716 Stevens Avenue at Westbrook College. Special exhibits; also a permanent collection including works by Van Gogh, Renoir, Degas, Prendergast, Picasso, Homer, and Wyeth.

Morse-Libby House, "Victoria Mansion" (772-4841). 109 Danforth Street, corner of Park. Open mid-June through Labor Day, Tuesday-Saturday, 10-4, closed holidays. About as Victorian as a mansion can be; a brownstone Italianate home built in 1859 for a Maine native who had made his fortune in the New Orleans hotel business. The interior is extremely ornate: frescoed walls and ceilings, a flying staircase with 377 hand-carved balusters of San Domingo mahogany, giant gold leaf mirrors, marble mantels, ornate chandeliers, stained glass, and more, more.

GREENSPACE   **Eastern Cemetery.** Congress Street and Washington Avenue, near the Portland Observatory on Munjoy Hill. More than 4000 souls are interred in this nine acres, and the headstones, dating back to the mid-seventeenth century, are embellished with angels and death's heads. Despite its derelict state it is utterly fascinating.

Fort Allen Park. The park dates from 1814 and is on a blustery point on Casco Bay, a sure bet for a fresh breeze on the hottest day, as is the adjacent sixty-eight acre **Eastern Promenade.**

Deering Oaks. A fifty-one acre city park designed by Olmstead, with a pond, swans, fountains, a playground, and a fine grove of oak trees.

Portland Head Light. This is the oldest lighthouse in Maine. It was first illuminated in 1791 per order of George Washington; grounds are open year-round, 8-7. Easy to find: take ME 77 south from Commercial Street for four miles. The lighthouse adjoins Fort Williams Park.

Two Lights State Park. Open April 15-November. No swimming, but forty acres of shore. Good for picnicking, fishing.

Gisland Farm Sanctuary (781-2330). Open year-round, Monday-Saturday 9-5, Sundays 1-4. 118 Old Route One, three miles east of Portland in the Falmouth headquarters for Maine Audubon. Seventy acres of trails, rolling fields, river frontage, and salt marsh; also a solar-heated educational center with exhibits, a shop, and special programs.

Scarborough Marsh Nature Center (883-5100). June 28-Labor Day, 9-5, closed Mondays. On Pine Point Road, ten miles south of Portland. This is the largest salt marsh (3000 acres) in Maine. The marsh itself is, of course, there year-round. **The Audubon Nature Center** offers canoe rentals, exhibits, a nature store, guided walking and canoe trips, and a full program of activities in summer.

Winslow Homer Studio (883-2249). By appointment only, summer months. The modest, shingled studio in which one of the world's foremost marine artists worked from 1883 until 1910. It is basically the way he left it, complete with tilt-table and easel. The studio is in Prouts Neck off ME 207, a short distance along the private Prouts Neck Association Road.

BOAT EXCURSIONS **Casco Bay Lines and the Calendar Islands.** Casco Bay Lines (774-7871), founded in 1845, claims to be the oldest continually operating coastal ferry company in the country. Back in 1895, the firm offered its patrons tickets priced from five to twenty-five cents, depending on the quality of the seat, for a play at the Gem Theater in Peaks Island. Besides the huge summer theater, Peaks—just a fifteen-minute ferry ride from Custom House Wharf—boasted a major amusement park, frequent balloon ascents, and a half-dozen big hotels. Today Peaks is a quiet Portland suburb, year-round home for some 1200 people. It is still a good place to bring a bike, since its circle road is paved, and the far side is relatively unpeopled and open to the Bay.

In all, Casco Bay Lines serves six of the 140 islands in the Bay. They were named the "Calendar Islands" by that famous promoter John Smith who claimed that there was an island here for every day of the year. The only other islands even relatively receptive to daytrippers are Chebeague, the biggest (five miles long, two miles wide), with its delightful Chebeague Inn; Long, with a state-owned beach and lunch counter, and Cliff—a ninety-minute ferry ride from Portland—the most remote of the serviced islands, with dirt roads ideal for walking. Casco Bay's service is year-round, but during the tourist season it calls its three-hour 10 AM and 2 PM runs a "cruise" ($6.55 adults, $4.65 children). It also offers a four-hour "Bailey Island Cruise" in summer months which continues on past Cliff and Eagle Islands to Bailey Island (see Brunswick). The line also offers seasonal sunset, moonlight, and other special tours.

House Island Tour and Clambake, Memorial Day to mid-October (799-8188, or write House Island Tours, Box 592, Portland, Maine 04112). Departing Long Wharf, Buccaneer Line transports you to House Island where there is a genuine Civil War fort (still complete with seventy gun casements, subterranean vaults, circular stairways, and tunnels), also a choice of sandy beaches and a dining hall in which clambakes—from chowder through blueberry cake—are served.

Atlantic Navigation Company (774-3578), offers seasonal harbor tours that are shorter, cheaper, and more visitor-oriented than those available from Casco Bay. Their boat is the *M.V. Longfellow;* tours range from a one-hour Historic Harbor Tour ($4 adult, $3 child) and a Luncheon Harbor Cruise (12:05-12:55, $2) to a two-hour Naturalist Tour ($5 adults, $3 children). The company also operates schooner yacht *Annie McGee,* available for two-hour sailings ($10 per person), as well as sunset and moonlight sails.

Deep-sea fishing is offered by the *Lazy Day* (774-0122) mid-June through late September, Monday-Saturday 9-4, $17 per person plus $1 rod rental; charters and clambakes also available. Contact Captain Rich, 128 Bentwood Street, Portland, Maine 04103.

BEACHES **East End Beach** below the Eastern Promenade is a real city beach but nevertheless safe and clean, and is the most convenient dunking spot. You can also take ME 77 south to Cape Elizabeth, where **Willard Beach** fringes a residential neighborhood (take Prebble Street). But the nearest genuine beach is **Crescent Beach State Park** on Route 77 (served by city bus lines), a mile of sand complete with changing facilities, playgrounds, picnic tables, and snackbar. A few miles further, ME 77 brings you to **Higgins Beach** in Scarborough, an extensive strand backed by summer cottages. Continue a few more miles along ME 77 and you come to **Scarborough Beach State Park,** a superb beach of which only a sixty-five-foot stretch is technically public, but—thanks to limited parking—the crowd is rarely excessive. There is also **Ferry Beach** (off ME 207), fringing the Prouts Neck Golf Course and also offering plenty of breathing space.

Just across the mouth of the Scarborough River, but many miles round as ME 207 and 9 go, is **Pine Point,** offering white sand and surf and possible free parking. **Old Orchard Beach** extends a full seven miles to the south. We should also mention that there is public swimming on Long Island and Chebeague (see Casco Bay Lines).

GOLF Right in Portland there is **Riverside Municipal** (797-3524 or 797-5588) at 1158 Riverside: eighteen- and nine-hole courses. In Scarborough there is **Willowdale Golf Course** (883-9351), eighteen holes.

THEATER **Portland Stage Company** (774-0465) performs at 15 Temple Street September-April, Tuesday through Friday evenings, weekend matinees. Reservations are necessary because of the 150-seat limits in this very professional group's downtown theater.

The Portland Players (799-7337) stage six productions each season

(September-June) at Thaxter Theater, 420 Cottage Road, South Portland.

Portland Lyric Theater (799-1421) is a community theater presenting three musicals each winter season at the Cedric Thomas Playhouse, 176 Sawyer Street, South Portland.

MUSIC AND DANCE   The **Portland Symphony Orchestra** (773-8191) performs in City Hall Auditorium, 389 Congress Street, October-April, Tuesday nights at 7:45, also at various other locations and times.

Portland String Quartet (773-0544) is a distinguished chamber group, which performs periodically in a variety of Portland places.

The Portland Concert Association (772-8630) presents top artists, usually four, in City Hall Auditorium in the course of the winter season.

Ram Island Dance Center (773-2562), 25A Forest Avenue, offers year-round weekend performances.

SPORTS   Cumberland County Civic Center (775-3481), a new 9000-seat arena, best known during winter months as the home of the Maine Mariners hockey team, also hosts a variety of other events.

Harness Racing (883-2020), US 1 in Scarborough (exit 6 off the Maine Turnpike). Early May to mid-September, nightly except Tuesday, Sundays at 2:30.

LODGING   There are more than 2000 hotel/motel rooms in and around Portland. The major chains are all here: **Howard Johnson's** (774-5861), **Holiday Inn** (775-2311), **Sheraton Inn** (775-6161), **Ramada Inn** (775-2311), **Quality Inn Friendship** (774-5891), and John Martin's Best Western **Merry Manor Inn** (774-6151). These all range from $40 to $60 per night in summer, less off season. There is also a **Susse Chalet Lodge** (774-6101) at $25 double, and the **YWCA** (772-1906) which charges $11 per person, double; the **YMCA** (773-1736) charges $14 per person. The **Eastland** (775-5411 and 800 341-0414), a 190-room downtown hotel, has been thoroughly restored and offers character and convenience at reasonable rates: $35 single, $41 double off-season, $55 and $59 in the summer. It's Top of the East Lounge is the highest spot in Portland. There are also some fine inns—as we understand the meaning of inn—in the area:

Homewood Inn (846-3315) in Yarmouth, June to mid-October. The Maine House, built in 1742, has four antiques-furnished rooms, and there are twenty-three attractive rooms and suites in all, scattered in five houses, plus a number of cottages with fireplaces. The Lodge houses the dining room, cocktail lounge, and a lobby and gift shop. In all there are forty rooms, $32 to $60 double, up to $142 for six people in a cottage. No meals included, but box lunches are available, and breakfast and dinner are served. There is a pool, nearby beach, tennis, lawn games, and bike rentals.

Black Point Inn in Prouts Neck (883-4311). Open from late June to Labor Day. Easily one of the most elegant inns in the state, a vintage 1878 summer hotel which is such a part of its exclusive community that guests are permitted to use the Prouts Neck Country Club's eighteen-hole golf course and fourteen tennis courts, also to rent boats or moor their own at the local Yacht Club. There are eighty rooms, poolside buffets with live entertainment, afternoon tea, evening cocktails and dancing, $100-120 per couple per day, three meals included. Open for groups off season.

Atlantic House (883-4381) at Scarborough Beach. Open mid-June through early September. A seventy-eight room, old-style summer hotel which was run by the same family until 1971, when Barbara and Dino Giamatti (brother of Yale's youthful president) bought it. They have added a liquor license in the dining room, but have otherwise preserved the old shoe atmosphere. In contrast to Black Point (see above), children are welcome here, given special programs, a dining hour, and of course superb Scarborough Beach—which is just out the door. High season rates are modified American plan (two meals), but in June and early September the dozen cottages go at bargain prices, no meals.

Higgins Beach Inn in Scarborough (883-6684). A 1920s, three-story, wooden summer hotel up the road from Higgins Beach. Open mid-May to mid-October with a pleasant dining room and public rooms, twenty-three basic guest rooms upstairs, moderately priced, also geared to families.

The Breakers Guest House (882-4820), right on Higgins Beach, is an overgrown summer house serving meals on its glassed porch and offering a variety of comfortable rooms, on a per week, MAP basis.

The Chebeague Inn By-the-Sea (846-9634). Open late May into foliage, $36 to $48 (for a two-room suite with bath) double. To our minds this is the place to stay in Portland. An 1880s, three-story summer hotel with fourteen second-floor rooms, all but the two-room suite sharing baths. The living room centerpiece is a mammoth stone hearth, and there are plenty of books and games; a cocktail lounge opens onto the wrap-around porch, and the pleasant dining room offers three meals a day. This, the largest island in Casco Bay, offers beaches, a nine-hole golf course, and roads suited to biking. You get there via Casco Bay lines, or a far speedier water taxi from Cousins Island.

COTTAGES   South of Portland cottages in the Higgins Beach and Pine Point areas can be found through the **Scarborough Chamber of Commerce,** 142 Free St., Portland (772-2811). **The Moorings By The Sea** in Pine Point (883-2032) offers one- and two-bedroom housekeeping cottages with fireplaces, also a guest house right on the beach. For listings on summer rental cottages in the Casco Bay Islands contact **Port Island Realty,** 377 Fore Street, Portland (775-7253).

RESTAURANTS **F. Parker Reidy's** (773-4731) 83 Exchange Street. Housed in the former Portland Savings Bank, it has a polished elegance, a distinguished menu, and moderate prices. Good for lunch and dinner daily, brunch on Sunday.

The Vineyard (773-5524) 111 Middle Street. A small, intimate winebar which many claim offers the best continental food in town. Just a few choices are offered daily, but they all tend to be exquisite. $20 plus per person for a three-course meal.

The Roma (773-9873) 769 Congress Street. Very formal and classic Italian, also seafood and steaks, lunch and dinner; cheaper downstairs in the Bramhall Pub (soups and sandwiches).

The Seamen's Club (772-7311) 375 Fore Street. Housed in an 1860s building with two splendid gothic windows on its airy second floor, this is a delightful, informal, and moderately priced place, open for breakfast, lunch, and dinner daily except Sunday, when there is brunch. The chowder is great, a meal in itself for lunch; the dinner menu runs from a $5.95 Rock Cornish game hen to a $10.50 seafood casserole. Since prices are the same downstairs and up, be sure to request the more distinctive upstairs room.

The Wine Cafe (772-8885) 154 Middle Street, lunch and dinner, a homey atmosphere created by old oak tables, inn-like anteroom, and good art on the walls. An imaginative, moderately priced menu and extensive wine list.

The Bakers Table (775-0303) 434 Fore Street, below the bakeshop which furnishes its own elaborate breads and desserts. Bouillabaisse is a specialty, along with other soups, chowders and dishes you don't find everyday. Customers queue for lunch in a cafeteria-style line to pick up elegant, moderately priced dishes; dinner is more formal and expensive, but still a good value.

Before the 1970s birth of the Old Port Exchange the big places in town to eat lobster were **Boone's** (774-5725) on Custom House Wharf—still going strong as it has been since 1896, serving lunch and dinner at competitive prices, and **DiMillo's Lobster House** (772-2216), 121 Commercial Street—at this writing vastly expanding its seating capacity into a former car ferry which has come to rest across the street. Families will do well to check out the **Village Cafe** (772-5320), closed Sunday but otherwise a great place to feed the children spaghetti or pizza while you enjoy first-rate seafood, all at reasonable prices. Smack on the water there is **J's Oyster** (772-4828) on Portland Pier, a smoky lounge, but one with windows overlooking fishing boats, and a genuine choice of moderately priced oysters and clams. The **Old Port Tavern** (774-0444), 11 Moulton Street in the basement of The Mariner's Church, was one of the first Old Port dining spots, a dark, brick-walled place featuring jazz and bluegrass in the evening, but also offering moderately priced lunches and dinner.

Elsewhere in the Old Port there is **Carbur's** (772-7194), 121 Middle Street, a classic hanging-plants-pub-style place with a twenty-page menu of sandwiches and light fare; **Horse Feathers** (773-3501) 191 Middle Street, serving moderately priced soups, steaks, chili and such; and the very elegant **34 Exchange Street** (775-1100) open for both lunch and dinner. There is also the pre-Old Port **Hole on Custom House Wharf,** open early for breakfast but closed after lunch (great chowder, clean, cheerful, both counter and table service, and unbeatable prices); and at 116 Free Street, between the Chamber of Commerce and the Civic

Center, there is **The Bag,** another pub-style standby for burgers, quiche, and the like. In the Marketplace mall, 164 Middle Street, there is **Ruby's,** good for soups, salads, and light exotica in a second floor greenhouse; deck dining in warm weather, and folk music at night.

We should also mention the **Gallery,** a glass-faced, waterside dining landmark in Falmouth that's at Handy Boat on ME 88, less than five miles north of Portland (781-4262). Seafood specialties for lunch and dinner year-round. At 540 Forest Avenue back in Portland, **The Great Lost Bear** (formerly "The Grizzly Bear") is a bare-brick-and-old-wood kind of place which makes an art out of serving burgers, salads, and vegetable dishes at moderate prices (772-0300).

Smith Farm in North Portland (797-3034) is open early June-mid-October for lunch and dinner. Basic New England dishes and homemade ice cream in a fine old barn located on ME 26 and 100, two minutes north of Maine Turnpike Exit 10.

Captain Newick's Lobster (799-3090), 740 Broadway in South Portland, isn't big on atmosphere but the price is right for lobster, and most meals cost under $7. Closed Mondays.

Ye Olde Pancake Shoppe, 617 Congress Street, is also a good family bet for breakfast and lunch (good for omelets as well as pancakes at reasonable prices), as are the **Deering Ice Cream Shops**—always good for soup, sandwich, and cone (sugar or plain).

On Cape Elizabeth there are two dining landmarks: **The Lobster Shack** (799-1677) faces the rocky shore at the tip of the cape, dining both inside and out. There is also the **Crescent Beach Inn** (799-2196), Route 77 near Crescent beach. We found the rooms uninviting, but the restaurant is cozy and has a strong local following.

SHOPPING Both Congress Street and the Old Port shops complement each other, the former offering solid department and chain store basics, the latter full of unusual hand-crafted, hewn and painted items. Most Old Port stores are owner-operated. With the exception of two mini-malls—the Middle Street marketplace (a former garage) and 10 Exchange Street (old commercial buildings)—these buildings have been bought and restored one at a time. We have come home from Portland laden with purchases ranging from an egg separator to a dining room table. I contend that Portland offers New England's best selection of winter clothing—from bargain-priced flannel shirts in **Benoit's Bargain Basement** to exquisite knits and parkas in the boutiques—and the prices are refreshing when compared to megalopolis prices.

Congress Street Shops include **Porteous, Mitchell and Braun** (772-4681), on Congress Street, a full service department store. **A.H. Benoit's** (773-6421) in Monument Square has quality clothing upstairs, bargains in the Free Street basement. **Owen Moore** (773-7221), 502 Congress Street, and **Carroll Reed** (774-3777), 510 Congress Street, specialize in quality sportswear.

In The Old Port Exchange, crafts shops that we swear by are the

Women's Exchange (quilts, sweaters, placemats) and the **Marketplace** (Maine-made pottery and glass), both on Exchange, and **Maine Potters Market** on Moulton Street. **Linekin Bay Fabrics** (35 Silver Street) sells richly colored material woven on the spot, and in the **Portland Art Building** (corner of Fore and Union Streets) you can frequently find affordable original paintings and sculpture. There are also a number of antiques shops, the most famous of them **F.O. Baily** on Middle Street. My own favorite is **Mainely Oak** on Fore Street, good for nicely re-finished oak pieces of all sizes and shapes.

There are a half dozen substantial bookstores within walking distance of each other, not counting the line of cookbooks at the **Whip & Spoon** on Commercial Street. There are also a good dozen boutiques selling cloth-ing, ranging from **Dunham's** classic tweeds to the unusual designs at **Amaryllis.** There are also entire shops dedicated to selling records, posters, ballet outfits, tobacco, wood stoves, canvas bags, cheese, woodenware, paper products, art materials, stencil equipment, games, potting supplies, herbs, and more, more, more. Beyond Portland Proper is **the Maine Mall,** Exit 7 off the Maine Turnpike, offering sixty stores. Also see Brunswick area for **L.L. Bean.**

Brunswick

Maine Street is handsome, a full twelve rods wide—the way it was laid out in 1717. This was an early commercial site near the junction of the Androscoggin and Kennebec Rivers, generating power for nineteenth-century mills. Turn off cluttered US 1 and drive through town to the campus of Bowdoin College, Maine's proudest educational institution, one blessed with a fine campus and two outstanding museums. Three peninsulas jut beyond Brunswick into Casco Bay, but these are essentially private, suburban places, with the exception of Orr's and Bailey Islands, linked to US 1 by ME 24, a good bet for a night's food and rest.

GUIDANCE **Chamber of Commerce,** 59 Pleasant Street (725-8797).

GETTING THERE Frequent service via **Greyhound.** Casco Bay Line ferry to Bailey Island in summer months. By car, take Exits 20-24 off I-95. Beware of the fact that Exits 21 and 22 are northbound only.

BOWDOIN COLLEGE Tours of the 110-acre, forty-building campus begin at Moulton Union. During the academic year they leave on the hour from 10 to 4; June through Labor Day they depart on weekdays at 9:30, 10:30, 11:30, and 2, 3, 4; on Saturday at 9, 10, and 11. The college number is 725-8731.

The College was founded in 1794, named for a Massachusetts governor, since Maine was still part of that state. Hawthorne and Longfellow were classmates here in 1825; other notable graduates include Franklin Pierce and Robert Peary. Current applications average 3500 each year for the 380 coed freshmen places. It isn't necessary to take a tour to see the sites:

Walker Art Building. (Open during the academic year Tuesday-Friday 10-4, Saturday 10-5, Sunday 2-5. July-Labor Day: Tuesday-Saturday 10-5, 7-8:30, and Sunday 2-5.) Designed by McKim, Mead and White, the building contains Colonial and Federal-era portraits by Stuart, Feke, and Copley, also a number of Winslow Homers, Fackens and works by other nineteenth-century American landscape artists, and collections from ancient to present times.

Peary-MacMillan Arctic Museum (same hours). A well-displayed collection of clothes, equipment, trophies, and other mementoes from expeditions to the North Pole by two Bowdoin alumni. Peary (Class of 1877) was the first man to reach the North Pole; MacMillan (Class of 1888) was his chief assistant, who went on to dedicate his life to exploring arctic waters and terrain.

SIGHTS TO SEE   Harriet Beecher Stowe House (725-5543), 63 Federal Street. A Federal-style house in which Henry Wadsworth Longfellow once lodged, but best known as the home of Harriet Beecher Stowe during the two years in which she wrote *Uncle Tom's Cabin* while her husband taught religion at Bowdoin. The building is now an inn and restaurant, with a fifty-unit motel attached, open year-round.

Pejepscot Historical Society Museum (797-4622), 11 Lincoln Street. Open year-round, Monday-Friday 1-4:30, and by appointment. Pejepscot is the Indian name for the lower Androscoggin, meaning, "crooked like a snake." The collection includes a military room and fire engines dating back to 1810.

THINGS TO DO   Thomas Point Beach (725-6009) at Cook's Corner, ME 24. Sequestered behind the sprawl of the shopping centers there is a public beach on tidal water, overlooking the New Meadows River. Open Memorial Day to Labor Day, 9 AM to sunset, with picnic tables, snack bar, and arcade, nominal fee.

Golf, Brunswick Golf Club. 18 holes (725-8224).

Desert of Maine in Freeport (865-6962). Mid-April to mid-October, 9-5 daily. An enormous patch of sand which was once the Tuttle Farm. Heavily farmed, then extensively forested to feed the railroad in the nineteenth century, the topsoil eventually gave way to sand—which spread—and spread until entire trees sank below its surface. It is an unusual sand, rich in mineral deposits which make it unsuited for commercial use, but interesting to rockhounds. Children love it. Reasonable fee. From I-95 at the Freeport exit, take Desert Road inland until you see the signs.

Winslow Memorial Park, Staples Point in Freeport (five miles off US 1 865-4921). Open Memorial Day to Labor Day, daily 8-10:30, swimming, camping, picnicking.

Mast Landing Sanctuary in Freeport on Mast Landing Road, an Audubon Sanctuary. 150 acres with self-guiding tours, picnicking.

Wolf Neck Woods State Park (865-4465). Open Memorial Day to Labor Day. Nature trails, picnicking.

Eagle Island in Casco Bay, off Harpswell. The former home of Admiral Peary here is not open but, if you can get there, the island is, complete with landing pier, nature trails, and interpretive panels.

Bailey Island. Connected to Brunswick via ME 24, which traverses Orr's Island enroute. A half-dozen motels, an outstanding inn (see Lodging), and a clutch of good seafood restaurants are all clustered on this rocky point. There is a fine shore walk, "The Giant's Steps," and Mackerel Cove is a departure point for deep-sea fishing boats with a record for landing record-breaking tuna.

BOAT EXCURSIONS   Deep-sea fishing. The *Striker* and the *Odyssey,* both based at Dockside Marina (833-6871) in Mackerel Cove, are both available for charter. The *Happy Hooker* offers deep-sea fishing trips out of South Harpswell (Captain Gerald Sullivan: 833-5447). *Odyssey* also offers

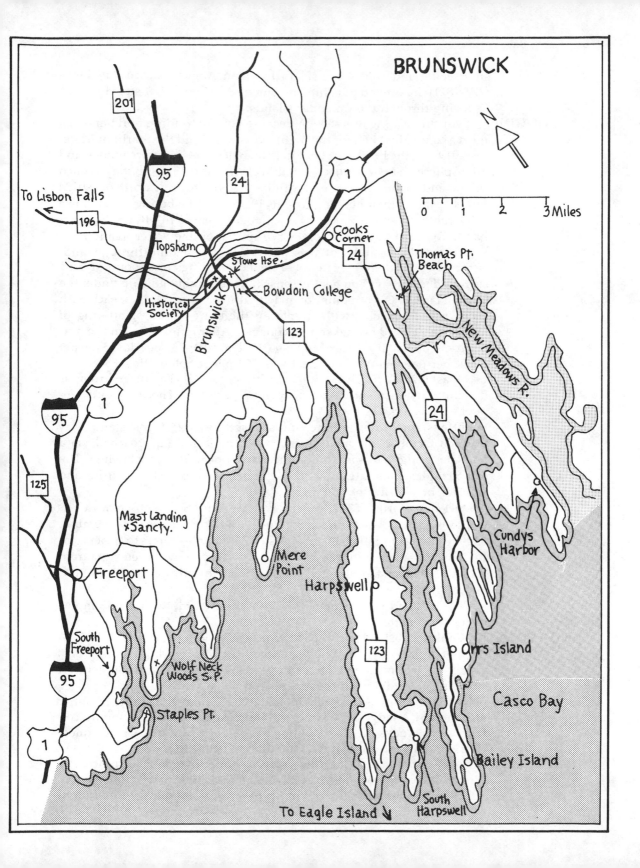

sightseeing and sunset cruises in July and August. **Casco Bay Lines** (774-7871) in Portland puts into the pier next to Cook's Lobster House on its swing through the Calendar Islands.

LODGING   If you are reading this section because you are heading north and just need a convenient bed for the night, we recommend the **Starlight Motel** (729-9195) in the lineup on US 1 in Brunswick, or—for more money and atmosphere—**Stowe House** (see above). If it is a high-holiday crunch period and all the US 1 motels are full, we advise turning north on ME 24 into Topsham, then heading up ME 196 toward Lisbon Falls. This is a truck route, lined with motels which never seem to fill. If, on the other hand, you are looking for someplace special on the water, read on:

Driftwood Inn and Cottages (833-5461). Open June through mid-October. A weathered cluster of shingled buildings on a point of land surrounded by bay. You get the sense here of a tight-run ship under the Conrad family. Guestrooms are in delightful summer houses, each with its own living room (with fireplace); there are also a smattering of moderately priced housekeeping cottages. After June 25, when the dining room opens, it's American Plan (three meals): $32 per day, $180 per week per person. Without meals it's $32 per couple with set rates for breakfast ($2.50), lunch ($5.50), and dinner ($6.95). The dining room is delightful, with splendid views, open to the public. There is a saltwater pool on the rocks below.

Little Island Motel and the Gull's Nest (833-2392), Orr's Island. May through October. Situated on its own little island (approached via a one-lane bridge), this is a nine-unit motel, one unit with a kitchen. The $50-55 high season rates include use of boats and bicycles. Muffins and fruit for breakfast. Refrigerators.

Dockside Marina (833-6656), on Bailey Island. Seven efficiency units overlooking the water, heated. Open mid-April to mid-November. $35-38 off season, $40-45 July, August. This complex caters to fishermen. It is owned, along with the marina and a reasonably priced restaurant (open 7 AM to 9 PM in summer, varying hours in spring and fall), by Stew and Marie Place.

Cook's Island View Motel (833-7780). A standard, twenty-unit motel, some kitchenettes.

RESTAURANTS   **Cook's Lobster House** (833-7356). Memorial Day to Labor Day. A barn of a place, right on the water, adjacent to a working fishing boat pier. *The* place to come for a seafood lunch or dinner; save your leftover French fries and muffin crumbs to feed the seagulls.

The Log Cabin (833-5546). Open March through November for lunch and dinner. A lodge-type structure, built as an enormous summer cottage, which looks like it should be in the north woods. A nice atmosphere and an extensive menu, children's menu, too.

Rock Ovens (833-5546). Mid-April to mid-November for lunch and dinner. A cozy atmosphere, slightly more expensive than the other two.

22 Lincoln Street (725-5893) in Brunswick. Year-round, closed Mon-

Fredrik D. Bodin

L. L. Bean in Freeport

days, specializing in $15-20 dinners geared to a discriminating local clientele.

The Bowdoin House, 115 Main Street (725-2314). Open year-round for lunch and dinner, moderately priced, children's menu.

J.L. Gambianno's Restaurant in Freeport (865-4823). Lunch and dinner year-round, a wide choice of antipasto, pasta, zuppe, and veal dishes; moderately priced; children's menu.

Harraseeket Lunch and Lobster Company (865-4888). South Freeport. Turn off US 1 at the giant wooden Indian outside the Casco Bay Trading Post. Open mid-May through September. A dockside pound at which you order lobsters and clams on one side, fried food on the other, eat at picnic tables (of which there are never enough at peak hours). Homemade pies are a specialty.

SHOPPING   **L.L. Bean** (865-3111). Open twenty-four hours a day, 365 days a year. More than a store—for millions of annual visitors, this is the gateway to Maine. Most shoppers arrive having already studied the mail order catalog and are purposefully buying—be it a $4 pair of thermal boot liners or a $300 tent. The store is a rehabilitated version of the boot factory built by Leon Leonwood Bean. Mr. Bean developed his boot—a unique combination of rubber bottom and leather top—in 1902. He began selling it by mail order but gradually began catering to the hunters and fishermen who tended to pass through his town in the middle of the night. L.L. Bean himself died in 1967, but his grandson Leon Gorman continues to sell 100,000 pairs of the family boots per year. Current stock ranges from canoes through weatherproof cameras, climbing gear, a variety of footwear and clothing (men's flannel shirts are big), and every conceivable gadget designed to keep you warm. There are irregulars and other bargains in the store itself, but this is no factory outlet.

Eastland Shoe Outlet (865-6314). A genuine factory outlet, good for top brand name shoes for the whole family, children too.

SPECIAL EVENTS   **The Maine Festival.** First weekend in August. "A Celebration of Maine's Creative Spirit" is a major cultural bonanza: dancers, musicians, humorists, dramatic groups, craftspeople, and various artists convene from every corner of the state to put on their own shows —which fill every corner of the Bowdoin campus, and every minute from noon to late evening. There is plenty here for children, plenty to eat, too. Tickets vary in price depending on the length of your stay.

Brunswick Music Theater (725-8768). Mid-June through August, evening performances at 8:30, Sunday matinees at 2:30, children's specials on Saturday morning.

Bowdoin College Summer Concerts (725-8731, extension 321). The Aeolian Chamber Players present a series of concerts.

Tuna Tournament at Bailey Island, last full week in July.

MID-COAST

Bath and Environs

Shipbuilding began in Bath with a thirty-ton vessel launched in 1607, and it continues with tankers and naval ships currently on the ways at Bath Iron Works—which employs roughly the same number of people employed by the sixteen shipyards here in the 1850s. Above the gates at the Iron Works a sign proclaims: "Through these gates pass the world's best shipbuilders." It's no idle boast. Many current employees have inherited their skills from a long line of forebears involved in producing a total of 5000 ships launched from this stretch of the Kennebec River over the years.

Obviously this is the place for a museum about ships and shipbuilding. The Maine Maritime Museum just happens to have one of the country's foremost collections of ship models, journals, photographs, and other memorabilia. Museum sites include a mansion and a church full of exhibits, and a shipyard full of more exhibits. The museum program includes an apprenticeship in which small craft are built. The museum tour—which absorbs the better part of a day—includes a cruise on the river past the ships currently under construction at the Iron Works.

Allow a full day for Bath. Over the past few years the old red brick city has undergone a renaissance, and now it is a place to shop and dine in its own right. While it is not a place to stay, there are nearby inns—as there are beaches and nature preserves—worth finding.

GUIDANCE   **Bath Chamber of Commerce** (443-9751), year round, 45 Front Street. Also: mid-June to mid-October, a US 1 (northbound side) information center is one of the state's busiest. It marks the gateway to Maine's mid-coast—also offers picnic tables and restrooms (both modern and old-style).

GETTING THERE   **Greyhound** offers frequent service, but you need a car. US 1 passes above the city (and the Kennebec) via the Carleton Bridge, and provides easy access.

SIGHTS TO SEE   **Maine Maritime Museum** (443-6311). Open year round, daily. Mid-May through October all sites are open daily 10-5. Phone to check off-season hours. The 1981 fees: $5 per adult, $2 for children under 16, maximum family charge $16. This includes access to the four museum sites as well as the twenty-five-minute ride aboard the *M/V Sasonoa*, and you can come back the next day free. The sites are:

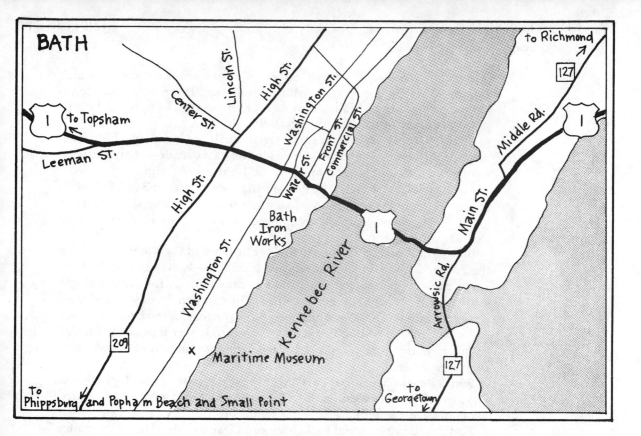

Sewall House, 963 Washington Street. A thirty-room, 1844 mansion. Exhibits focus on the years in which the Sewalls made their own fortune, building the bulk of the country's four-masted barks, cannily switching to steel-hulled versions at the right time, and, incidentally, helping the Hawaiian Islands get annexed by country. There is a hands-on children's room with bells to pull and helm to man.

Winter Street Center, 880 Washington Street. An 1843 Gothic revival church which once served as spiritual center for the city's sea captains, but which was about to be razed in 1971, when local preservationists rallied to save it. Displays trace the history of shipbuilding in town. You learn that State O'Mainers were such skilled shipbuilders by the time the local lumber supply was exhausted that the timber was actually brought to them; late nineteenth-century Maine vessels tended to be made of Georgia pine. There is a grand parade of ship models: clipper ships, Down Easters and multi-masted schooners (designed to ferry coal and local exports such as ice, granite, and lime).

Percy and Small Shipyard, 263 Washington Street. The only extant shipyard in America which has produced large wooden sailing ships. The buildings here house photos and models of the multi-masted vessels produced on the spot between 1894 and 1920. In the restoration shop next door, visitors can watch ongoing work on historic vessels under renovation.

Apprentice Shop, 375 Front Street. Visitors are welcome to watch boatbuilding by apprentices who are engaged in an eighteen-month "labor for learning" (no tuition, no pay) program. The goal is to perpetuate the art of wooden boat building.

Front Street. A commercial strip built grandly in the city's nineteenth-century heyday, restored in the past decade—complete with benches, landscaping, and appropriate lighting and signs.

The Chocolate Church. The Performing Arts Center of Bath (442-8455) offers year-round presentations: summer theater, concerts, a variety of guest artists, also an art gallery housed in a chocolate-colored, Gothic Revival church.

Bath Iron Works. Not open to the public beyond the water views from the *Sasonoa* (see above), but since the company's 400-foot-high shipways crane looms over the city, and because this is the largest single employer in Maine, it deserves a word. The company is descended from a firm founded in 1884, and has been filling orders for the US Navy since 1891. During World War II it actually produced more destroyers than all of Japan, and it continues to fill Navy orders faster and at a lower cost than any other firm.

Fort Baldwin Memorial Park in Phippsburg, site of the Popham colony, which tried to weather the winter of 1607-8, but gave up and sailed away aboard the pinnace Virginia, built on the spot.

Fort Popham Memorial Park. Memorial Day to Labor Day. Picnic sites are scattered around the ruins of the 1861 fort, which overlooks the beach.

THINGS TO DO **Popham Beach State Park** (389-1335). An immense expanse of sand, also a sand bar, tidal pools, and smooth rocks. Never fills up, but can be windy. $1.50 day use fee in 1981, standard state facilities.

Reid State Park in Georgetown (371-2302). Open Memorial Day to Labor Day. $1.50. Fourteen miles south of US 1 on ME 127. Bath house, snack bar, 1½ miles of sand in three distinct beaches which seldom fill—but the limited parking area does fill by noon on weekends in season. You can choose between surf, and slightly warmer sheltered backwater for children.

Merrymeeting Bay and Swan Island. Upstream from Bath, the Kennebec mingles with five other rivers to form a 4500-acre bay, much loved by birders as a prime stopover on the Atlantic Flyway. The area is accessible to the public from ME 201 in Topsham, and from ME 24 in Bowdoinham. Camping is actually permitted on Swan Island at the northern end of the bay. Ferry service from Richmond and a half-hour bus tour of the **Steve Powell Wildlife Management Area** can be arranged by writing Wildlife Division, Department of Inland Fisheries and Wildlife, 284 State Street, Augusta, Maine 04333.

LODGING **Crane's Fairhaven Inn** (443-4391). Open year-round. Hidden away on the Kennebec River as it meanders down from Merrymeeting Bay, this 1790s house has nine pleasant rooms, four with bath, all very neat, antiques, a warm hearth, and gourmet breakfasts. $20 single, $3 extra for breakfast.

Rock Gardens Inn, Sebasco Estates (389-1339). Mid-June through September. On the grounds of **Sebasco Estates,** a large, self-contained golfing resort, this is a small inn (four rooms in the inn, nine more in surrounding cottages) with a charming dining room. Overlooking the water and offering use of the tennis, golf, and other facilities at the adjacent resort, it is also handy to Popham Beach.

Grey Havens Inn in Georgetown (371-2616). Open Memorial Day to Columbus Day. The same Mr. Reid who donated the neighboring state park built this turreted, grey-shingled summer hotel with a deck-like porch which commands a sweeping view of Sheepscot Bay. Inside, the feel is unexpectedly homey and imaginative. There is a huge rock fireplace, an old-style dining room which manages not to be stiff, and twenty-four upstairs rooms, ranging from small doubles ($36 per night) to large turret rooms ($65 per couple), breakfast included. The dining room is open Tuesday-Saturday by reservation; its moderately priced menu features fresh seafood and organically grown fruit and vegetables. Swimming is just up the road at Reid State Park, and a lobster pound and rental boats can be found at the nearby village of Five Islands.

New Meadows Inn (443-3921). Open year-round, with the exception of the ten cottages which close mid-October, open late May. An adequate motel a few miles south of Bath (take the New Meadows exit off US 1) with a good family restaurant, open for lunch and dinner, children's menu.

Cottages for this area are listed in the Maine Publicity Bureau's *Maine Guide to Camp and Cottage Rentals.* (Also see Cottage Rentals in "What's Where.")

RESTAURANTS **Wife of Bath** (433-3036). Open year-round, closed Monday, Commercial Street, Bath. Overlooking the Kennebec from the modernistic Bathport complex, this establishment is open for lunch and dinner with an ambitious menu that changes monthly. Moderately expensive, but well worth it. Light meals, drinks, and entertainment are upstairs in the Alewife Saloon.

J. R. Maxwell (633-5203). Year-round, 122 Front Street in Bath in a renovated 1840s hotel. Basic chicken, steak, and seafood with blasted brick atmosphere at moderately expensive prices, children's menu.

Kristina's Bakery (442-8577). Corner of High and Center Streets in Bath. At this writing open daily for lunch, and Thursday-Saturday for dinner. You can get a hamburger on a homemade roll, but the specialties are salads, sandwiches with generous greens, quiche, omelettes, special breads, and desserts. A small, pleasant restaurant with a big reputation, reasonable prices.

Souperwoman, 34 Center Street in Bath. Year-round, weekdays for breakfast and lunch. Reasonably priced homemade soups, salads, and desserts.

Lobster House at Small Point (389-1596). Open summer season, ME 126 from US 1, a classic lobster pound specializing in seafood dinners, homemade pastry, beer and wine served, moderate prices.

Spinney's Restaurant and Guest House (389-1122). Open May to Labor Day, at the end of ME 209 at Popham Beach. Our kind of beach restaurant: counter and tables, pleasant atmosphere with basic chowder and sandwich menu, also hot plates, reasonably priced. The cottages out back are geared to fishermen who frequent this end of the beach.

SPECIAL EVENTS   July 4 weekend and week: **Bath Heritage Days;** elaborate Independence Day celebration, a fair in Waterfront Park, a variety of happenings. Mid-August: **Annual Antiques Show** sponsored by Bath Junior Hospital League; **The Great Kennebec River Boat Race,** a power boat marathon down the lower reach of the Kennebec.

Bodin/Dudley

Wiscasset

Wiscasset is Maine's gift to motorists toiling up US 1. For pilgrims who have endured hours of interstate and commercial clutter, here is finally a line of unmistakable sea captains' mansions, and a Main Street full of picturesque brick buildings, slanting toward the Sheepscot River. The inevitable traffic crunch invites you to slow as you near the bridge, the better to view wrecks of two schooners—the *Hesper* and *Luther Little*—a delight for camera clickers.

Still shire town of Lincoln County, Wiscasset is only half as populous as it was in 1850. As the abundance of wooden mansions attest, this was a thriving port after the Revolution and before the War of 1812. Many fine old buildings are open to the public, and many more house antique shops and restaurants. Lodging is limited. Most visitors stay in the Boothbays—from which this is a place to catch the bus for a sense of local history.

GUIDANCE   A leaflet "Visitors Guide" is available from the Association for Wiscasset Area Regional Development, PO Box 291, Wiscasset 04578.

GETTING THERE   **Greyhound** stops at the Wiscasset Newstand, Main Street (882-7148). From Portland's Jetport there is limo transport (1-800-482-7494). Air charters are available from **Wiscasset Airways** at the municipal airport on ME 144 (882-5089).

GETTING AROUND   You need a car, but it is possible to use this as a waystop enroute to Monhegan—come by bus, spend the night in town, and take a taxi to the dock to board the *Balmy Days* (see Boothbays).

SIGHTS TO SEE   **Lincoln County Museum** (882-6817). Open mid-June-Labor Day, Monday-Saturday 10-5, Sunday 2:30-5, and by appointment the rest of the year. Nominal fee. The museum is composed of a chilling 1811 jail with damp, thick granite walls (in use until 1953), and the jailor's house with displays of tools, costumes, and other memorabilia.

The Maine Art Gallery (633-5055). Warren Street in the old academy (1807); exhibits by Maine artists and special programs year round. Free. Open late June-Labor Day, Monday-Saturday 10-4.

The Nickels-Sortwell House. June 1-September 30, daily 12-5, closed Monday. $2. A classic Federal-era mansion, corner of Main and Federal Streets. It served as a hotel for many years. Some furnishings date from the early twentieth century, when it was owned by a Cambridge, Massachusetts mayor. The elliptical staircase is outstanding.

Fort Edgecomb State Memorial. Off US 1 just north of the bridge. An octagonal block house (1809), open seasonably (25c for age 12 and on), but the beauty of the place is its exterior and the grounds, which make it an ideal picnic site (for the same reasons that it was an obvious fort site—it overlooks a narrow passage of the Sheepscot River).

Musical Wonder House (882-7163). June-Labor Day, Monday-Saturday 10-5, Sundays and Holidays 1-5, 18 High Street. Guided tours through a fine old house filled with musical machines. $5.

Castle Tucker (882-7364). July and August, Monday-Saturday 11-4, and by appointment. An extremely unusual 1807 mansion overlooking the harbor, Victorian furnishings. $1.

Lincoln County Courthouse. Open business hours, built 1824. The oldest functioning courthouse in New England, an imposing structure on the Common.

Lincoln County Fire Museum. Open July-Labor Day, weekdays 10-4, and by appointment. Exhibits include an 1803 hand tub, also stages, and a hearse.

Pownalborough Court House (882-6817). Open July and August, Wednesday-Sunday, 11-4. Worth the eight-mile drive north on ME 27 to Dresden. The only surviving pre-Revolutionary courthouse in Maine, it conveys a sense of this country along the Kennebec in 1760, when this was an outpost tavern and dwelling as well as courtroom. It is a dramatic, three-story building, still isolated, with fascinating exhibits.

World's Smallest Church, ME 218. Just room for two worshippers, maintained as a memorial to a former Boston Baptist minister.

Maine Yankee Atomic Power (882-7153). New England's largest nuclear generating station has an elaborate visitors' center, open Monday-Saturday 10-5, Sunday 12-5. Take ME 144 off US 1, three miles west of town.

LODGING **Ledges Inn and Restaurant** (882-6832), year-round. An old mansion that has seen better days. Clean but plain, and noisy, since it is located right on US 1 at a point where trucks must shift into low gear to go downhill. Four rooms, two with private path ($27), two with shared ($22). A short walk from the bus stop.

The Roberts House (882-5055), bed and breakfast, Main Street. Year-round. A 1799 house with three rooms, two with double beds, one with twin. Guests make themselves at home; breakfasts are filling and include homemade bread; $30 double, $20 single.

Squire Tarbox Inn (882-7693), open May 22-October 12. On Westport Island, ten miles south of US 1. A quiet, pleasant retreat in a Federal-era home: eight guestrooms, three of them in the barn. Very clean, attractive, with a big reputation for owner Anne McInvale's cooking, served to guests only; $30 single, $42 double, including breakfast but not dinner. A set dinner is $14.50 in 1981.

Riverside Inn and Cottages (882-6364), open all year. Across the bridge in North Edgecomb, smack on the river, a new, box-like building

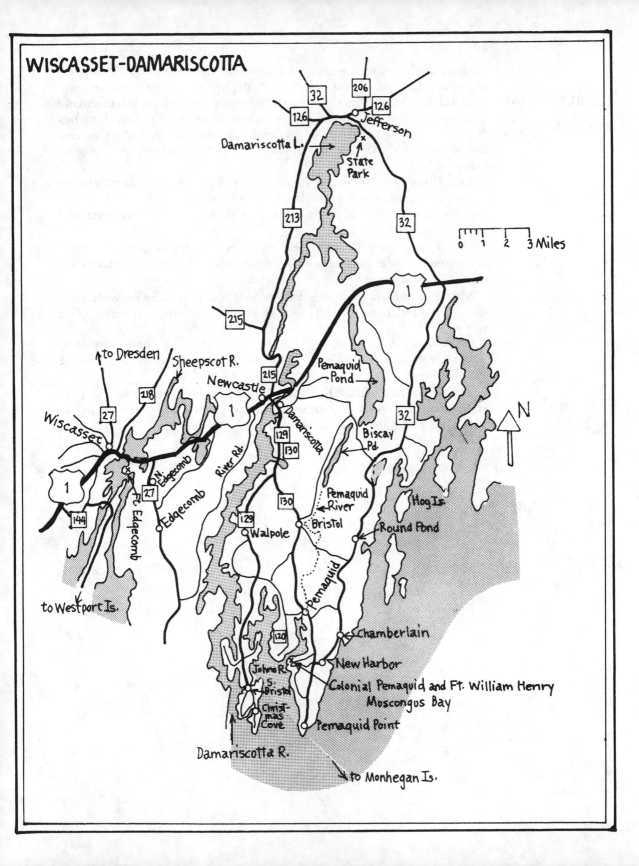

WISCASSET-DAMARISCOTTA

32
206
126
126
Jefferson
Damariscotta L.
x
State Park
213
32
0 1 2 3 Miles
1
215
to Dresden
Sheepscot R.
Pemaquid Pond
Newcastle
215
32
218
27
Wiscasset
Damariscotta
Biscay Pd.
129
130
N. Edgecomb
River Rd.
27
Edgecomb
Ft. Edgecomb
130
129
Pemaquid River
Bristol
Hog Is.
Walpole
Round Pond
1
144
Pemaquid
to Westport Is.
120
Chamberlain
New Harbor
Johns R. S.
Bristol
Colonial Pemaquid and Ft. William Henry
Moscongus Bay
Christmas Cove
Pemaquid Point
Damariscotta R.
to Monhegan Is.

N

containing fifteen efficiencies and combines in one complex. A scattering of older, seasonal cottages. $10-35, depending on unit and season.

RESTAURANTS   Le Garage (882-5409). Year-round except January. Water Street. An old auto repair shop with a glassed-in porch overlooking the river. Lunches (crepes, omelets, soups) are $2-4, and dinner is under $10 in an airy blue-and-white room with classical background music. Exceptional value.

Tree House Tavern (882-6070) on Water Street. A cozy tavern atmosphere, lunch and dinner, sandwiches and specials.

Tat's Diner (882-7700). Main Street. Closed Sundays. Counter and booths, good for breakfast.

Muddy Rudder (882-7748). Seasonal, US 1, North Edgecomb. Lunch and dinner, moderately expensive, basic fish and steak, but nice riverside site, deck dining.

Montsweag Farm Restaurant (443-6563). US 1 midway between Bath and Wiscasset. Long established, large but charming, friendly, good value.

McLellans Seafood (882-6000). US 1 in North Edgecomb, seasonal. Extremely reasonable lobster, both cooked and ready to go, shaded picnic tables.

Ice Cream: **The Milk Shed,** Middle Street, 11-9 daily. Basics, plus make-your-own sundaes. **Round Top Ice Cream** (based in Damariscotta) also maintains a seasonal stand near the bridge.

Damariscotta Area

The Damariscotta area, including Newcastle, Bristol, New Harbor and Pemaquid, typifies the best of coastal Maine. There is something here for everybody and not too many bodies to get in the way of enjoying it.

Damariscotta's musical name means "meeting place of the alewives" and there are, indeed, alewives to be seen by the waterfall at Damariscotta Mills in spring—not far from a spot on which generations of Indians heaped oyster shells from their summer feasts. The Indians also had a name for the peninsula jutting ten miles seaward from this spot: "Pemaquid," meaning "long finger."

Pemaquid loomed large on sixteenth- and seventeenth-century maps, because its protected inner harbor was the nearest mainland haven to Monhegan Island, a fishing stage for European fishermen since the 1500s. It was from these fishermen that Pemaquid Indian Samoset learned the English with which he welcomed the Pilgrims at Plymouth in 1621. The following winter, the Pemaquid settlement supplied the Plymouth one with supplies enough to see it through to spring. Pemaquid, however, lacked a Governor Bradford to write down its history; although it is occasionally referred to as this country's first permanent settlement, its status remains murky.

The site of Maine's "Lost City" is delightful, surrounded on three sides by Johns River (an arm of the bay), where lobster boats and sailing craft are moored. At one tip of the mini-peninsula stands a round stone fort, and near it a square, decidedly spooky, old garrison house. In recent years more than 40,000 artifacts have been unearthed in the adjacent meadow, many of them now displayed in Colonial Pemaquid, a fine state-run museum which has been set up beside a lobster pound. A cemetery full of crooked slate headstones completes the scene.

Since the late nineteenth century, when steamboats put into New Harbor, this area has been a summer resort. It is blessed with beaches, both fresh and saltwater, and with fascinating coastal rocks, especially at Pemaquid Point where the fine old light towers above them. Cottages are scattered throughout the area, and there are some exceptional inns.

GUIDANCE **The Damariscotta Region Information Bureau,** Maine 04543 has two locations: one on Business Route 1 at Church Street (563-3175), and one on US 1 in Newcastle (563-3176). Both are open mid-June to late September, 10-6, closed Sunday, but can be reached by mail year-round.

The Bureau keeps tabs on vacancies. In June it will also match inquiries with available cottages in the area extending from Jefferson to Pemaquid Point.

GETTING THERE   **Greyhound** buses stop in Damariscotta. Airport transportation to Portland Jetport (Delta and Bar Harbor Airlines) is available (800-482-7494). A few inns on the peninsula will pick guests up in Damariscotta, but basically this is the kind of place that requires a car—or a boat—to get around.

SIGHTS TO SEE   *Churches.* This particular area possesses an unusual number of fine old meeting houses and churches, all of them open to the public. **St. Patrick's Catholic Church,** Academy Road in Newcastle (posted from Newcastle Village), is open year-round, daily to sunset, and is the oldest surviving Catholic church (1808) in New England, and an unusual building: brick and very narrow with a Paul Revere bell; pews and stained glass date from 1896; there is an old graveyard out back, and forest all around.

The Old Walpole Meeting House in South Bristol (563-3983), ME 129, open on July and August Sundays at 3 PM for services, and by appointment. A fine 1772 meeting house, restored to its original shape with box pews and a pulpit with a sounding board.

The Old German Church, also built in 1772 (832-5100), is open July and August daily: 1-4, free and fascinating; an inscription in the cemetery reads: "This town was settled in 1748 by Germans who immigrated to this place with the promise and expectation of finding a prosperous city, instead of which they found nothing but wilderness." Bostonian Samuel Waldo—owner of a large tract of coastal land in this area—had obviously not been straight with the forty German families he imported to settle. This was the first Lutheran church in Maine, long since gone native (Congregational).

Still another 1770s church—**Harrington Meeting House** in Pemaquid on ME 130—is open July and August, Monday, Wednesday, Saturday: 2-5, 50c. It has been restored as a museum of "Old Bristol," including all the peninsula.

Fort William Henry. May 30-Labor Day, daily: 10-6; 25c adults, Route 130. This is a replica of the third in a series of four forts built on this one site to fend off pirates and Frenchmen. In 1630 a stockade was built, but it was sacked and burned by pirate Dixie Bull. In 1677 Governor Andros built a wooden redoubt manned by fifty men, but this was captured by Baron Castine and his Indians in 1689 (see Castine). The original of this fort, built in 1698, was to be "the most expensive and strongest fortification that had ever been built on American Soil," but it was destroyed by the French a year later. Fort Frederick, built in 1729, was never attacked, but during the Revolution locals tore it down lest it fall into British hands.

Colonial Pemaquid. Memorial Day to Labor Day, 9:30-5:30, adults 50c, children 25c. Just up the road from Fort William Henry. After the

Harrington Meeting House

neighboring fort had been torn down this was a little-noticed corner of town, and in the early nineteenth century local farmers filled in the cellar holes of the seventeenth-century settlement. Excavations over the past decade have been made through the efforts of Rutgers University Professor Helen Camp, who noticed clay pipes and other artifacts in a newly plowed field near the fort. She submitted these findings to the Smithsonian Institute, which verified their importance. The state has since purchased this neck of land, including its lobster pound. Inside the present museum building (which once housed the pound's female employees) you view a diorama of the original 1620s settlement, and artifacts such as a sixteenth-century German wine jug and slightly later tools and pottery, Spanish oil jars, and wampum—all found in the cellar holes which you can see outside.

Pemaquid Point Lighthouse and Fishermen's Museum (677-2726), end of ME 130. The museum, housed in the former lighthouse keeper's home, is open Memorial Day-September, Monday-Saturday; 10-5, Sunday: 11-5 and by appointment. The point is owned by the town, which charges a 35c per person parking fee (free under age twelve). The lighthouse, built in 1827 and automated in 1934, is a beauty, looking even more impressive from the rocks below than from the parking lot. These rocks, wonderfully varied and filled with tidal pools, can occupy children and adults alike for an entire day; they stretch a half mile to Kresge Point (where you can park free). The museum has fine photographs and ship models, as well as other artifacts related to the Maine fishing industry, and a description of coastal lighthouses. The complex at the Point also includes the Pemaquid Art Gallery and public toilets.

Thompson's Ice House, ME 129 in South Bristol. One of the few surviving commercial ice houses in New England, a 150-year-old family business using traditional tools for cutting ice from the adjacent pond.

Old Rock Schoolhouse. Follow signs from ME 130 and 132 in Bristol. Open in summer months, Tuesday and Friday: 2-4. Dank, haunting, rural stone schoolhouse at a long-overgrown crossroads in the woods.

Chapman-Hall House Late June to early September, daily except Monday: 1-5; small fee. Corner of Main and Church Streets in Damariscotta, a restored, mid-eighteenth-century home with its original kitchen and herb garden.

Damariscotta Shell Heaps What is left of these famous mounds is on private land. Inquire at the Information Bureau.

SWIMMING   **Pemaquid Beach Park,** a town-owned area, open Memorial to Labor Day: 9-6; with rest rooms, a bath house, snack bar, and picnic tables: 75c adults, free under age twelve. Nice, but it can be windy, in which case try the pebblier but more sheltered (free) beach down the road.

On the peninsula there is public swimming at **Biscay Pond** off ME 32, and at **Bristol Dam** on ME 130, five miles south of Damariscotta.

Damariscotta Lake State Park, ME 32 in Jefferson, is a fine sandy beach with changing facilities, picnic tables, and grills up at the northern end of the lake.

GOLF   **Wawenock Country Club** (563-3938), open May-November, nine holes. ME 129, seven miles South of Damariscotta.

CANOEING   **Pemaquid River Canoe Rental** (563-5721). Route 130 across from Bristol Dam, open May-October, 7-7. Canoes rented by the hour, day, or week to be used on the Pemaquid River, which links Bristol Dam with Biscay Pond and Pemaquid Lake.

Audubon Ecology Camp. For details about the two-week summer sessions on Hog Island, a quarter mile off shore at the head of Muscongus Bay, write: Camp Registrar, National Audubon Society, 950 Third Avenue, New York, New York 10022.

LODGING   **Gosnold Arms** in New Harbor (677-2103). Mid-June through September; meals end Labor Day. New Harbor itself is a picture perfect clutter of lobster boats and pleasure craft. The inn is a rambling white clapboard complex: an old farmhouse with a long, welcoming porch (much of which serves as an extension of the dining room), an attached barn, and scattered cottages. Sixteen rooms have been fitted into the barn around a pleasant gathering space complete with huge fireplace.

The farmhouse itself has three upstairs rooms, and then there are the cottages, ranging from a one-person former ship's pilothouse to the original steamboat freight office. There are no efficiencies. Guests breakfast and sup in the dining room, which is also open to the public (dinner entrees are $8-10). Rates range from $28 per person to $64 per couple, two meals included, less $12 per couple without meals.

The Bradley Inn, Pemaquid Point (677-2105). Mid-May until mid-October. Twelve upstairs rooms in a pleasant old summer hotel which prides itself on its dining room; a pleasant walk from the lighthouse in one direction, from Kresge Point in the other: $29 single, $32 double without meals.

Newcastle Inn, River Road in Newcastle (563-8878), open all year. A middle-of-town, comfortable kind of inn, with 24 rooms: $20 double with shared bath, $27 with private bath, breakfast not included but served (no other meals).

The Brandon-Bunker Inn (563-5914). May-October, Route 129 not far south of Damariscotta. An 1820 home with eight artfully furnished rooms, four in the main house, four more in the attached barn, also two efficiency units in an adjacent coach house. There is handy fresh water swimming, and golf across the road; breakfast included in $35 double (private bath), $30 (shared bath), $20 for a single room with shared bath.

Christmas Cove Coveside Inn (644-8282). June through September. Holly red, with a mansard roof, and five old-fashioned rooms (ten more in the motel which hangs out over the water across the road). This is an extremely attractive inn which must be booked far in advance. Meals are served in the Dory Bar and Shore Restaurant in a separate building down the road. $32 to $34 per room in the inn, $38 in the motel, no meals included.

Hotel Pemaquid. A century-old, classic summer hotel, run down until 1981, when it was purchased by a group of Portland businessmen. When we stopped by, the place was under renovation, to reopen for the 1982 season with twenty-eight rooms, roughly $28 per couple.

Damariscotta Lake Farm in Jefferson (549-7953). Sited at the junction of Routes 32, 126 and 213 at the head of Damariscotta Lake, these lined-up one-, two- and three-bedroom efficiency cottages with screen porches go for $120-180 per week; there is a private, sandy beach, boat rentals, and a restaurant serving the supper meal only, but ice cream all day. Open year-round weekends; daily June-September from 11:30.

The Tern Inn, Bristol (563-5296). A big yellow Victorian house on ME 130 near Pemaquid Beach. It offers nine rooms, five in the house and four motel units, $34 per couple with private baths, $22 shared.

Ocean Reefs Lodge, Chamberlain (677-2396). A guesthouse with a nice site up ME 32 from New Harbor: $22 per person, $30 per couple, continental breakfast included; less of a value, I felt, than the Gosnold Arms.

Down Easter Inn, ME 130 just south of Damariscotta (563-5332). A gracious old manor house with rooms in the back and a new motel wing.

COTTAGES   All of these must generally be booked by March of the season, but you can luck into a cancellation.

Harborside Cottages (677-2701). May through October. Right on the harbor, six with two bedrooms and Franklin stoves, four with one bedroom: $140-$180 per week.

Thompson House and Cottages (677-2317). Four apartments, one- and two-bedrooms: $125-175, in an annex to the handsome main house; and a number of cottages scattered along the harbor and back cove: $310 per week, and out on the ocean: $410. Those on the cove and ocean seem to be a good value.

The Jamestown, a variety of apartments and rooms in one building overlooking the water near Fort William Henry; all share a lounge: from $75 per week for a third-floor efficiency to $185 per week for a cottage.

Ye Olde Forte Cabins (677-2261), mid-May to late October. A parade of snug cottages up and down the grassy knoll beside Fort William Henry; all share a "cookhouse:" $112 to $185 per week.

RESTAURANTS   **New Harbor Co-op,** "owned and operated by fishermen" (677-2791), summer season, daily: 11-7:30. An unbeatable location with a deck right above the harbor, and uniformly the lowest-going boiled lobster and steamed clam prices that we have found in Maine; indoor dining for chilly weather; no beer or wine, but you can bring your own.

Christmas Cove Dory Bar and Shore Restaurant (644-8540). June through September. Out of the way, but a nice excuse to drive down to the tip of ME 129, actually an island connected to South Bristol by one of the world's smallest drawbridges. The cove is so named because explorer Captain John Smith so named it on December 25, 1614. The restaurant, connected with the nearby inn, serves three daily meals and is a beloved local standby, known for baked mussels and seafood pies.

The Cheechako (563-3536), off Elm Street at Lewis Point in Damariscotta; April to mid-October, closed Mondays, lunch and dinner; a long-established dining room with a pleasant, low-key atmosphere, a distinguished seafood menu, and a loyal following.

Pine Grove Family Restaurant (563-3765), year-round, three daily meals, US 1 north of Damariscotta. A pleasant dining room with moderate prices and the motto: "Where friendliness adds flavor to your food." Service can be slow, but there is a takeout window for those in a hurry.

Small Brothers (677-2200), next to the New Harbor Co-op (see above). Open late May to mid-October, daily: 11-8. More expensive than its neighbor, but offering a real dining room, liquor, and a variety of basic foods (sandwiches or specials such as meatloaf, fish cakes, and stews).

The Gosnold Arms (see Lodging), also in New Harbor, offers a genuine dining room; dinners served either in the nineteenth-century house or on its porch; moderately priced.

The Bradley Inn (see Lodging) at Pemaquid Point is open to the public for lunch and dinner, desserts a specialty.

The Sea Gull Shop at Pemaquid Point (677-2374). May 11-October 15, 8-8. A good place for breakfast, but better for other meals before they hiked their prices ($6.50 for a lobster roll). There is even a charge for the restrooms. If you can get a table in the tiny Monhegan Room (facing out to sea), it's all worthwhile. The food is basically good.

Pemaquid Fisherman's Co-op, seasonal, daily, 8-4:30, on Pemaquid Harbor off ME 120; another basic boiled-lobster-and-steamed-clam place with picnic tables, but not even any butter.

Clarissa Illsley Tavern, junction US 1 and Business Route 1 north of Damariscotta (563-5500). Year-round, dinner only, big but lots of charm and good value; a complete dinner (including appetizer, salad, entree, and dessert) for $6, carafes of wine, children's menu.

Round Top Ice Cream. Memorial Day to Labor Day, Business Route 1 north of Damariscotta, 11-10:30. This is the original Round Top—on the grounds of the farm, where it all used to happen (an expanded creamery is now just over the hill). In addition to the creamy ice cream in dozens of flavors there are hot dogs only; but an outstanding roadside stand just down the road sells burgers and corned beef sandwiches—which can be topped off with a cone under the umbrella-topped tables here.

Cohen's Deli and Bakery (563-4334) in Damariscotta, 7:30-5; a few tables, otherwise a takeout specializing in imported foods and quality sandwiches.

Clark's Spa, Main Street, Damariscotta. There is an old-fashioned soda fountain here, an excuse to come into the shop, which specializes in books on Maine, fishing licenses, and a myriad of reading and writing basics which may not be out on display, but can be plucked out of the walls on request.

SHOPPING   Damariscotta/Newcastle—two towns connected by a bridge—add up to one of the better spots along the coast to look for antiques. The nineteenth-century brick buildings along Damariscotta's Main Street also house a number of fascinating shops. Across from Clark's Spa (see above) is the **Maine Coast Book Shop** (one of the best in the state). There is also **The Lincoln,** an old-fashioned movie house, and on Water Street there is the **Victorian Stable** (seasonal), its box stalls and tack room filled with the work of more than 100 Maine craftsmen.

SPECIAL EVENTS   Oyster Festival, second week in July: oysters fixed every way (especially au naturel), music, crafts, and a canoe race down the Damariscotta River.

Boothbay Harbor Region

The water in Boothbay Harbor is more than a view. It is something you must cross—via a footbridge—to get from one side of town to the other. It is something you explore on a choice of more than thirty excursion boat rides, something you test gingerly with your toes along quiet inlets, and enjoy in hidden, warm water ponds.

Boothbay Harbor is the liveliest of Maine's mid-coast resorts. Enticing shops line its crooked streets, and there are plenty of dining spots, even a few offering nightly music. But what the Boothbays are best known for is boats. Boats are built, repaired, and sold on this scraggly peninsula, and Boothbay Harbor itself—with due respect to Marblehead, Massachusetts—calls itself "Boating Capital of New England." Certainly it offers the region's greatest number and variety of pay-as-you-go trips.

Excursion rides range from an hour's sail out into the harbor, to a forty-one mile cruise up to the Kennebec to see ships under construction at the Bath Iron Works. You can also ride out to Monhegan, an exquisite island with public paths through the woods and along precipitous cliffs. And if you want to pursue giant tuna, stripers and blues, there are a half dozen deep sea fishing boats, complete with electronic fish-finders.

Until this century the Boothbays relied on the construction and operation of sailing vessels for both livelihood and transport. Even today the harbor looks complete only during Windjammer Days, when it is filled with sails of a dozen passenger-carrying schooners and hundreds of smaller sailing craft.

It's obvious from the very lay of the village that men have always walked around town and boated to other destinations. The village of Boothbay Harbor packs its lodging and dining places into an amazingly small piece of waterfront. The remaining, extremely convoluted coastline of the peninsula takes a day to explore by car, and you see little more than pine trees. That's because the area's self-contained resorts are all sequestered on "heads" and "points." Other inns and cottages, naturally, also hug the ocean.

Good public beaches are, unfortunately, something that the Boothbays lack entirely. But the resorts and many of the more expensive motels have pools. Better yet are the warm water lakes and ponds, accessible from dozens of rental cottages, a few cottage colonies, and motels.

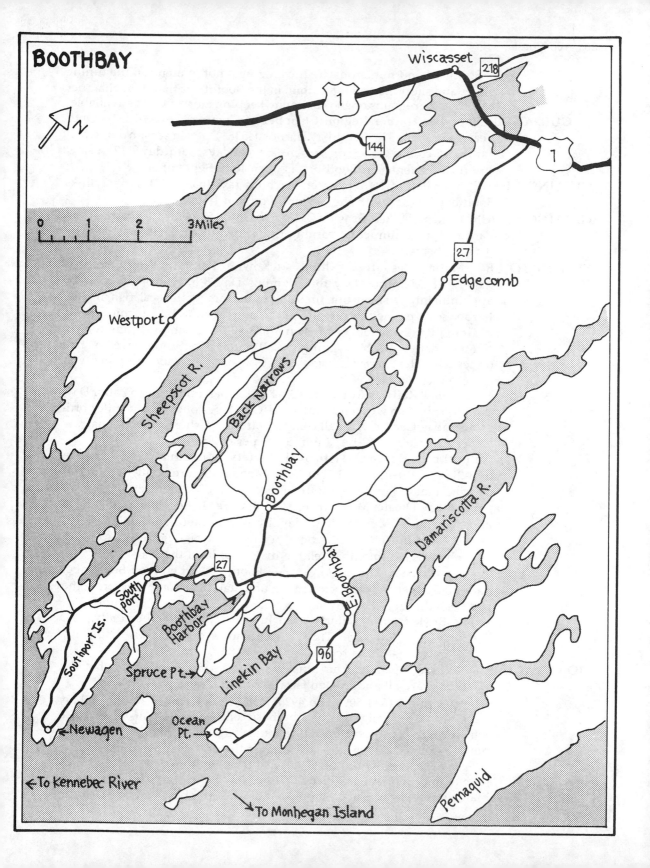

BOOTHBAY

N

0   1   2   3 Miles

Wiscasset

1

218

1

144

27

Edgecomb

Westport

Sheepscot R.

Back Narrows

Boothbay

Damariscotta R.

27

E. Boothbay

South port

Southport Is.

Boothbay Harbor

96

Spruce Pt.→

Linekin Bay

←Newagen

Ocean Pt.→

Pemaquid

←To Kennebec River

→To Monhegan Island

So varied and numerous are the lodgings, not to mention the dining places and shops geared to visitors, in the Boothbays that their chamber of commerce remains open year-round keeping tabs on what's available.

GUIDANCE   Boothbay Harbor Region Chamber of Commerce (633-2353). Open year-round, Box 356, Boothbay Harbor 04538. Open in season daily (May through October 31) 9-7; off season 9-5 weekdays, Saturday 9-12. A small information center in Boothbay is open June-September.

GETTING THERE   Greyhound to Wiscasset. **Archie's taxi** (633-2221) service links Boothbay Harbor with the bus and Portland Jetport.

GETTING AROUND   Rental bikes: **Seaside Cycle,** 3½ Union Street, Boothbay Harbor. **Parking:** good municipal parking right downtown, facilitates daytripping on boats.

SIGHTS TO SEE   Marine Resources Exhibit, McKown's Point in West Boothbay (289-2291). Memorial Day to Columbus Day 8-5, rest of the year by appointment. A small but first-rate aquarium with local fish inside, harbor seals penned in outside pools, a great spot for a picnic, free.

Grand Banks Schooner Museum (633-4727). Open mid-June to September, daily. 9 A.M.-evening. $1.50 adults, 75c under twelve, free under five. The *Sherman Zwicker* is a Nova Scotia schooner which you can clamber over.

Boothbay Railway Museum (633-4727). Open mid-June to Labor Day, daily 9-5:30, then weekends until mid-October. Route 27, one mile north of Boothbay Center. A small complex offering a short ride on a narrow gauge steam train, $2 per adult, $1.25 per child.

Boothbay Region Historical Society Museum, Hyde House (633-2244). Mid-June to Labor Day, Monday-Saturday 10-12 and 1-4, closed Sunday. Local memorabilia. 50c adults, 25c children.

Boothbay Theater Museum (633-4536), Corey Lane. Open mid-June to mid-September, Monday-Saturday, by appointment only. Billing itself as the "only museum of its type in the US," this eighteenth-century home houses exhibits that tell the history of local theater. Fee.

Auto Museum, Route 2 (633-6160), Boothbay. Open June-September daily 10-5, weekends in October. An unusual collection of cars from the late 1940s through the early sixties. $2 adults, $1 children, free under 5.

The Brick House Gallery, open July to mid-September daily, 11-5 weekdays, 2-5 Sundays. Three juried shows each season displaying works by artists of the region.

BOAT EXCURSIONS   We mean it. You must board a boat to find out what the Boothbays are all about. Don't wait until the last day.

Argo Cruises (633-5090 and 4925). May 20 to October 20. Eight daily trips in season, ranging from the basic one-and-one-half-hour cruise which circles Southport Island, to cruises up the Kennebec to Bath, or north to Pemaquid. In July and August there are supper sails.

Balmy Days (633-4027). 9:30 AM day trips to Monhegan Island (mid-June to mid-September), Pier 5. This is the daytripper's boat to one of Maine's most beautiful offshore islands, also the best way to reach the island for an extended stay. The trip takes one-and-one-half hours each way and there are four hours to spend walking the island paths before having to return. At this writing the fare is $15 per person, round trip.

Maranbo II (633-2284) departs Chimney Pier daily, rain or shine, May-October. One-hour tours of the harbor: $4 adult, $2 child; also a Sunday church boat to All Saints by the Sea in Southport.

Cap'n Fish Boat Trips (633-3244, 2626, and 3636). Mid-May to mid-October, one, two, and three-hour boat excursions from Pier Three.

DEEP-SEA FISHING   *Fish Hawk, Mystery, and Buccaneer* are all operated by Captain Bob Fish (see numbers above). There is also the *Gertrude "R"*, a charter boat (Captain Arno Rogers: 827-7160), the *Codfather* which features an electronic fishfinder (Captain Bill Bibber: 633-6200), as does the *Capella* (Captain Ben Lewis: 633-3562); there is also charter boat *Shark II* (Captain Barry Gibson: 633-2316).

SAILING   Friendship sloop *Eastward* offers day and half-day sails (Captain Roger Duncan: 633-6200), as does the forty-four-foot yawl *Nightingale* (633-4480), forty-four-foot ketch *The Quest* (633-2756), schooner *Goblin* (Jack Kemble: 633-6003), and trimaran *Wind Dance* (633-4027). From Halladay Marine in West Boothbay Harbor (633-4767) you can also rent Tartan sailboats of varying sizes, take lessons, or charter a cruise.

GOLF AND TENNIS   **Boothbay Region Country Club** (633-9885) on Route 27 offers nine holes, lessons. **Boothbay Region YMCA** (633-2855) is an exceptional facility (Route 27 in Boothbay Harbor), open to nonmembers in July and August, with special swimming and other programs for children, well worth checking out if you are in the area for an entire week. The "Y" also maintains public tennis courts in the Back Narrows section of Boothbay.

SWIMMING   The beaches are all private, but visitors are permitted in a number of spots. Here are four: (1) Follow Route 27 towards Southport, beyond the Townsend Gut Bridge to a circle (white church on the left, monument in the center, general store on right), turn right and follow Beach Road to the beach, which offers roadside parking and calm, shallow water. (2) Right across from the Boothbay Harbor Yacht Club (Route 27, south) just beyond the post office, at the far end of the parking lot. This property is owned by the club, which puts out a float by July; there are ropes to swing from on the far side of the inlet, a grassy area to sun in, and a small sandy area beside the water, but it is too deep for small children. (3) Barretts Park, Lobster Cove (turn at Catholic Church), a place to picnic and get wet. (4) Grimes Cove, a little beach with rockclimbing at the very tip of Ocean Point.

LODGING   The Chamber of Commerce guide lists forty-six cottages and colonies, eight guesthouses, and thirty-two hotels, motels, inns, and resorts. And of course there is more of everything. But the Boothbays are far from cluttered. Lodging facilities are salted along the shore, around hidden ponds, up dirt roads, and down deep coves. The most famous inns and motels are expensive in high season, but there is an unusually wide range of prices here, and the fact that the Chamber of Commerce is open year-round facilitates finding a cottage for July in March. Cottagers can also take advantage of the first-rate laundromat and supermarket just outside the village of Boothbay Harbor.

RESORTS   **Spruce Point Inn** (633-4152). June to Labor Day. Sited on its own 100-acre peninsula, the tip of Spruce Point. Most of its rooms are scattered in cottages and larger "lodges;" just twelve are in the main inn, which also houses the dining room. Tennis, golf, sailboats, and lawn games are available. $90-100 double, MAP.

Linekin Bay (633-2494). Mid-June to Labor Day. A dozen rooms in five lodges, plus thirty-three cabins, some with Franklin stoves or fireplaces. A pool. Weekly rates $238 double, AP.

Newagen Inn (633-5242). June-September, secluded amid the pines at the tip of Southport Island. A total of fifty rooms between the main inn and cottages, some with fireplaces. A pool, lawn games; rates range from $15 for a single to $48 double in an oceanfront cottage with fireplace; breakfast and dinner served.

Ocean Point Inn, Lodge, Cottages and Motel (633-4200). June 27-October 15. Off by itself on a peninsula at the entrance of Linekin Bay, this complex offers seven rooms in the inn, eleven more in the Lodge, nineteen in the motel, and eight cottages. A restaurant, pool, lawn games, and boat excursions. Prices vary from $24 for a cottage without kitchen to $60 for one with (sleeping four people).

INNS   **Albonegon** (633-2521). July-Labor Day. A "determinedly old-fashioned" haven from the twentieth century, part of the gingerbread-style summer colony on Capitol Island (linked to the real world by a small bridge). The twelve rooms are clean and sea-bright, with sinks, shared baths, and a blueberry muffin breakfast included in the $18 per adult price ($12 per child under six). There is a comfortable, old-shoe atmosphere; guests are permitted to use the nearby beach, and to bring in lobster to eat in the dining room.

Spruceworld Lodge (633-3600). July and August (groups in June and September). There are twenty-nine rooms in the 1920s "rustic" lodge, also two log cottages—also a pleasant beach, a pool, tennis, and a nature trail. $27 double, $44 for a family of four, continental breakfast included.

Thistle Inn (633-3541). Open year-round, 53 Oak Street. Ten rooms with shared baths, a pleasant and friendly atmosphere, but frequently noisy because of the downstairs pub. $12-14 single, $14-20 double.

Lawnmeer Inn and Motel (633-2544). May to late September, Route 27 at Townsend Gut in Southport. The thirty old-fashioned rooms in the inn are $27 in season, the cottage and motel units—all with decks and waterfront views—are $37. The restaurant (see Food) is locally respected, open for three daily meals.

GUESTHOUSES   **Oakledge** (633-2366). Mid-June to mid-October, 41 Oak Street. Three pleasant rooms rented by Mrs. Eva Holbrook. $16-18.

Captain Sawyer's Place (633-2474). April through October, 87 Com-

Boston Globe/Joseph Dennehy

mercial Street. A yellow captain's house with a widow's walk, right downtown, private baths. $33 double in high season, lower weekly rates; also efficiencies in the **Admiral's Quarters,** a nearby motel. Open year-round.

Hilltop House (633-2941). McKown Hill. Four rooms with shared baths at $21, also doubles with baths at $29.40 and $18.50, also one efficiency. Great view, pleasant.

Topside (633-5494). McKown Hill. Memorial Day to mid-October. A big old house plus a small motel, $25-45 in season.

Welch House (633-3431). April-November. A grand view, like the other two McKown Hill guesthouses. Eight rooms with shared baths in the house itself, eight more with private baths in the newer Sail Loft, a great porch and sundeck from which to survey the harbor scene below; $30 range.

MOTELS   "Resort motels"—the kind with color tvs in every room, balconies, oversize beds, pools, and games, are the specialty of the town, costing between $40 and $75 per couple per night in high season, no meals. Since they are described in countless guides, and this book focuses on a different breed of lodging, we will simply list them: **Brown Brothers Wharf** (633-5440), **Fisherman's Wharf Inn** (633-5090), **Rocktide Motor Inn** (633-4455), **Ocean Gate Motor Inn** (633-3321), **Tugboat Inn** (633-4434), **Cap'n Fish's Motel** (633-3636), and **Smuggler's Cove** (633-2800).

Smaller, moderately priced motels include: **The Harborage,** 73 Townsend Avenue (633-4640). Open all year, an overgrown house with ten units in the middle of town, overlooking the water; $35 double, $45-50 for efficiencies.

Town House Motel (633-4300). Open year-round, 71 Townsend Avenue, central. Rooms with private bath, efficiency units, $28-48 high season.

Mid Town Motel (633-2751). Open mid-April to mid-November. Twelve units and one cottage. Centrally located and pleasant. $33.

The Pines (633-4555). Mid-May to mid-October, secluded site literally in the pines on Sunset Road, tennis, rooms with decks, $40 double.

COTTAGES   **Highmeadows Cottage Colony** (633-4141), seasonal. Trevett Road. A former children's camp converted to comfortable, clean, housekeeping cottages set in manicured grounds, with lawn games and access to a fresh water pond, also up the road from a picnicking site on a salt water inlet. One of the nicest places our family has ever stayed. Weekly rentals under $200.

Knickerbocker Lake Cottages. During off-season these must be reserved by writing or phoning their owner, M. A. Blycher, in Springfield, VA (5234 Inverchapel Road, 703-321-7242). Well worth the trouble of lining up, these are two-bedroom cottages on a lake, complete with sandy beach and boats.

We cannot honestly describe the remaining thirty-four cottages listed in the Chamber guide, not having inspected them. But many sound extraordinary, and some February or March we will mail our querying postcards to most of them, then see what is available in July and August at prices we can afford—that's the way the system works. But there are always last-minute cancellations, so check with the Chamber even in August, and you may luck into your dream cottage.

RESTAURANTS   **Robinson's Wharf** at Townsend Gut, Route 27 (633-3830). Mid-June to Labor Day, lunch and dinner daily, children's menu. Sit outside next to the boats, watching the traffic through the gut; the prices are right, the lobster is fine, and the desserts are memorable.

Lawnmeer Inn dining room (633-2544). Mid-June to late September, across from Robinson's Wharf (above). Moderately priced and outstanding for dinner, pleasant atmosphere, child plates.

Thistle Inn Pub (633-3541). 53 Oak Street, year-round. A great pub atmosphere; hearty dishes and moderate prices.

Rocktide Restaurant (633-4455). Mid-June to Columbus Day weekend. Formal dining. Pricey but worth it. Fish and steak specialties. ·Entertainment; also a luncheon dock.

Ebb Tide (633-5692). Downtown, year-round. Next to Gilchrist's, with whom it shares the same management, but we prefer the atmosphere and prices here. Omelets and fried fish all day, $1.65 to $3.60.

Fisherman's Wharf Inn (633-5090). Late May to mid-November, three daily meals, geared to bus groups but right on the water, nicely prepared seafood and basics.

Lobsterman's Wharf (633-3443). Route 96 in East Boothbay. Adjacent to a boatyard, a restaurant rather than a lobster pound, but with some atmosphere. Pizza, burgers, salads, limited menu, moderate prices.

Smuggler's Cove, an 1820 house in East Boothbay (632-2800). Mid-May to mid-October, very pleasant. Broiled fish, chicken, and steak, moderate prices, children's menu.

The Blue Ship (633-7404). Mid-June to Labor Day, daily, three meals. Great for breakfast (try the honey buns), a nice, cheery old-fashioned Maine dining room with polished wooden tables, ladder-back chairs, and a view of the harbor beyond the municipal parking lot. Good for salad platters and seafood in the $10 range. Don't miss the walnut pie with whipped cream. Round Top Ice Cream is served at parking lot level from The Hold.

Green Shutters Inn (633-2646). By reservation only. Both meat and seafood specialties, home baking their pride.

For breakfast we also have to recommend the **Broken Anchor** off Townsend Avenue at the parking lot, 5 AM until 3 PM year-round, until 8:30 PM in summer. Not fancy, but a good family restaurant. **Sappy's Doughnuts** across from the Gulf Station in the Harbor is open 4 AM to 6 PM daily, producing forty-five different kinds of doughnuts and outstanding coffee. There is also **Everybody's** in the shopping center next to Finast just outside the village, junction 27 and 96. No atmosphere, but good plain food at reasonable prices.

LOBSTERS AND CLAMS   **Boothbay Region Lobstermen's Cooperative** (633-4900), Atlantic Avenue (east side), serves up the basics: boiled lobsters and steamed clams to be eaten at waterside picnic tables.

Ken Gray's Clam and Lobster Bakes (882-5490), Boothbay Harbor. $15 for two lobsters and fixings.

Seth's Old Fashioned Lobster Fest (633-4925). Cruise out on *Minikin II* and go ashore at Southport for the bake. Two lobsters: $16.

ENTERTAINMENT   **The Carousel Music Theatre** (633-5297). Open late June through Labor Day, six nights a week. Light dinners and cocktails are served by the cast before they hop onto the stage to present reviews of Broadway show tunes. **Playhouse 27** on Route 27 (633-6185). Italian food, but the big thing here is live, nightly entertainment.

McSeagulls (633-4041). Open year-round. A waterside restaurant which livens up around 9 PM, when young singles congregate for exceptional desserts: strawberry crepes, cheesecake, and such.

Jordan's Downstairs, 49 Commercial Street (633-2600). Live music nightly during the summer season in a bar-like setting with a small dance floor, an older crowd than McSeagulls.

Deckhouse Lounge at the Tugboat Inn (633-4434). A marvelous view and nightly entertainment, good for a nightcap.

SHOPPING   The village of Boothbay Harbor is a browser's delight. Crafts shops include: **A Silver Lining** (working metalsmiths); **Left Bank** (contemporary stained glass); **Hassenfus Glass Shop** (glass-blowing); **Tigger Leather** and **Keepsake Leather; Andersen Studio** (ceramic sculpture); **Nathaniel Wilson** (sailmaker, canvas products); **Madras Mousse** (hand-made musical instruments); **The Studio of Francis Hook** (figurines). There are also more than a dozen gift shops.

SPECIAL EVENTS   Early April. **Fishermen's Festival,** which includes a shrimp princess pageant, relay races, clam shucking, net mending contests, and a blessing of the fleet.

Second week of July. **Windjammer Days** are the big event of the year, featuring a fabulous parade of boats. Also a colorful parade of floats, bands and beauty queens up Main Street, church suppers, band concerts, street dances, too.

Late July. **Antiques shows** at the Boothbay Regional High School.

Early August. **Tuna Tournament.**

Fall Foliage Weekend Festival and Country Fair on Columbus Day weekend. Pancake breakfasts, church suppers, crafts, antiques.

Rockland Area

Two peninsulas divide Muscongus Bay from Penobscot Bay. One is the fat arm of land on which the villages of Friendship and Cushing doze. The other is the skinnier St. George Peninsula. Port Clyde at St. George's tip, departure point for the year-round mailboat to Monhegan, is a village with decent places to eat and sleep, as is Tenants Harbor, a short way up ME 131. The peninsulas are divided by the ten-mile-long tidal St. George River, at the head of which sits Thomaston. This beautiful old town has produced its share of wooden ships, but it has been upstaged by Rockland, the largest distribution center in the world for lobster, also home for an active fishing fleet and the trade center for Penobscot Bay. And in Rockland there is the Farnsworth Museum, filled with water-colors and oils by some of the best of the eighteenth- and nineteenth-century artists who have painted the Maine Coast (it's famed for its collection of works by all three Wyeths). Rockland is also home base for ferries to the islands of Vinalhaven, North Haven, and Matinicus, and for a number of seasonal Windjammer cruises, as well as some unusual daytrips in Penobscot Bay.

GUIDANCE **Rockland Area Chamber of Commerce,** Public Landing, Rockland 04841 (596-6631), summer season daily 8:30-6, otherwise weekdays 9-5. The chamber serves as an information source for the area covered in this chapter; cottage listings for North Haven, Vinalhaven, and the Owls Head to Cushing area are also available.

GETTING THERE Knox County Airport at Owls Head, just south of Rockland, has daily service to Boston and other points via **Bar Harbor Airlines. Greyhound** bus has frequent daily stops in Rockland. For taxi service contact Rokes and Harvey (594-5525). Also check with Knox County Airport (594-4131) about charter flights to Boston.

SIGHTS TO SEE **The Farnsworth Museum** (598-6457). Open year-round, daily June through September (10-5, except Sunday 1-5), otherwise closed Mondays, 19 Elm Street. Lucy Farnsworth was a spinster who lived frugally in just three rooms of her family mansion. When she died in 1935 neighbors were amazed to find that she had left $1,300,000 to establish the present museum. It is a handsome building, but the big lure are paintings like *Christina's World* and *Her Room* by Andrew Wyeth, also posters and book illustrations by his father N.C. Wyeth, and oils by his son Jamie. Winslow Homer is also well represented, and there are

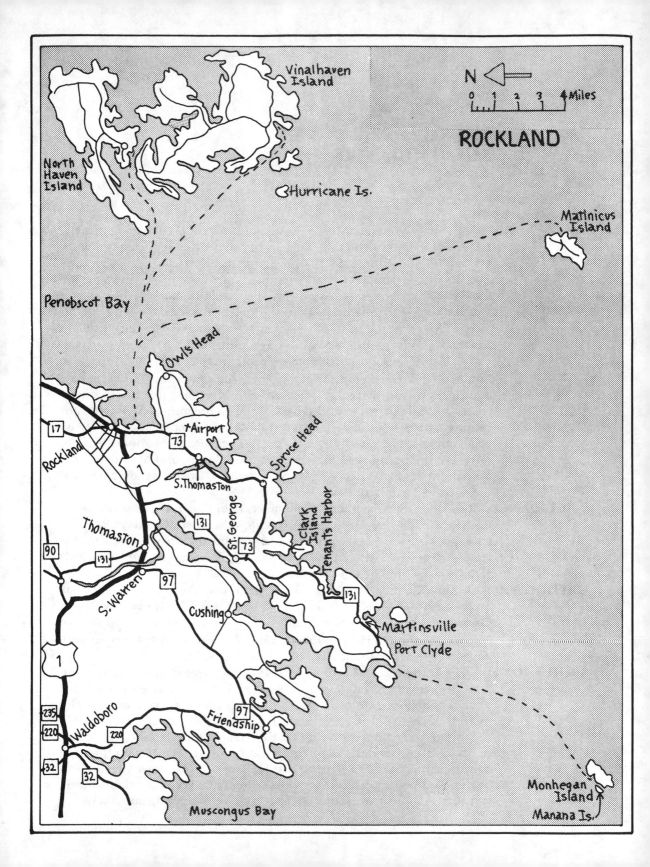

changing exhibits, a program of lectures and concerts, also a museum store. **The Farnsworth Homestead** up Elm Street (June to mid-September, Monday-Saturday 10-5, Sunday 1-5, $1 admission) was built in 1840 and is lavishly furnished in Victoriana, all of it original.

Montpelier, in Thomaston (354-8062). Memorial Day to Labor Day, daily 10-5, $1 adults, 25c children. This is not the original, but a splendid reproduction of the grand mansion built on this spot in 1794 by General Henry Knox, the portly (five-foot-six, 300-pound) Boston bookseller who became a Revolutionary War hero, then our first secretary of war. He married a granddaughter of Samuel Waldo, the Boston developer who owned all this area, and built himself as elaborate a mansion here as any to be found in the new republic. It has an oval dining room facing on the St. George River, high ceilings, and long windows, not to mention a semi-flying staircase. By 1871 it had, however, degenerated into a tenement and was torn down, then rebuilt as a Depression project at a cost of $300,000 (financed by magazine publisher Cyrus Curtis).

Owls Head Transportation Museum (594-9212). Mid-May through mid-October, daily 10-4, then five days a week until December, also special weekends. $3 adults, $1 children, $1.50 senior citizens. Adjacent to the Knox County Airport off ME 73 at Owls Head, south of Rockland. Founded in 1974, this has quickly become one of the country's outstanding collections of antique planes and autos, unique because everything works, as you can see on weekends when you can watch a 1901 Oldsmobile or a 1918 "Jenny" airplane put through their paces. In all there are more than twenty aircraft and three dozen shiny cars—dating from 1898 through the 1920s into early stationwagons. There are also wagons, motorcycles, and bikes. Inquire about special weekends (when admission is higher), when a variety of vehicles perform; the Red Baron's Fokker triplane is traditional star of the Memorial Day Weekend. All vehicles have been donated or lent to the museum, which is a largely volunteer effort.

Owls Head Light. North from the museum a rough dirt road diverges from the main route, leading to a good parking area complete with toilets. The 1825 lighthouse is impressive, set atop sheer cliffs, but with safe trails down one side to the rocks below, good for scrambling and picnicking.

Shore Village Museum (236-3206 or 594-4950). Year-round, Limerock Street in Rockland, June through October, Monday-Friday 10-5, Sunday 1-5; rest of the year Monday-Friday 1-4 and by appointment. Exhibits include Coast Guard memorabilia and Civil War artifacts, a delight for small boys of every age.

Friendship Museum (July to Labor Day, Monday to Saturday 12-5, Sunday 2-5). Free. The former schoolhouse contains local memorabilia, including an exhibit on Friendship sloops.

BOAT EXCURSIONS   *M/V Katahdin,* a 385-passenger excursion boat built in 1974 to be the *M/V Viking Queen* in Portsmouth, N.H., moved to Rockland the spring of 1982. In spring and fall she offers whale watching cruises. From June 11-September 10 there are three daily excursions and in late September-early October foliage cruises are offered. The Summer Day Cruises (10 AM and 2 PM) cost $6 per adult, $7 with a stopover in Vinalhaven; the dinner cruise, with live entertainment, costs $15 per person. Contact **Penobscot Bay Line,** PO Box 1112, Rockland.

WINDJAMMERS   Rockland is the second largest windjammer port after Camden. All these schooners offer six-day-long sails in and around the islands of Penobscot Bay: Schooner *Isaac H. Evans,* PO Box 482, Rockland (594-8007); Schooner *Lewis R. French,* North End Shipyard, Rockland (594-8007); Schooner *Harvey Gamage,* 39 Waterside Lane, Clinton, Connecticut (203-669-7068); Schooner *J. E. Riggin,* PO Box 571J, Rockland (594-2923), and Schooner *Victory Chimes,* PO Box 368, Rockland (596-6060). For further details see Windjammers under "What's Where."

 Mussel Ridge Cruises (596-0381 or 594-8749). Seasonal excursion boat cruises to Matinicus Island and on to Matinicus Rock, known as one of the few nesting places for puffins; shorter cruises through Mussel Ridge Channel, a run which takes you by the Owls Head Lighthouse and off around Spruce Head.

DAY SAILING   Schooner *Maryleigh* offers three-hour sails from the Black Pearl Restaurant (236-4867) in Rockland: $15 per person, half price for children under twelve. Sixteen-foot sailboats can also be rented here: $12 for two hours to $145 per week.

DEEP-SEA FISHING   Charter boats include *Henrietta* (Captain John Earl: 594-5411), *Shamrock* (Captain Bill Cargan: 594-5995), and *Dolphin,* a partyboat out of South Thomaston (Ernest Rackliff: 594-9362).

SPECIAL ISLAND PROGRAM   **The Hurricane Island Outward Bound School** (594-5548) offers five- to twenty-six-day courses, May to October. Hurricane Island at the mouth of Penobscot Bay serves as base for sailing, rock climbing, and outdoor problem solving. For details write the school, Box 429, Rockland, Maine 04841.

LODGING   The **East Wind Inn** (372-8800 or 372-8908) in Tenants Harbor. Open year-round, a nineteenth-century shoreside hotel recently restored and winterized, very much a part of its surroundings: a salty village centering around the wharf and Cod End Fish Market (at which lobsters and clams can be consumed in comfortable chairs, set among potted flowers and water tanks full of fish for children to examine). There is also a good little library, and beyond the village there are beaches, rock cliffs, tidal pools, old cemeteries, and the kind of country described in *Country of the Pointed Firs.* Sarah Orne Jewett lived just a few bends down ME 131 in Martinville while writing the book. The East Wind Inn itself is very clean and well run, with seventeen pleasant harbor-view rooms and three meals a day served in its restaurant (open to the public); uncomplicated fish dishes are the specialty. The 1982 rates are $38 per night, $230 per week, double May through October; and $32 per day, $192 per week double off season. There are also rates for singles and suites; meals are extra.

The Ocean House (372-6691) in Port Clyde, open May 15-October 12, is an adequate roadside inn, the only place in the village to stay if you want to drive up the evening before taking the ferry over to Monhegan. Rates in 1981 were $21-23 double with shared bath. The small dining room is very attractive, serving breakfast 7-11, lunch until 3 PM and dinner, 5-9 (no liquor license).

The Craignair Inn (594-7644). Open March until December 1, serving breakfast and dinner to guests only, off by itself on Clark Island (accessible from ME 73 from Rockland, ME 131 to ME 73 from Thomaston). Sited on a granite ledge by the shore, its unusual architecture is explained by the fact that it was built to house workers at the nearby quarry. The sixteen rooms are simply but nicely furnished and shared baths are the rule; downstairs common rooms are charming, especially the dining room with its blue trim, tablecloths, and china. There are wildflowers on the table, and name cards. In 1981, high season, $57 double with two meals, $41 with breakfast only. Cheaper in June and September. Bikes

Gordon Pine

View of Tenants Harbor

are available, but walking is the thing to do, down the miles of paths meandering off from the inn.

GUESTHOUSES   **Mill Pond House** in Tenants Harbor. Marilyn Korpinen offers three rooms in her home, from which she also runs a beauty shop; $20 single, $25 double including Continental breakfast. **Bed and Breakfast** are offered at a turn-of-the-century salt water farm in Cushing Maine. Kathie Canonica, Davis Point (254-8825); $32 double, $18 single, including a full breakfast; cottage also available.

COTTAGES   A tempting list of cottages, primarily in the Owls Head, Spruce Head area, is available from the Rockland Area Chamber of Commerce (see Guidance).

FOOD   **Moody's Diner** (832-7468). Open daily and nightly (except midnight to 5 AM Friday and Saturday nights), US 1 in Waldoboro. Unbeatable breakfasts, constant specials, memorable desserts, and digestible prices in a clean, warm and wooden old classic of a diner—a very family-run enterprise.

The Dip Net Coffee Shop. Seasonal, 8 AM-4 PM in Port Clyde. Counter only with fifteen stools; the idea is to park and buy your ticket for the 10 AM Monhegan boat—then unwind over a breakfast of homemade coffee cake, muffins, or better yet, fresh strawberry pie. The lunch menu runs to chowder, quiche, lobster stew and a tantalizing lineup of desserts. The owner used to run Yorkie's in Camden.

Black Pearl (594-2250), year-round at the Public Landing in Rockland, is locally respected.

George's Bank (594-5900), year-round, Main Street, is a pleasant dining room in what was the old Depositors Trust, a sign of the re-emerging downtown; along with **Salad Patch** (594-2496), year-round, Main Street, a good place for lunch.

Also see **The East Wind Inn** under Lodging.

SHOPPING   **Maine State Prison Shop,** US 1 in Thomaston, maintains a shop year-round. Daily 9-8, and 9-5 on Sundays, good for a wide variety of wooden furniture—coffee tables, stools, lamps, trays—and a choice of small souvenirs, all carved by inmates. Prices are reasonable, profits go to the craftsmen. A dozen antique shops can also be found between Thomaston and Rockland.

EVENTS   **Maine Seafoods Festival.** Four days including the first weekend in August. This is probably the world's biggest lobster feed, prepared with the help of the world's biggest lobster boiler; patrons queue under a huge tent on the Public Landing to heap their plates with clams and shrimp along with lobster and all the fixings. King Neptune inaugurates the event; the Maine Sea Goddess is judged and crowned, and there are a number of contests (like clam shucking and sardine packing), also a roadrace and a midway.

Friendship Sloop Days, late July.

July Fourth celebrations in Thomaston and Vinalhaven.

THE ISLANDS

MONHEGAN   This island is barely a square mile, yet it boasts 600 kinds of wildflowers, more than 400 years of history, and unequaled beauty. Two-thirds of
Monhegan is, moreover, wild land, laced with foot paths which run
along dramatic cliffs and through meadows, tall stands of pine where
birdcalls and the sound of crunching needles blend with clanging buoy
bells.

"Beached like a whale," one mariner in 1590 described it: the
150-foot-high headlands sloping down to coves, low and quiet at its tail.
Miraculously, this beauty survives. "Prospect Hill," the only attempted
development, foundered around 1900. It was Theodore Edison, son of
electricity's discoverer, who amassed property enough to erase the last
traces of Prospect Hill, and to keep the island's 125 cottages bunched
along the sheltered Eastern Harbor. In 1954 Edison helped organize
Monhegan Associates, a non-profit corporation dedicated to preserving
the "natural, wild beauty" of the island. Ironically, this is one of the
country's few communities to shun electricity, and there are just a few
trucks to haul lobstering equipment and summer visitors' luggage to and
from the dock and the island's three inns and sprinkling of seasonal
cottages.

Daytrippers and visitors without cars come on the *Balmy Days* (see
Boothbay Harbor), and longer-term visitors take mailboat *Laura B*
(reservations necessary; phone Captain James Barstow: 372-8848) from
Port Clyde, where parking is $1.50; the ticket for the one-hour mailboat
voyage is $12 round trip, no charge for children five and under. This
mailboat sails year-round, twice daily in season. When you make a
reservation, request a copy of the outstanding booklet, *An Introduction to
Monhegan Island,* by Alta Ashley (the island's retired physician and
current reporter and naturalist in residence). Doctor Ashley advises all
visitors to come properly shod for the precipitous paths and equipped
with sweaters and windbreakers; she also cautions against wading or
swimming from any of the tempting coves on the backside of the island.
Anyone staying overnight should bring a flashlight. Heavy rubber boots
are also a good idea.

The Lighthouse, built 1824, automated in 1959, offers a good view.
The former lighthouse keeper's house is now the **Monhegan Museum**
(July-Labor Day 11:30-3:30), displaying flora, fauna, and something of
the geology, lobstering, and artistic history of the island, including
documents dating back to the sixteenth century.

Cathedral Woods of spruce and fir balsam, carpeted with needles and
mossy rocks; there is a distinctly fairy tale quality to this area.

The Headlands. Pick up a good trail map at one of the island's three
stores and follow the paths carefully along the dramatic cliffs. (Daytrippers should take the Burnt Head trail out and loop back to the village via

Lobster Cove, rather than try a longer circuit). **Manana Island** off Middle Beach (at which a skiff can easily be found to take you across) is the site of a famous rune stone with inscriptions purported to be Norse or Phoenician. **Lobster Cove**, at the tail of the island, is a good spot for birdwatching (600 species recorded spring and fall). **Pebble Beach** at the northern end of the island is good for picnicking, and both seal and birdwatching.

For rainy days there is an exceptional library, **The Island Spa** (good for browsing but only open two days a week), and artist's studios are open (a listing available on the island informs you which studios are open on which days); works by local artists are also hung in the **Plantation Gallery** across from the **Periwinkle Coffee Shop** (offering three daily meals in season).

The Trailing Yew, run for fifty years by Josephine Day, is the favorite place to stay of artists who come year after year. In all, fifty very basic rooms are scattered between the main house, adjacent buildings, and cottages on the grounds and up the road. Expect shared baths, kerosene lamps, good food, and reasonable prices. Guests gather before meals around the flagpole outside the main building to pitch horseshoes and compare notes; dining is family style at shared tables.

There is also the **Island Inn,** which has electricity and six doubles with private baths, a number of others with shared baths. Downstairs are two small living rooms and the dining room, which serves three daily meals—all open, as are those at the Trailing Yew, to the public. There is **Monhegan House,** too, a picturesque old place with the lowest prices on the island, but offering no meals. A list of rental cottages is available from the postmistress. There are also a few rooms to be found—the only lodging available off season—in private houses. At this writing, the only island phone is a marine radio phone situated near the Monhegan Store (selling most basics, also wine and beer). Better service is expected, but your best bet for reserving a room (which should be done in spring) is writing to the above inns.

VINALHAVEN   In contrast to Monhegan—a small, hilly island which catches lobster all winter and tourists all summer—Vinalhaven is a large (eight miles long) island with a year-round fishing fleet, still limited quarrying, and some summer residents. Visitors can stay at the small **Tidewater Motel** (863-4856); or at the **Bridgeside Inn** (863-4354), which offers seven rooms, all nicely furnished, open June through August. It serves three tasty meals a day, but to guests only (moderately priced). There are restaurants in town, but daytrippers would do well to bring a picnic to eat at **Round Pond** or **Grimes Park.**

In 1880, when granite was being cut on Vinalhaven to build Boston's Museum of Fine Arts and New York's Court House, there were 3,380 people living on Vinalhaven, a number now reduced to 1211—a mix of descendants from eighteenth-century settlers and the stonecutters who came here from Sweden, Norway, Finland, and Scotland. The summer people here and on North Haven are an unusually well-heeled, old shoe

Charles Carey

White Head on Monhegan Island

group. The roads are paved, and for bicyclists this makes a fine daytrip. There are ample swim spots (both pebbly beaches and defunct quarries), and nature conservancy areas in which to berry, bird and generally unwind for weeks on end. The **Vinalhaven Historical Society Museum** in the old town hall displays photos and mementoes from the island's granite and fishing industries. The car-carrying ferry *Governor Curtis* from Rockland to Vinalhaven takes one-and-one-half-hours; inquire for current schedule and rates with the State Ferry Service in Rockland (594-5543).

MATINICUS   From Rockland you can also take a twenty-three-mile ferry ride aboard the *Deborah Jane* (372-6280) to the most remote of all Maine islands served by regularly scheduled ferry. I must admit that of all the islands this is the one I have never visited; there is one guest house (366-3663) and camping is permitted with special permission; there is also a small village and two beaches.

The Maine State Ferry *William Silsby* also serves Matinicus one day a month (594-5543).

Camden/Rockport/Lincolnville

All I could see from where I stood
Was three long mountains and a wood;
I turned and looked another way,
And saw three islands in a bay.

The opening lines from Edna St. Vincent Millay's "Renascence" describes a view which can still be shared by anyone who pays 75c to drive the short road up Mount Battie. Below, the town of Camden is laid neatly on a curving shelf between the abrupt hills and Penobscot Bay.

Camden is midway between Portland and Bar Harbor. Few motorists pass through without pausing at least to stroll the town dock area. The unusually picturesque harbor is filled with sailing craft, rimmed with restaurants and boutiques. It is difficult to spend an hour in Camden without realizing that the town is special.

Camden's early business was building and sailing ships. The town's first schooner was launched in 1769, and the *George G. Wells*, the first six-masted vessel in the world, was launched from Holly Bean's yard in 1900.

It was the steamboat, however, which shaped the Camden of today. As a stop on the Boston-Bangor line, its fame spread. Soon the town "where the mountains meet the sea" had attracted a wealthy, cultured group of summer residents, primarily from Philadelphia and Boston, who built their summer mansions along the shore here and in the neighboring town of Rockport, a far sleepier resort village just to the south. Fostered by long-time summer residents, the two towns together now offer a quantity and quality of music, art, and theatrical productions surprising for towns their size. In recent years an unusual number of crafts shops have also opened, along with summer programs for photography and dance.

But Camden is best known as home for Maine's windjammer fleet, the country's largest concentration of passenger-carrying schooners. A sizeable sailing fleet has been carrying tourists from Camden up and down the Maine coast, in and around the islands of Penobscot Bay, since the 1930s.

Camden itself remains one of the few places in New England which you can enjoy without a car. Thousands of people come by bus each year just to board the windjammers and sail away for a week. Others come

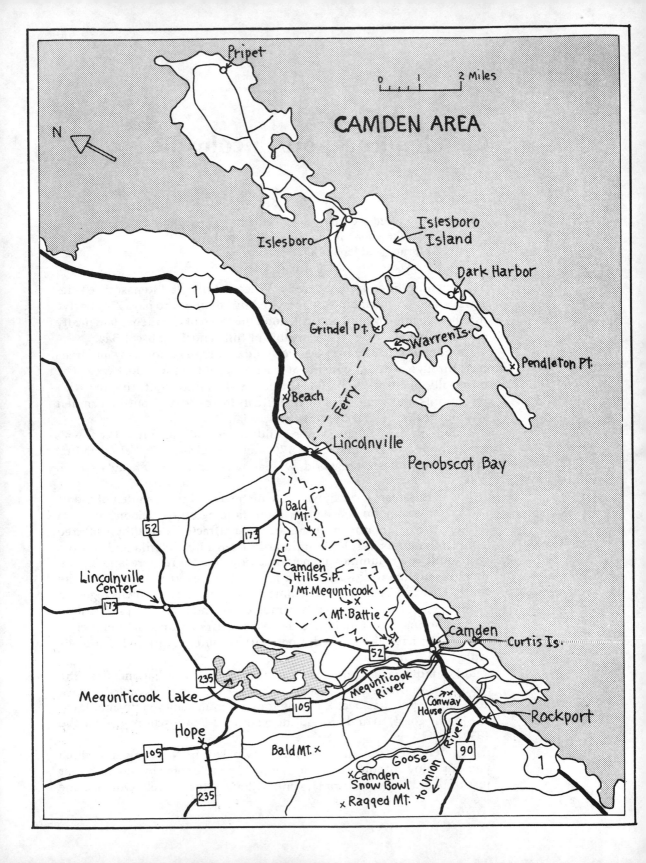

Pripet

0   1   2 Miles

CAMDEN AREA

N

1

Islesboro
Islesboro
Island

Dark Harbor

Grindel Pt.
Warren Is.
Pendleton Pt.

Beach

Ferry

Lincolnville

Penobscot Bay

Bald
Mt.

52

173

Camden
Hills S.P.
Mt. Mequnticook
Mt. Battie

Lincolnville
Center

173

Camden
Curtis Is.

52

235

Mequnticook
River

Conway
House

Rockport

Mequnticook Lake

105

Hope

105

Bald Mt.

Camden
Snow Bowl

Ragged Mt.

Goose

to Union

River

90

1

235

and rent a bike, the better to get to Camden Hills State Park, to Rockport, or to the island of Islesboro—accessible by ferry from Lincolnville Beach. From Islesboro you can continue on to Warren Island, a state park with picnic tables, trails, and tent sites. For campers and hikers there are also the twenty-five miles of trails and 112 campsites in 6500-acre Camden Hills State Park.

There are a few fine, medium-sized and small inns in Camden, queen among them the Whitehall Inn, a rambling white presence just north of town with a parlor in which Edna St. Vincent Millay was "discovered" by a wealthy patron who heard her read "Renascence."

GUIDANCE The **Rockport-Camden-Lincolnville Chamber of Commerce** (236-4404) PO Box 246, Public Landing, Camden 04843, is open year-round, daily Memorial Day-Labor Day 9-5; weekends 10-4 in September. Otherwise, weekdays from 9-2:30, also open weekends in September and October. The Chamber keeps tabs on available vacancies during high season, also on what's open off season and what cottages are for rent, a list which is ready for requests by January. Also be sure to secure the chamber's excellent "Directory," and the brochure produced by the Camden Historic Society, outlining biking and walking tours.

SIGHTS TO SEE **Conway House and Mary Meeker Cramer Museum,** Conway Road. Open July and August, Monday-Friday: 1-5. Fee. The late-seventeenth-century house is furnished to period, and its barn holds collections of carriages, sleighs, and early farm tools. There is a blacksmithy and museum displaying ship models, Maine paintings, and local historical memorabilia.

Maine Coast Artists, Russell Avenue in Rockport (236-2875), June to mid-September, daily: 10-5; Sundays: 1-5. The gallery sponsors several shows a season; all works are by established Maine artists. Arts programs for adults and children are also offered.

GREENSPACE **Camden Hills State Park** (236-3109) includes Mount Megunticook, one of the highest points on the Atlantic seaboard, also some of the most rewarding hikes. From Megunticook Street in Camden itself you can climb to the summit of Mount Battie (never crossing the auto road), or you can assail the sheer heights of Maiden Cliff, or the summits of Mount Megunticook, Bald Rock, and Ragged Mountains. At the park entrance, pick up a "Hiking at Camden Hills State Park" map. There is also a shoreside picnic area across from the park's main entrance. The twenty-five miles of hiking trails are suitable for cross-country skiing, given snow.

Marine Park in Rockport. A nicely landscaped waterside area with sheltered picnic tables and a set of restored lime kilns on the banks of the Goose River, reminders of the era in which the town's chief industry was processing and exporting lime. You read that in 1816 some 300 casks of lime were shipped to Washington to help construct the Capitol. Today the site is best known as a viewing spot from which to watch Andre the Seal perform at 4 PM. Andre is immortalized in the statue at the park's center.

Vesper Hill Chapel in Rockport. This is the site of an old hotel; the delightful spot, a small chapel complete with wooden benches facing the sea, was landscaped by volunteers.

Merryspring Foundation. A sixty-six-acre preserve bisected by the Goose River, accessible via Conway Road from US 1 in Rockport, and Simonton Road in Camden. The foundation is dedicated to planting and preserving flowers, shrubs, and trees in this natural setting, and to interpreting them through workshops and special events. A fee is charged in season.

Islesboro. A ten-mile-long, string bean-shaped island with a lighthouse and adjacent Islesboro Memorial Museum (June-September, Tuesday-Sunday, 10-4) at Grindle Point where the ferry lands. The public beach is at Pendleton Point, far tip of the island. At Dark Harbor there is a natural pool, linked to the sea but calmer and warmer. Lunch and lodging are available at the Islesboro Inn (see Lodging). The Islesboro Historical Society Museum is open May-mid-September, daily: 10-4. This is a great biking island.

Warren Island. There are more than seventy acres, but just a half dozen campsites (first come, first serve). Accessible by public launch from Camden Hills State Park. For launch information, check with the ranger there, or phone the park from Grindle Point on Islesboro.

Curtis Island. A small speck of an island with a lighthouse, off Bay View Street in Camden; a public picnic spot, if you can get yourself out there.

Bok Amphitheater. A gentle, manicured slope behind the Camden Library and down to the high water mark of the harbor, site of Camden Shakespeare Company productions, also a good place to sit anytime.

SWIMMING   Saltwater swimming in Camden at **Laite Memorial Park and Beach,** at **Lincolnville Beach,** and in Rockport at **Walker Park.**

Freshwater swimming at **Megunticook Lake** (Barrett Cove Memorial Park and Beach off ME 52), and the **James Brown Bathing Beach** on the Megunticook River (Moyneaux Road).

BOATING   **Windjammer Cruises** (236-4867), mid-June to mid-September. At present seven schooners and a ketch are based in Camden, and one schooner in Rockport. For brochures about a dozen of the current fifteen vessels carrying passengers, write to Maine Windjammer Association, Box 317T, Rockport, Maine 04876. See the Windjammer section in "What's Where" for a detailed listing. From Camden you can board the *Mattie, Mercantile, Mistress, Mary Day, Stephen Taber, Adventure,* and *Roseway* for six-day cruises. From Rockport you can sail on the *Timberwind.* All schooners charge between $350 and $400 for the voyages.

Dirigo (236-4200), a thirty-foot Friendship sloop offers half- and full-day sails, also lobster bakes.

Arete (236-2938). A twenty-eight-foot ketch available for cruises and instruction.

The schooner *Isaac H. Evans*

The Betselma, a motor launch, offers daily tours of the harbor, June through September: $3 per adult, $2 per child; also evening cruises, charters.

Arcturus (236-3430). Full- or part-day charters, six people maximum, a cabin cruiser.

Fiberglass sailboats can be rented at Willey Wharf (236-3256).

Camden Yacht Club Sailing Program, Bay View Street, July and August, sailing classes available for children and adults—boat- and non-boat owners.

Maine State Ferry Service at Lincolnville Beach (789-5611) operates the *Governor Muskie;* during summer months there are nine daily trips to Islesboro, eight on Sundays, 25 minutes each way; cars, bikes, passengers.

SPORTS   **Goose River Golf Club** (236-8488). Nine holes, carts.

There are two public tennis courts at Camden Snow Bowl on Hosmer's Pond Road.

Camden Snow Bowl (598-2511). A ski area operated since 1981 by the Samoset Resort. Eight miles of terrain, 950-foot vertical drop, one chair, two T-bars, 20% snowmaking coverage on 1300-foot-high Ragged Mountain; a day lodge, alpine and cross-country rentals, night skiing, packages with the Samoset, ten miles away.

ENTERTAINMENT   **Camden Shakespeare Company** (236-8011), PO Box 786, Camden. July-Labor Day, nightly performances, also special matinees for children; all performances in the amphitheater on Atlantic Avenue.

Bay Chamber Concerts (236-2248). July and August, a series on nine Thursday evenings, concerts in the Rockport Opera House.

The Bay View Cinema (236-8722). Daily, a mixed bag of old favorites, current, foreign, and art films.

SPECIAL PROGRAMS   **The People to People Dance Company** (236-3771). July and August. Classes in African, jazz, and modern dance.

The Maine Photographic Workshop (236-3581), Rockport, Maine 04856. A nationally respected, year-round school offering three-month programs, two-week programs in basic and intermediate photography, also weekly "crash courses," and a variety of special interest courses. The school helps students find lodging space in and around Rockport.

LODGING   **Whitehall Inn** (236-3391). Memorial to Columbus Day weekend. The main building rambles off the original 1834 sea captain's house, and the forty-one rooms (most in the main building but some in the "Annex," a former mansion across US 1) are furnished with antiques; the public rooms are elegant without being stiff; there are puzzles on the tables, a library of inviting books, and a telescope to survey the bay. In the evening humorists, magicians, and musicians perform in much the same spirit that Edna St. Vincent Millay (whose diploma hangs on one wall) recited her poetry on that night that changed her life. Guests can also cruise off to **Little Green Island**, the inn's private nature preserve. High season (mid-June to October) the rates are $40 single, $42 double,

MAP (two meals); off-season bed and breakfast rates are lower; three meals a day are served in the pleasant dining room.

Aubergine (236-8053). Mid-May to October. A shingled, 1890s hotel with just six airy rooms, each painstakingly furnished with such touches as matching paper and spreads. Better known as a restaurant, but not a bad place to stay, either. $25-35 single, $35-45 double, breakfast included.

Camden Harbour Inn (236-4200). Year-round, 83 Bay Street, another 1890s inn. High season rates are $24 to $56 which, we feel, gives you less for your money than you get at the Whitehall. But the view is great. From November through late May this is the only inn in town, and the rates are $18-33.

The Owl and the Turtle Bookmotel (236-4769), year-round, 8 Bay View Street. The three guestrooms here are convenient to the dock, shops, bus—and to the thousands of books in the rest of this exceptional store, ideal for bookish adventurers.

Islesboro Inn (734-2221). Mid-June to mid-October. A gracious mansion of an inn to which many patrons come by yacht to stay and take advantage of the adjacent nine-hole golf course and the inn's own clay tennis court. There are fourteen guest rooms, just four with bath, but seven with working fireplaces. Biking, beaching, berrying, and birding are the other things to do. Call for current rates. **High Tide Inn** (236-3724). Mid-May to mid-October. We must confess to never having seen this facility, but the Chamber of Commerce assures us that "it has been there forever and we have never had any complaints." There are waterside cottages as well as the inn itself, moderately priced.

Samoset Resort (594-2511), year-round. A new resort, built on the site of a classic old wooden one which burned. It turns a blank, warehouse-style face to the parking lot and the lobby is straight from midtown Manhattan. But the 150 rooms all have private baths, color tv, climate control and balconies, and a high percentage face the sea. There is a glass-roofed indoor pool, an outdoor one, tennis courts, a health club. Obviously geared to groups and conventions. It is good value if you take advantage of its myriad packages—like $88 per person (double occupancy) for two nights, three days, including breakfast and greens fees; or, in the winter, $227.50 per person for five nights, including all meals and lifts at the Camden Snow Bowl which the inn now manages.

RESTAURANTS   **Aubergine** (236-8053). 6 Belmont Avenue, April 15-November 1. Dinner from 7 PM by reservation. Generally accepted as one of the top restaurants in Maine. An airy, spacious dining room with limited seating and a "new style" French menu which changes monthly, but which might include medallions of lobster with mussels and duck with fresh peaches. Fresh flowers on the tables and crisp napkins and cloths tend to complete the sense of perfection, and the bill is digestible.

Swan's Way (236-2171). Frequently there are customers on the steps waiting to get into this genial dining room, which opens at 5 PM, closes at 12:30 AM. It is small, very good, and accepts no reservations. The specialties are coffees, light dinners, and memorable desserts.

Yorkie's Restaurant (236-3156), 44 Chestnut Street, famed for its baking; good for breakfast, lunch, and dinner; moderate prices, great atmosphere.

The Helm Restaurant (236-4337). April to late-October, 11:30 AM-8:30 PM, closed Mondays, US 1 in Rockport overlooking the Goose river. Its French owners Caluse and Madeline Broutin, do an outstanding job with coquille St. Jacques, mussels, and trout meuniere, as well as meat dishes; moderately priced, with a child's menu also. Probably the only take-out window in Maine at which you can order real French onion soup to complement a peerless crabmeat roll.

Whitehall Dining Room (236-3391). Late June to mid-October; breakfast, dinner. See Lodging. If you can't stay in the inn don't miss a meal in the attractive dining room.

Lobster Pound Restaurant (789-5550). Early May to Columbus Day. At Lincolnville Beach. You can order seafood newburg or steak, as well as the basic crustacean you select from a tank. Depending on the weather, you can dine beside the fireplace or on picnic tables on the wharf: $6.25-14.45, child's plate from $3.25.

Homeport Lobster Company (236-8256) is right on the dock at Harbor Square, Bayview Street, Camden. Lobster and clams live and to go or consume. Moderate prices.

Cappy's Chowder House (236-2254), year-round, from 6 AM-7:30 PM in summer, 4 PM in winter, corner of Main Street and the Public Landing. Nice decor, good chowder, unpretentious, tasty fare, reasonably priced.

The Waterfront Restaurant (236-3737). Year-round, daily. Salads and sandwiches for lunch. Nice touches like wildflowers on the tables, good relishes, dressings, and homemade bread. Swift service both inside and on the harborside deck (under a free-form canvas awning). Most dinner entrees under $10.

Mainely Grain (236-2856). A retail store selling hundreds of grains, but with a table or two at which to sample delicious soups, vegetarians whole-wheat pizza, and other delicacies which can also be transported to the amphitheater or harborside to enjoy.

The Eating Gallery (236-3911). 31 Elm Street, closed Sunday and Monday. Mussels in unusual sauces, but basically not a seafood nor a high volume restaurant, open for lunch and dinners, $6-12.

Peter Ott's Tavern and Steak House (236-4032). Bay View Street, steak and seafood, moderately pricey.

Rockport Corner Shop (236-3324). Year-round, 6:30 AM to 3 PM weekdays, 7 AM to 2 PM weekends. Corner of Main and Central Streets. An exceptional eating spot with very white walls decorated with photographs from the Workshop across the street, for which it is an obvious social center. Fresh coffee cakes are baked each morning, all salads are made with garden-grown vegetables, even the tomatoes in the tomato sauce. Omelets, lentil burgers, chowders, and fresh fruit pies are specialties. While there is a vegetarian leaning, there are also meat and fish dishes. Herb teas and good coffee, no liquor, reasonably priced.

Sail Loft (236-2330). Year-round, daily lunch and dinner, Sunday brunch, on the water. A large old dining room right on the water, locally respected for its daily specials which are truly specials: such as medallions of veal Oscar, local crab imperial, and local sole with mussels and shrimp. Moderately expensive.

Camden Harbor Inn (236-4200). 83 Bay View Street, year-round. The specialties are fresh seafood prepared with imagination; the dining room has both a splendid view and an ample hearth. Dinners cost around $10.

SHOPPING   Camden has always had a few pleasant summer-resort style shops, but it is just in the past years that craft shops and boutiques have burgeoned around the harbor, adding up to Maine's biggest concentration of such shops beyond Portland.

The Owl and the Turtle Bookshop and Tea Room (236-4769). Year-round 9-5, also evenings and Sundays in summer. Six rooms full of books, including special ones devoted to arts and crafts, marine, sports, young adults, and children's titles, also a major search service for out-of-print books.

The Smiling Cow. Open April through October, 8 AM-9 PM, with slackening hours off season. Three generations ago, a family consisting of a mother and five children converted this stable into a classic summer gift shop, but one with unusual warmth and scope. Customers can help themselves to tea and coffee on a back porch overlooking the harbor.

Perspectives (236-8470). 4 Bay View Street. Year-round, 10-5. A cooperative of local artisans, whose work is sold.

Unique 1 (236-8717). 2 Bay View Street. The specialties are woolen items, all locally made, handloomed and 100% Maine wool, also pottery and an assortment of other locally crafted items.

Anne Kilham Designs (236-8127), 142 Russell Street, Rockport, is the home/studio of an increasingly famous local artist whose cards, calendars, block prints, and drawings—all depicting Maine flowers and scenes—are sold in stores throughout the state and via a mail order catalog. Phone before coming, because Anne may or may not be there, but she welcomes visitors during regular business hours.

"Harbor Square" by the water, and **Highland Mill Mall**, a converted textile mill full of shops on Mechanic Street, also house specialty shops. **The New Leaf Book Shop** (236-2030), 23 Main Street, Rockport, is another fine bookstore, specializing in books by and for women, and in alternative energy and health care. It offers a pleasant front stoop to read on.

Brott Gallery (236-2692), 6 Bay View Street. Year-round but just Saturdays in Winter. Diane Brott's outstanding crocheted hats and Gordon

Brott's fine pieces of sculpture are sold along with work by other local craftspeople.

SPECIAL EVENTS   June: **Annual North Atlantic Festival of Story Telling** at the Rockport Opera House.

July 4: Public feeds, road race, parade, and fireworks.

Mid-July to mid-August: Friday noon **concerts** at St. Thomas Church, Chestnut Street, Camden. Free.

Mid-July: **Open House and Garden Day,** sponsored by Camden Garden Club; tour of homes and gardens; $5. **Arts and Crafts Show** in the Bok Amphitheatre, Camden.

Mid-August: **Union Fair** in Union; old-style agricultural fair featuring blueberries.

Late August: **Downeast Jazz Festival** at the Camden Opera House.

DOWN EAST

The Searsport Area

Searsport has about the same number of people as it did in 1845—when it managed to launch eight brigs and six schooners. It continues to be an enterprising place.

Driving up US 1, you think you are through it quickly: a few blocks of nineteenth-century brick buildings, a gas station or two, and a thickening of "Antiques" signs. The fact is that this is now Maine's second-largest deepwater port and there are enough shoreside sea captains' mansions to suggest its past importance. The story is told in the Penobscot Marine Museum, which focuses on Penobscot Bay—around which more than 3000 different vessels have been built, beginning in 1770.

Besides building boats, the city of Belfast has had a history of unusual diversification—including a highly successful sarsaparilla company, a rum distillery, and a city-owned railroad; most recently it has been known for poultry and shoes. A commercial rather than a resort center, it is a good place to shop.

Bucksport, north of Searsport and at the mouth of the Penobscot River, is dominated by the St. Regis paper mill (established in the days when this was the end of the long log run), and by Fort Knox—New England's biggest fort, a memorial to its smallest war.

Pleasant inns are scattered throughout this area, which makes a logical hub from which to explore the region from Camden to Bar Harbor, Lake St. George and Augusta.

GUIDANCE   There are two information booths serving this area maintained by the **Belfast Chamber of Commerce** (338-2896), one on US 1 just south of town (northbound lane), the other on Rte 3; the chamber is open year-round, weekdays: 9-5; or write to Belfast, Maine 04915. A leaflet guide, including information about antique stores, is also available from **Searsport Chamber of Commerce,** PO Box 269, Searsport, Maine 04974.

GETTING THERE   **Greyhound** bus stops in Belfast, Searsport, and Bucksport. **Bar Harbor Airlines** serves Knox County Airport near Rockland, and Hancock County Airport in Trenton. Rental cars are available from both points.

EXCURSIONS   Windjammer *Syvania W. Beal* departs Belfast June through September for six-day cruises; built of oak in 1911, rebuilt in 1979, she takes 18 guests, a crew of four, $350; contact Captain John Worth (548-2922) or Box 509, Belfast.

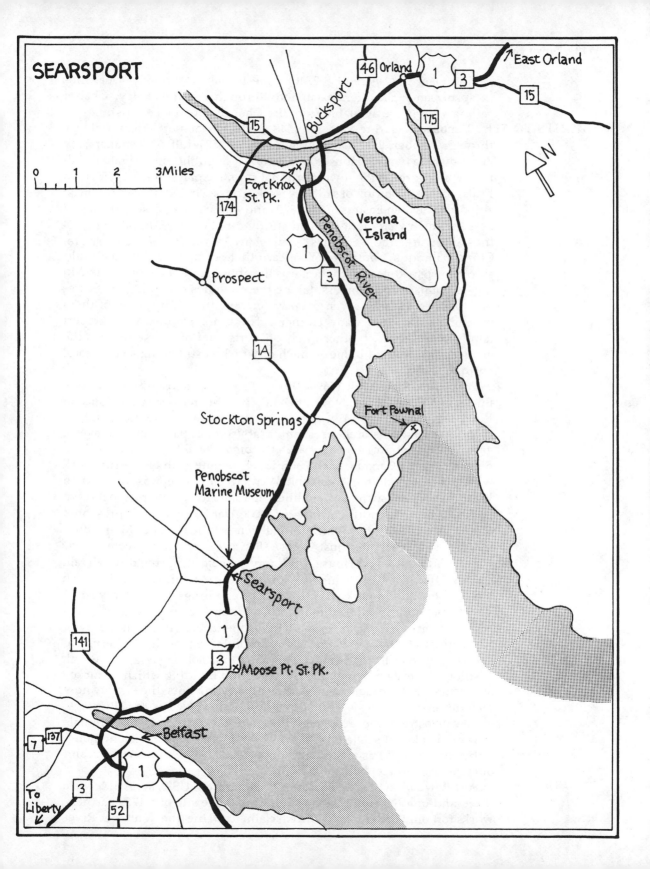

SEARSPORT

0 1 2 3 Miles

East Orland

Orland

46

1 3

15

Bucksport

175

15

Fort Knox St. Pk.

174

Penobscot River

Verona Island

1

3

Prospect

1A

Stockton Springs

Fort Pownal

Penobscot Marine Museum

Searsport

1

141

3

Moose Pt. St. Pk.

7 137

Belfast

1

To Liberty

3

52

N

Motor launch *Osprey* (338-2740), June 19-Labor Day daily, weekends in spring and fall, offers excursions through Penobscot Bay. Charter sailing vessels are available from the Chance-Along (see Inns).

SIGHTS TO SEE   Penobscot Marine Museum (548-6634) in Searsport. Memorial Day through October; 9:30-6, except Sundays 1-5; $2 adult, $1 teenagers, 50c ages seven to twelve. Housed in a complex of public and private buildings which formed the town's original core. Displays in the 1845 Town Hall trace the evolution of sailing vessels from seventeenth-century mast ships to the Down Easters of the 1870s and 1880s: graceful, square-rigged vessels which were both fast and sturdy cargo carriers. In other buildings there are fine paintings, scrimshaw, a variety of lacquerware, Chinese imports, and more. You learn that Searsport didn't just build ships; townspeople owned the ships they built, and sailed off in them to the far points of the compass, taking their families along. In 1889 Searsport boasted seventy-seven deep water captains, thirty-three of them manning full-rigged Cape Horners. There are pictures of Searsport families meeting each other in far-off ports, and of course there is the exotica they brought home— much of which is still being sold in local antique shops.

Fort Knox State Park (469-7719) in Prospect, across the river from Bucksport. Open May 1-November 1 daily: 10-6; fee per car, off US 1 on Route 174. Built in 1844 of granite cut from nearby Mount Waldo, it includes barracks, storehouses, and a labyrinth of passageways, even a granite spiral staircase. There are also picnic facilities. It was to be a defense against Canada, in the boundary dispute with New Brunswick which was called the Aroostook War. The dispute was ignored in Washington, and so the new, lumber-rich state took matters into its own hands, arming its northern forts in 1839. Daniel Webster represented Maine in the 1842 treaty which formally ended the war, but Maine built this fort two years later, just in case. It was never entirely completed.

Perry's Tropical Nut House. US 1 north of Belfast, spring through fall, daily 9-5, until 9:30 PM in high season. A nutty store in every way which has become a landmark since its 1920s beginnings—during a year in which the South produced more pecans than it could sell, a situation which inspired a Belfast man (with investments in Southern nut groves) to sell pecans to the new tourist traffic up US 1 in Maine. Irving Perry was soon doing so well that he moved his shop to the old cigar factory which it still occupies, along with the original shop building which he tacked on. He traveled through South America collecting nuts (the display now includes every species of nut known to man), as well as the alligators, monkeys, ostriches, peacocks, gorillas, and other dusty stuffed animals now on display. It's all a bit fusty now, and Perry himself is long gone, but everyone still has to stop and pose next to the various exotica and outsized carved elephants out front.

Fort Pownall in Stockton Springs, marked from US 1, accessible via a three-and-one-half-mile access road. This is the site of a 1759 earthenworks fort built to defend the British claim to Maine (the Kennebec River was the actual divider between English and French territories). It was burned twice to prevent its being taken; a restoration is under way, and it makes a fine picnic spot.

Bucksport Historical Society Museum (459-2591). Main St. in Bucksport, housed in the former Maine Central railroad station. Open July and August, Thursday-Saturday: 2-4:30, and by appointment. Nominal admission.

Craig Brook National Fish Hatchery in East Orland (469-2803), daily: 8-4:30. Turn off US 1 to Route 46 in Orland, just north of Bucksport. Opened in 1871, this is the oldest salmon hatchery in the country. Situated on the shore of a lake, it offers a visitors' center with aquaria, also a nature trail, picnic tables, and a nineteenth-century ice house.

Cemeteries. In Searsport, the Bowditch Cemetery on US 1 has an unusual number of memorials to mariners lost at sea or buried on foreign shores. It is named for the famous Nathaniel Bowditch of Salem, Massachusetts, author of the navigational guide by which most seamen of his era sailed, the idea being that if he helped them navigate this world's water, he could do so in the next as well.

In the Bucksport Cemetery, near the Verona Bridge, a granite obelisk marks the grave of Colonel Jonathan Buck, founder of Bucksport, and a judge who condemned a mentally retarded resident to death for killing a woman whose body had been found, minus one leg. The man protested his innocence, and when, in time, the judge died and was buried beneath this obelisk, the outline of a leg soon appeared in the stone and reappeared whenever erased. It's still there.

Searsport Historical Society (548-2915), US 1. Open July-September: 1-5 and by appointment. A local collection of artifacts, clothing, maps, and town records.

THINGS TO DO   **Moose Point State Park.** US 1 south of Searsport: picnicking and cookout facilities in an evergreen grove and open field overlooking Penobscot Bay.

Swimming. Lake St. George State Park. Route 3 inland to Liberty. Open May through October; lifeguard, changing facilities, picnicking, and thirty-one camping sites. At City Park, US 1 south of Belfast, you can picnic and at least cool off at the gravel beach on Penobscot Bay.

Tours of the St. Regis Paper Mill (469-3131) are offered weekdays in summer, 9-3; the mill turns more than 400 cords of wood to paper daily.

LODGING   **The Homeport Inn** (548-2259), US 1 in Searsport. Open all year. An 1863 captain's mansion, complete with widow's walk overlooking the bay. Owned by Dr. and Mrs. Johnson, who offer three guestrooms in the spirit of sharing their fine home; $30 per couple, $17 per person, breakfast included in 1981. Each room is different, one has a working fireplace.

Chance-Along Inn (388-4785), US 1 in Belfast, year-round. A gambrel-roofed turn-of-the-century home offering five double rooms and one single, two shared bathrooms. It is an unusually homey place, geared to the sailors who come to take a concentrated weekend or week of sailing instruction, but a comfortable place for anyone to repair to, to sit in front of the fire, play the piano, put together a puzzle. Pets and children are welcome. Sailing weekends are $78 per person, $100 per couple, lodging and breakfast included with use of the boat and instruction; bed and breakfast prices are reasonable.

The Yardarm Motel and Restaurant (548-2404), US 1 in Searsport, mid-May to mid-October. More like an inn than a motel, this complex consists of an 1868 captain's house with an attractive dining room, a well-named "elbow room" bar, and a string of eighteen nicely furnished, spacious rooms along the back; there are also two guest rooms upstairs in the house. Everything is immaculately clean, and the restaurant (open to the public) serves creditable breakfasts and dinners. Moderately priced.

Carriage House Inn (548-2289). Open all year. Directly across US 1 from the Homeport, another mid-nineteenth-century mansion with four guestrooms, one suite, and two more guestrooms in the making. Breakfasts are a pride and are included in the price: $18-22 single, $26-30 double.

Jed Prouty Tavern, Main Street in Bucksport (469-3113). There are just eight rooms upstairs in this middle-of-town inn; plain but clean: $16 single, $20 double. See Restaurants.

RESTAURANTS   **Jed Prouty Tavern,** Main Street in Bucksport (496-3113). Open for breakfast, lunch, and dinner; diners choose between the formal dining room and the informal, reasonably priced coffee shop, which is ideal for families en route up or down US 1; the menu is large, food is good and moderately priced; beer and wine are served.

Pirates' Cove on Verona Island (469-7860). May 21 through November: 9-5 daily. A mid-nineteenth-century house on an island at the mouth of the Penobscot River; moderately expensive, children's menus.

Belfast Cafe, 90 Main Street (338-2949), corner of High and Main Streets in Belfast. Pocket sandwiches, salad, coffee house atmosphere with weekend entertainment, a full bar.

City Boat Landing in Belfast (338-2574). Dinner only: 5-10; seafood and steaks, a pub-like atmosphere right on the water, moderately expensive.

The Lobster Shack (548-2448). Open 8 to 8 in summer, varying hours in spring and fall. Trundy Road off US 1 south of Searsport Village; reasonable priced lobsters; **Superior Shellfish** will pack lobsters for travel or ship them anywhere in the world.

ANTIQUE SHOPS   More than thirty dealers can now be found in town, and a listing is available from the Chamber of Commerce. We do not pretend to have visited every one, but we did like **Better Day Antiques** (548-2467), specializing in Victorian pieces. There is also **Rudder House Antiques** (548-2570), a furnished house full of items for sale, and **Red Kettle Antiques** (548-2978), specializing in antique dolls and country furniture.

SPECIAL EVENT   **Belfast Bay Festival** in mid-July: barbequed chicken, many events.

The East Penobscot Region

The peninsulas along the eastern rim of Penobscot Bay are not for everyone. This was a lively commercial area in the age of sail; then, a busy resort area when steamboats docked at Castine, Sargentville, and Stonington. But today tourists whiz on by, up US 1 to Mount Desert. Few stray as far off the highway as Blue Hill (thirteen miles south on Route 15), or Castine (seventeen miles down Route 175 and 166), let alone ever reaching Stonington (thirty-two miles off the beaten track down at the tip of Deer Isle). The result is that a number of villages, although now technically linked to US 1 by bridges, retain the atmosphere of islands. Lodging, though limited, ranges from waterside tent sites to exquisite inns.

Days are spent blueberrying, sunning on smooth rocks and shingle beaches, deep sea fishing, sailing, or maybe taking the ferry from Stonington to Isle au Haut, a little-visited corner of Acadia National Park. Nightly entertainment is limited to chamber music concerts in Blue Hill or Castine, or whatever happens to be the presentation at Haystack Mountain School of Crafts in Deer Isle. On rainy days there are a surprising number of art galleries, crafts shops and historical societies to visit.

GUIDANCE There is no year-round, or even part-time, chamber of commerce beating the drums to lure tourists. Local map/guides are printed with no address. During high season the **Deer Isle-Stonington Chamber of Commerce** maintains an information booth on Route 15 at Little Deer Isle, open when it's open. The Blue Hill inquiries are referred to the Town's Clerk's "office" (374-5645), which happens to be the counter at Candage Hardware where Genette Candage works with her husband Rufus, who—since he is a realtor on the side—is a good source for local cottage rentals. You might also try the Stonington town clerk (348-2579). For the Blue Hill peninsula and down, the booklet to secure is the *Bay Community Register*, describing who is what and what is where each year, published by Penobscot Bay Press, Stonington, Maine 04681. *Island Ad-Vantages*, the region's weekly newspaper—also in Stonington—is always the best source of what's going on everywhere except Castine—for which you must secure a copy of the weekly *Castine Patriot*.

GETTING THERE **Delta Airlines** to Bangor International, or **Bar Harbor Airlines** to Hancock County Airport near Ellsworth; rental cars at both points. For

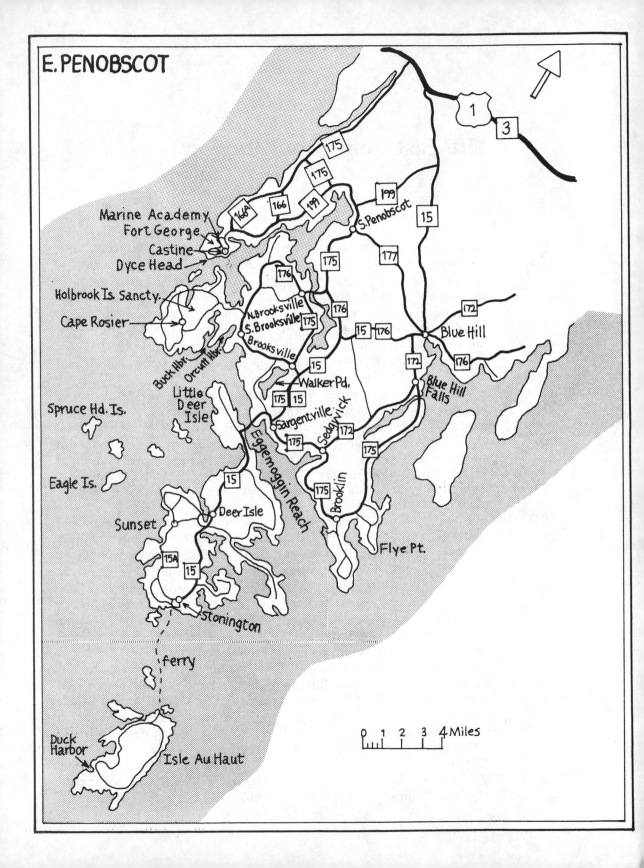

E. PENOBSCOT

taxi service contact Bar Harbor taxi. Nearest bus service is Bucksport (Greyhound).

GETTING AROUND   **Downeast Transportation** (667-5796) offers year-round service, Tuesday and Thursday, linking Ellsworth and Stonington via Blue Hill, Brooklin, Sedgwick, Deer Isle, and Sunset; it's timed to connect with the morning and noon ferries to Isle au Haut.

CASTINE

Castine must be treated separately because it is physically separate, with a different history and feel from anywhere else in the world. According to the historical markers which pepper its tranquil streets, it has been claimed by four different countries over the years. Founded by a Frenchman as Fort Pentagoet in 1613 (says a plaque on Perkins Street), it was subsequently a trading post for the Pilgrims, but soon fell into the hands of Baron de Saint Castin—a young French nobleman who married a Penobscot Indian princess and reigned as a combination feudal lord and Indian chief over Maine's eastern coast for many decades.

Since no two accounts agree, I won't attempt to describe the outpost's constantly shifting fortunes—even the Dutch owned it briefly. Nobody denies that in 1779 residents (mostly Tories, fled here from Boston and Portland) welcomed the invading British. The Commonwealth of Massachussetts retaliated by mounting a fleet of eighteen armed vessels and twenty-four transports with 1000 troops and 400 marines aboard. This small navy disgraced itself absurdly the day they sailed into town on July 5, 1779. The British Fort George was barely in the making, manned by 750 soldiers with the backup of two sloops. But the American boats, all of which were actually privateers, refused to attack and hung around in the bay long enough for several British men-'o-war to come along and destroy them. The surviving patriots had to walk back to Boston, and many of their officers—Paul Revere included—were court-martialed for their part in the disgrace.

Perhaps it is to spur young men on to avenge this affair that Castine has been picked as home of the Maine Maritime Academy—which occupies the actual site of the British barracks, and keeps a World War II troop ship anchored at the town dock, incongruously huge beside the graceful white clapboard buildings bred of a very different maritime era. Castine had its shipbuilding days in the mid-nineteenth century, when it claimed to be the second wealthiest town per capita in the USA. Its genteel qualities were recognized by summer visitors who later came by steamboat to stay in the eight hotels; many soon built a number of seasonal mansions. Just two small hotels survive, but two of the mansions are now inns. Every room in town is usually taken for the summer—by June.

SIGHTS TO SEE   **Fort George,** open May 30-Labor Day, daily: 10-6. The sorry tale of its capture by the British during the Revolution (see above), and again during the War of 1812, when redcoats occupied the town for eight months, is told on panels at the fort—an earthenworks complex of steep grassy walls and a flat interior on which you frequently find Maritime Academy cadets being put through their paces.

Wilson Museum, open May 27 through September, Tuesday-Sunday: 2-5. Free. More than a town historical society, the museum displays an extensive collection of Micmac and Penobscot Indian sweet grass baskets, also bags made from porcupine quills and elaborately beaded pouches, other clothing. There are also farm tools, a few period rooms, a mineral display, working smithy, and the town's old summer and winter hearses. The eighteenth-century John Perkins House next door is open only Wednesday and Sunday during July and August, and there is a $1 fee to tour it.

State of Maine, the training ship for the Maine Maritime Academy (326-4311). Open year-round, daily: 9-4. Free. Visitors are welcome to clamber aboard and tour the ship. Inquire about the Allie Ryan Maritime Collection at the Academy.

Backshore Road and English Canal. During the War of 1912 the British dug a canal across the narrow neck of land above town, thus turning Castine into an island. Much of the canal is still visible, and at its western terminus there is a fine swimming hole.

Withevie Park is an extensive wooded area webbed with paths, up behind and at the western end of town.

Dyce's Head Light, western end of Battle Avenue, is now obsolete, but there is a path down to it and the ledges are fun to climb.

GOLF AND TENNIS   A nine-hole golf course and four clay tennis courts are both available at the **Castine Golf Club** on Battle Avenue.

SAILING   *Heritage,* a handsome forty-three-foot ketch, offers half-and full-day sails in July and August when she is not on week-long cruises (there are berths for four guests). The crew are owners Kathy and Gene Spinazola (469-2793). Day sails are $35 per person; week-long cruises are $435 per person.

Small craft rentals are available from **Eaton's Boat Yard,** Sea Street (326-8579).

SPECIAL EVENTS   Concerts are scheduled at **Downeast Chamber Music Center,** Maine Maritime Academy, in July and August (326-4310).

LODGING   **Pentagoet Inn** (326-8616). Open year-round. There are fourteen rooms in this turreted, gabled old hotel, accommodating twenty-eight guests (shared baths). It manages to be at once cozy and airy and is imbued with the ebullient spirit of owner Natalie Saunders. Breakfast is served, and dinner is a five-course, sit-down event for which you must sign up during the day; brunch is served Sundays; $36 double with a private bath, $30 with a half, and $30 with a shared bath. Pets and children welcome.

Holiday House (326-4335). June to October. An 1893 summer "cottage" with eight, sea-bright rooms, furnished in antiques. It is Verna

Allen's home, slightly worn around the edges, but comfortable with an unbeatable location; $42 double. Breakfast is served.

Castine Inn (326-4365). A wooden 1890s summer hotel in the middle of town with twelve guest rooms, one with a fireplace, and a pleasant diningroom. Since new owners are in the process of taking over at this writing, we can make no judgments.

The Manor (326-4861). May 15-October 15. An impressive mansion up on Battle Avenue, built for a commodore of the New York Yacht Club. It was owned by Sara Brouillard's parents until they sold it to Paul Brouillard—who then married Sara. Together the couple have restored the ten guest rooms: $30 double, $50 for a suite with a fireplace, breakfast included.

Castine Cottages (326-8809). June-September. Six housekeeping cottages on Route 166, nicely furnished, waterfront with a superb view, pine-paneled living rooms, fireplace heaters; $170-190 per week. For a brochure write Lloyd and Suzanne Snapp, Box 224, Castine.

FOOD   **The Pentagoet Inn** (see lodging)

Lafferty's (326-4776). A pub atmosphere with brick walls, in the basement of an old commercial building, right down on the dock; open for lunch and dinner; a good people-meeting place with adequate food and a lively bar.

Salty Breeze, a seasonal takeout at the dock, good for breakfast and lunch since there are picnic tables on the spot, overlooking boat traffic.

Tozier's Market, Water Street, is a grocery store selling hot coffee, pastries, and sandwiches; and the **Variety Store,** corner of Maine and Water, is an old-style pharmacy with a good soda fountain.

BLUE HILL

The town is named for a high, blueberry-coated hill behind it. It is graced with no fewer than seventy-five buildings on the National Historic Register: old mansions, and 1840s academy, and fine commercial buildings. It is known for the quality of its pottery makers and for the summer chamber concerts presented at Kneisel Hall.

SIGHTS TO SEE   **Jonathan Parson Fisher Memorial.** Open July to mid-September, Tuesdays and Fridays: 2-5, Saturdays: 10-12. A house built in 1814 by Blue Hill's first pastor, a Harvard graduate who augmented his meager salary with a varied line of crafts, also by teaching (he founded Blue Hill Academy), farming, and writing. His furniture, paintings, books, journals, and windmill are exhibited.

Holt House is open July and August; Tuesdays and Fridays: 1-5. The Blue Hill Historical Society collection is housed in this restored Federal-era mansion, noted for its stencilled walls.

MUSIC   **Kneisel Hall** (374-2811 after June 24) is a summer school for string and ensemble music; faculty present a series of seven Sunday concerts and five Wednesday evening concerts beginning the first week of July. There are also periodic student recitals.

Blue Hill Chamber Ensemble (667-2014) presents off-season concerts at the town hall.

POTTERY **Rowantrees Pottery** (374-5535). Year-round, daily in summer with Sunday: 1-5, otherwise Monday-Friday: 9-3:30, fifteen-minute tour, appointment preferred but not necessary. Pottery on sale, tableware and decorative pieces. Founded in 1934 by Adelaide Pearson who was encouraged by Mahatma Gandhi to produce pottery as an expression of art. The glazes are outstanding, gathered from the town's abandoned copper mines, quarries, and bogs.

Rackliffe Pottery (374-2297). Year-round, Monday to Saturday: 8-4. A half-hour tour, pottery sold at the store; also wheel-thrown dinnerware made from native clay, local ingredients in the glazes.

SPECIAL EVENTS **Blue Hill Fair.** At the fair grounds, always the last weekend in August: harness racing, a midway, livestock competitions, one of the most colorful old-style fairs in New England.

Blue Hill Days. Late July or early August: lobster dinners, entertainment.

Young Fools Renaissance Fair. At Rowantrees Pottery, early August: crafts, food, entertainment.

LODGING **Blue Hill Inn** (374-2844). A classic old tavern, complete with two doors. Within walking distance of downtown shops, but on a quiet, elm-lined street near the academy. Owners Jean and Fred Wakelin have added sophisticated touches to its simple interior, and it works. There are eight rooms, $36 single; one free day for a week's stay. Breakfast and dinner are served. Guests have golf, tennis, and beach privileges.

FOOD **Firepond** (374-2135), mid-June to mid-October, Main Street. Excellent food and service, reservations suggested. Housed in an old mill and blacksmith's shop, serving lunch, dinner, also hors d'oeuvres and cocktails. Respected as one of the best restaurants in the state; entrees are in an $8-$12 range.

Blue Hill Inn (374-2844). Dinner is open to the public by reservation; one entree is served per night, promptly at seven, in the inn's attractive dining room; BYOB.

The Sea Gull (374-5168). Lunch and dinner. The specialties are fried seafood, $5-9, with wine and cocktails served in the bar.

Blue Hill Lunch, Water Street, year-round. A tiny, congenial place serving tasty, inexpensive lunches with terrific desserts. Sandwich, coffee and dessert will run $3-4.

STONINGTON

Stonington's buildings are scattered around the harbor on the smooth, pink granite rocks for which it is famous. The many-colored houses are hedged with flowers, and the whole town resembles a giant rock garden. The harbor is filled with lobster boats, not pleasure craft. There is a weathered sardine-and-shrimp-packing plant, a boatyard, and a lobster

Lobster Boat

co-op. Main Street is picturesquely shabby, but offers unexpectedly fine shopping—between crafts shops, galleries and two competing, old-style "dry goods" stores.

BOAT EXCURSIONS *Palmer Day II* (367-2207), July 4-Labor Day. Captain Reginald Greenlaw offers morning deep-sea fishing trips to groups of a minimum of twelve who happen to book for the same time: $15 per person, rod reel and bait included. He also offers afternoon sightseeing excursions through the Penobscot Bay Islands, feeding his pet seal en route, and giving a spirited narration throughout the sixteen-mile cruise; $5 per adult, $3.50 under ten. Inquire about cruises to Vinalhaven, North Haven.

Mailboat to Isle au Haut (367-2468). Captain Herbert Aldrich leaves Stonington at 7 AM and 11 AM year-round, also at 5 PM mid-June to mid-September on Tuesdays and Thursdays. Isle au Haut (pronounced "Eel-o-ho") is six miles long and three wide; all of it is private except for

2800 acres of National Park. During summer months a ranger meets the boat at Duck Harbor, orienting passengers to the seven hiking trails, the picnic area, and drinking water sources (otherwise a pamphlet guide serves the purpose). Camping is forbidden save in the three Adirondack-style shelters, each accommodating six people mid-May through October; reservations must be made for these through Acadia National Park headquarters (see Bar Harbor) or at regional headquarters in Boston (617-223-0058).

SIGHTS TO SEE   Ames Pond, east of town, a pond full of pink and white water lillies in bloom June to early September. There is also a miniature village of sixteen buildings, which a local resident has made and set out in his garden for all to see, on Route 15 east of town.

LODGING   Captain's Quarters Inn and Motel (367-2420). Open year-round. A lineup of several waterfront buildings creatively renovated into suites and housekeeping units. There is a deck with grills to cook up the lobsters which can be bought at the co-op down the street. Rates vary from $25 to $100 in high season; guests are advised to obtain a room plan along with the rate sheet before making a reservation.

Boyce's Motel (367-2421) is an adequate motel with some efficiencies.

RESTAURANTS   Fisherman's Friend Restaurant (367-2442), 6:30-8; BYOB. One of the best values in Maine: simple decor, just up the hill from the harbor, on School Street. Dinner entrees run $3.95 to $7.95 for the Fisherman's Platter, which is enough to share among friends. Everything is fresh-caught and homemade.

Connie's Restaurant. Seasonal. 7 AM-8PM. Upstaged by its competition but also good, serving fish and lobster caught by proprietor Barbara Bridges' husband and son; choose dining room or takeout.

Gretchen's Pantry (367-5553). Seasonal, dinners only by reservation: "homecooking with a flair" served in the pleasant dining room of an old house in downtown Stonington.

SHOPPING   On Stonington's Main Street there are two "department stores": **Epstein's,** and **Freedman** (open daily and run by two elderly brothers Henry and Israel, selling "nothing that isn't American made") **"Some Stuff",** also on Main Street, displays the work of forty-five Penobscot Bay artists and craftspersons, including graphics, fabric, pottery, and weaving, with special exhibits running through the summer.

BETWEEN BLUE HILL AND STONINGTON

No peninsula is more crumpled and convoluted than the land between Blue Hill and Stonington—really many islands connected by bridges and causeways. The inns described below, the crafts centers, and other sights are salted through this area—providing many excuses to drive down almost every road, each of which seems more beautiful than the last, lined with lupine and firs, and cut unexpectedly by deep coves.

SIGHTS TO SEE   Holbrook Island Sanctuary. A state wildlife sanctuary of more than 1230 acres, accessible only by car from North or South Brooksville. No camping permitted, but there is a lovely picnic area adjacent to a pebble beach, as well as hiking trails.

Salome Sellers House, Route 15A in Sunset, (348-2505 or 348-2886). Open July to Labor Day: Wednesdays, Saturdays, Sundays: 2-5. This is the home of the Deer Isle-Stonington Historical Society, an 1830 house displaying ships models, Indian artifacts and old photos; interesting and friendly.

Haystack Mountain School of Crafts (348-6946), in Deer Isle. Three-week sessions, specializing in one of a variety of crafts, attract some of the country's top young artisans each year, mid-June through Labor Day; evening programs of music and faculty lectures are open to the public; visitors are also welcome Thursday-Sunday: 1-4 to view craftsmen at work and to see their work displayed in the striking wood-and-glass building overlooking the Bay.

CANOEING   No rentals, but the reversing falls at South Blue Hill (white water) and the area between Snow Cove and the Bagaduce Estuary in Brooksville are very popular with canoeists and kayakers.

SAILING   **Deer Isle Sailing Center** (348-2339) is a sailing camp for boys and girls which also offers charters. Contact Captain Selin, Box 62, Deer Isle, Maine 04627.

SWIMMING   There is sand by the Deer Isle Causeway on Route 15, and at Sylvester's Cove in Sunset. Freshwater swimming is available at Walker Pond.

GOLF AND TENNIS   **The Island Country Club** (348-2379) in Deer Isle welcomes guests. Mid-June to Labor Day, nine holes. Horseback riding: **Round Pond Riding Stables** in Deer Isle.

BOAT EXCURSIONS   The **mailboat** for Eagle Island leaves Sylvester's Cove in Sunset daily, June through mid-September, at 8:15 AM, stopping at Spruce Head Island, arriving at Eagle at 10 AM; for details contact Captain Robert Quinn (348-2817).

LODGING   **Breezemere Farm** (326-8626), South Brooksville ME 04613, overlooking Orcutt Harbor. Pleasant, and handy to Buck Harbor, one of the prettiest natural harbors on the entire coast. The inn has seven immaculate rooms in its 1850 farmhouse, plus four attractive cottages. There is a huge fieldstone hearth in the living room, also game and reading rooms to fend off the fog; $36 to $39 per person, gourmet dinner and farm breakfast included, BYOB, dinner for the public by reservation.

The Lookout (359-8344), May through October on Flye Point in the town of Brooklin, has changed little over the years. It is an old-fashioned country inn off by itself; just thirty guests can be accommodated in the rooms above the restaurant (highly esteemed locally), and in a few cottages.

Oakland House (359-8521). June 20-September 10 in Sargentville. A picturesque old place with a mansard roof, run by Jim and Sylvia Littlefield as it was by Jim's forebears back to 1889; his family has actually been living on this choice piece of property by Eggemoggin Reach since 1776. Meals are served in the delightful old dining room, but there are no longer any guest rooms upstairs. Guests are scattered in the dozen cottages and large guesthouse. During high season there is a minimum stay of four days, and the rate is $245 to $320 per week with three daily meals; in the off season, when meals are not being served, the cottages' (which have fireplaces) rates are $150 to $175 per week. Guests have use of rowboats, access to both saltwater and freshwater beaches, lawn games, and hiking trails. The inn boasts a seventy percent repeat business each summer.

Goose Cove Lodge (348-2508) in Sunset, open mid-June to mid-September. Set in seventy wooded acres with splendid bay and ocean views, this is a spread-out resort with a dining room and common rooms in a spacious main lodge. The seven cottages and two duplex cottages all have decks, and fireplaces or Franklin stoves, as do most of the motel units. There are marked hiking trails, a beach, and boats. There is a sense of remoteness, yet you are handy to Stonington. Rates are $240 to $350 per week, two meals a day included.

Eggemoggin Inn (348-2540), Memorial Day to October. A spacious old house in which Sophie Broadhead offers nine airy guest rooms, some of them so huge that our family of five managed to fit into one quite comfortably. You can sit here for hours and watch the boat traffic up and down the Reach, and there is an endless single beach to stroll, as well as a shoreside path. Children feel welcome in the parlor, where there are plenty of books and games and guests tend to talk to each other as they would in a private home. Rates are $30 to $40 per room, whether you are a single person or big family. The full breakfast is $2.50 extra.

Pilgrim's Inn (348-6615), open late May to late October. A very elegant inn housed in a 1793 gambrel-roofed house overlooking the harbor in Deer Isle village. There are twelve guest rooms, three with bath. The furnishings are beautiful and the food is excellent; rates are $330 per person per week, two meals included. The inn is up for sale at this writing.

FOOD   **Eatons Lobster Pool Restaurant** (348-2383) is open seasonally, Monday-Saturday: 5-9; Sunday: 12-9, BYOB. Be sure to order lobster a la carte and by the pound, instead of the higher priced "lobster dinner." The restaurant is still in the family which settled the spot, and it is the area's premier lobster pound; it offers a full menu and a fine view.

Bagaduce Lunch, just across the river from North Brooksville, is the closest lunch counter to the Brooksville and Cape Rosier area. Open seasonally, delicious fried clams. **The Country View,** on Rte. 15 in Sedgwick, is not far away and offers similar fare.

SHOPPING   This area is such a crafts center that "Directions", the leaflet guide "to Maine's Professional Craftspeople," is published in Stonington. The following are a few of the many local studios and shops:

North Country Textiles (326-8222) in South Penobscot, Route 175, is open summer months, displaying beautifully designed and woven clothes by four local weavers.

Hance Pottery/The Weave Shop. Open year-round 1-4. Functional pottery of a very high quality, also attractive woven wraps.

Pearson's Jewelry, Old Ferry Road off Route 15 in Deer Isle (348-2535), year-round, weekdays: 10-3. Ron Pearson has an international reputation for creative designs in gold and silver jewelry, as well as delicately wrought table-top sculpture in other metals.

Appel-Sedgwick Pottery (359-8986) in Sedgewick, Route 175, year-round. Outstanding pottery by Ezra and Jane Appel. He does the more functional pieces, she the more decorative.

Brooklin Crafts (359-2124). Memorial Day to Labor Day, Tuesday-Saturday: 10-5. A storefront shop in the village of Brooklin carrying the work of five craftspeople: weaving, pottery, batik, and porcelain.

Mount Desert

This is New England's second-largest island, one conveniently linked to the mainland and laced with roads for touring by car, plus fifty miles of carriage roads just for exploring by bike, horse, or ski, and another 142 miles of hiking paths.

Mount Desert's beauty cannot be overstated. Its seventeen mountains rise abruptly from the sea and its interior contains five large lakes, numberless ponds and streams, an unusual variety of flora and fauna, also more than 300 species of birds.

It was named L'Isle de Monts Deserts by Samuel de Champlain in 1604 and settled early in the eighteenth century, but it remained a peaceful, out-of-the-way place until a bridge was built in 1836. Artists began crossing the bridge immediately, followed by summer rusticators. Then millionaires by the scores began arriving by steamboat—more than 200 grandiose cottages were built on the island by the time the stock market crashed. Many of these were destroyed by the fire which wiped out most of Bar Harbor in 1947, but a number still survive, some as inns and two as the nucleus of the young College of the Atlantic, a pioneering environmental studies center.

The legacy of these turn-of-the-century cottages is Acadia National Park. Harvard University president Charles W. Eliot, Edsel Ford, John D. Rockefeller, Jr., and others began assembling parcels of land that were donated to the federal government in 1915 for the first national park east of Mississippi, now a 44,000-acre preserve.

Today you can enjoy an overview of the park's delights from the comfort of a seat in the park visitors center at Hulls Cove. Some three-and-one-half million people see this film every year and then drive the twenty-mile loop tour which includes the summit of Cadillac Mountain, the highest point on the eastern seaboard north of Brazil.

Each summer roughly 100,000 visitors take advantage of the rich program of hikes, nature walks, bike tours, and cruises offered during summer months by the Park Service. The number who actually strike off on their own (using the excellent printed guides available) find plenty of solitude as well as beauty.

Acadia National Park is sixteen miles wide and thirteen miles long, but it seems far larger, primarily because it is almost bisected by fjord-like Somes Sound. Bar Harbor is the big town: a jumble of motels, inns,

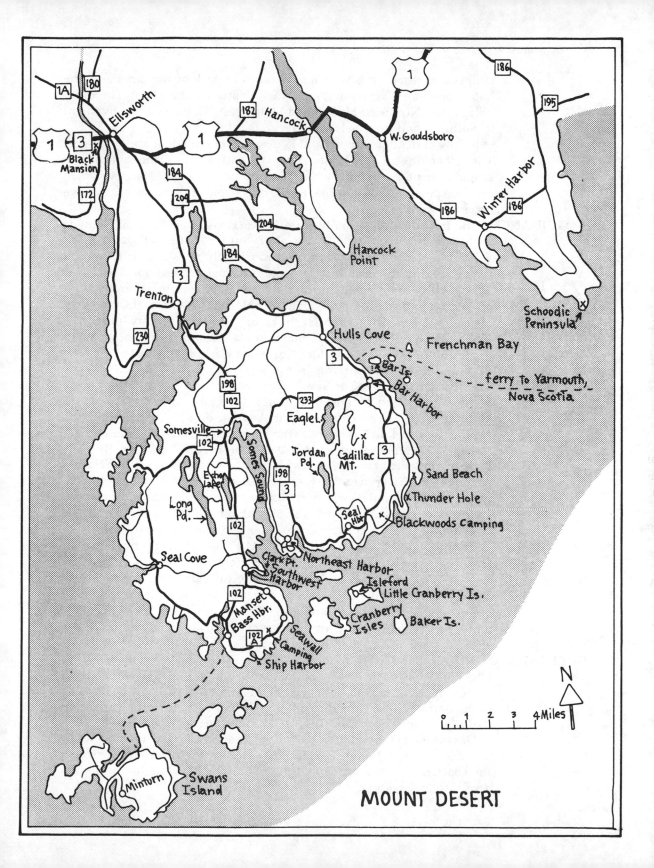

MOUNT DESERT

shops, and restaurants within easy reach of park headquarters on one hand, and the *Bluenose* ferry to Nova Scotia on the other. The other villages are Northeast Harbor and Southwest Harbor, both convenient to nothing, and extremely snobby.

In July and August the island is expensive, crowded, and exquisite. The rest of the year is off season. If you take advantage of the solitude and bargains available in June (which tends to be rainy), or February (which can be spectacular if you like to ski cross-country), be sure you have access to a fireplace.

GUIDANCE   The **Island Information Bureau** (288-3411) is open daily mid-June to mid-September on Route 3, just after you cross the causeway. It is a walk-in center, offering restrooms and friendly assistance with lodging on any part of the island. A separate information desk for Bar Harbor (288-3414) is maintained in the *Bluenose* ferry terminal, Route 3. For off-season information write to the **Bar Harbor Chamber of Commerce,** Municipal Building, Bar Harbor, or phone weekday mornings (288-5103). Southwest Harbor maintains a seasonal information booth on Route 102 (244-3772), as does Northeast Harbor, adjacent to the town dock and municipal parking area (276-5040).

GETTING THERE   By car from Boston or New York there are two routes. One is via the Maine Turnpike to Bangor, then Route 1A to Ellsworth, and Route 3 to Mount Desert. The other takes you to Augusta on I-95, then Route 3 (the Acadia Trail) east to Bar Harbor. The latter has the edge for scenery. Bar Harbor is 276 miles from Boston, 482 miles from New York City. By plane there are excellent connections with most eastern cities via **Bar Harbor Airlines** which services the Hancock County Airport at Trenton (between Ellsworth and Bar Harbor). Rental cars are available at the airport. Taxi service from the airport is also available (288-3888). Bus service is **Greyhound,** via Bangor (288-3666). Many visitors arrive by ferry from Yarmouth, Nova Scotia, served by the *M.V. Bluenose,* run by Canadian National Marine (800-341-7981 for most East Coast inquiries; 800-432-7344 in Maine, or 288-3395). The car-carrying ferry runs June 20-September 28, departing every morning at 8 A.M. It takes just six hours to get to Yarmouth and costs $18.50 per adult, $9.30 per child under thirteen, free under five; $43 per car; cheaper before June 20 and after September 28, when the ferry runs every other day.

GETTING AROUND   In Bar Harbor mopeds can be rented from **Mopeds of Maine** (288-4387) on Main Street, and bikes from **Maine Bicycle Touring Company** (288-5483) on Cottage Street. **National Park Tours** (AT8-3327) offers narrated bus tours through Bar Harbor and along the Park Loop daily in season, departing Testa's, 53 Main Street; $5 per adult.

Downeast Transportation (667-5796) is attempting to offer regularly scheduled service linking Bar Harbor with Ellsworth and with the rest of the island, as it does for Schoodic Point and the Blue Hill-to-Stonington area (see Excursions).

ACADIA NATIONAL PARK   The park maintains its own visitors center at Hulls Cove, June to Labor Day: daily, 8 AM-9 PM, in May and through October: 8-5. The center then closes, but the park headquarters at Eagle Lake (Route 233) is open weekdays: 8-4:30, also on weekends if visitation warrants. The year-round phone is: 288-3338. For more information about the park write to: Superintendent, RFD 1, P.O. Box 1, Bar Harbor, Maine 04609. The handsome glass-and-stone visitors center, set atop fifty steps, shows its fifteen-minute introductory film every hour on the hour. This is also the place to pick up a free map or cassette tape tour ($6.95 to rent for twenty-four hours), and to sign up for the various programs offered. It's advisable to get there before 10 AM in July and August, also to buy the excellent $1 AMC map/guide to Mount Desert.

Horseback Riding. Wildwood Stables (276-5091) is open May 15-October 15; guided trail rides departing every hour ($6 per hour), and carriage rides in an old wagon ($3 per person, and frankly, Mr. Rockefeller's vehicle *must* have had better suspension; I can't imagine how he enjoyed jolting along through the woods like this).

Canoe Rentals. Wilderness Paddlers, Pond's End (244-5854). Seasonal, at the north end of Long Pond, two miles west of Somesville; $11 per morning, $12 per afternoon, $18 per day.

Biking. Carriage Road tours are outlined in much of the free literature. Both the Maine Bicycle Touring Company and the Bicycle Shop, in Bar Harbor as well as the Park Service offer guided tours.

Birding. There are special programs led by naturalists. Also see Birding under "What's Where".

Camping. There are two campgrounds within the park—Blackwoods (open all year and handy to Bar Harbor) and Seawall (near Bass Harbor), open June 15-September 15; there are sites between the two; $4 per night, $2 for a walk-in tent site. Check with park headquarters on reservation policy.

Ski Touring. More than twenty-six miles of the carriage roads are maintained as ski touring trails; request a "Winter Activities" leaflet from Park Headquarters.

Snowmobiling. The motor roads are reserved for snowmobiles.

Special evening programs are scheduled for 8:30 PM nightly during July and August at the amphitheaters in Blackwoods and Seawall campgrounds.

SIGHTS TO SEE   **Sieur de Monts Spring and the Robert Abbe Museum of Stone Age Antiquities,** open May to October. The museum has an exceptional collection of New England Indian artifacts: sweet grass baskets, moccasins, a birchbark canoe, dioramas of Indian life during all seasons. You can drink from the fine spring and walk in the **Wild Gardens of Acadia,** displaying 300 species of native plants, all labeled. (The museum is posted from Route 3 as well as off the Loop.)

Sand Beach. Misnamed because it is really composed of minute shells, this is a great beach to walk—and to take a dip if you don't mind fifty-degree water (there are changing rooms, life guards). Take time to walk the Ocean Path along the rocks.

Thunder Hole. The water rushes in and out of a small cave—which you can view from behind a railing. The adjacent rocks can keep small children scrambling for hours.

Jordan Pond House. The fine old restaurant here, which burned in 1979 and reopened in 1982, specializes in popovers for tea—when it's so popular that you will have time to walk around the pond after submitting your name and before being seated. It is also open for dinner.

Cadillac Mountain. From the smooth summit you look out across Frenchman's Bay in which the islands look like giant steppingstones. This is the spot for a picnic, so come prepared. There is no place to buy food within the park.

Ship Harbor, near Bass Harbor, Route 102A, offers a fine nature trail that winds along the shore and into the woods, by "stations" which interpret what you see; it is also a great birding spot.

Cranberry Isles. There are five of these islands off Northeast Harbor, accessible by regular mail launch, but most enjoyable when you come on one of the naturalist-led trips to Baker Island and on to the **Islesford Historical Museum** on Little Cranberry Island (open daily, July and August: 10-4). The museum traces the area's history from 1604; there are some juicy smuggling stories told here about the War of 1812.

Schoodic Peninsula. More than an hour's drive from Bar Harbor, this isolated point of land beyond Winter Harbor is basically undeveloped; there are just five miles of trails. A rough dirt road leads to the summit of Schoodic Head (an unmarked left after the Frozier picnic area), and while you can walk out to Moose Island at low tide it is not encouraged because of the fragility of arctic fauna.

Isle au Haut. See Stonington, from which it is accessible on the mailboat. Roughly six by two miles, the island is heavily wooded, with a 554-feet peak; some 300 people live here in the summer, a dozen in winter; two-thirds of the island is part of Acadia National Park. There are hiking trails and very limited camping.

Jackson Laboratory (288-3371), mid-June to mid-September; a lecture and film program is presented Tuesday, Wednesday, and Friday at 3. This is the largest center for mammalian genetics in the world. Cancer, diabetes, and birth defects are among the problems intensely researched.

Wendell Gilley Museum (244-7555). Route 102, in Southwest Harbor. Open summer months daily: 10-5, except Sunday: 12-5; by appointment the rest of the year. A dramatic new building housing a collection of bird carvings and painting with the emphasis on local species.

The Bar Harbor Historical Museum (288-3838) is open mid-June to mid-September; Monday to Saturday: 1-4, Wednesday and Friday: 10-2, and by appointment. Free. A fascinating collection of early photographs of local hotels, steamers, cottages, the cog railroad, and the big fire of 1947.

Stanwood Museum and Birdsacre Sanctuary (667-8460 and 8683). Trails open all year; museum open mid-June to mid-October, daily: 10-4; otherwise by appointment. Although just off Mount Desert on Route 3, this is such an exceptional place it can't be missed: a forty-acre nature preserve which is a memorial to Cordelia Stanwood (1865-1958), a pioneer ornithologist, nature photographer, and writer.

John Black Mansion (667-8671). Open mid-June to mid-October; Monday-Saturday: 10-5; adults $2, children $1. In Ellsworth, off Mount Desert, but a place not to miss en route: an outstanding Georgian mansion built in 1862 by John Black, who had just married the daughter of the local agent for a Philadelphia land developer, owner of this region. This wedding present is said to have been built with bricks brought by sea from Philadelphia, and it took Boston workmen three years to complete it. There is a fine garden and a carriage house full of vehicles.

Mount Desert Oceanarium (244-7330). May to mid-October, daily except Sundays: 9-5. There are more than twenty tanks full of fish; $2.50 per adult, $1.50 ages five to twelve. Clark Point Road in Southwest Harbor.

COMMERCIAL ATTRACTIONS **Aqualand Wildlife Park** (288-3898). Seasonal, Route 3, 9:30-dusk; $3.95 per adult, $2.95 per child, free under three. There is also the **Seal Cove Automobile Museum,** open daily in season: 12-5.

BOAT EXCURSIONS **Frenchman Bay Boating Company** (288-5741), next to the Municipal Pier in Bar Harbor. Open Memorial Day to October: two-hour cruises, half-day deep-sea fishing trips, and sails aboard *Bay Lady*.

Beal and Bunker Company (244-3573 or 7457), in Northeast Harbor at the Sea Street Pier, run the mail boat and ferry service to Isleford and the Cranberry Islands; they also offer seasonal whale watch and seabird cruises.

Islesford Ferry Company (244-3366), June 26 to Labor Day, offers daily cruises to Islesford (two-and-one-half hours) and to Bakers Island (four-and-a-half hours), also a two-hour sunset cruise in July and August.

Sunrise Lobster Fishing Tours (276-5352/5853). Seasonal. Trips in a thirty-six-foot lobster boat from the Northeast Harbor town dock.

Gayle II whale-watching and all-day cruises (244-7312). This is a twenty-six-foot cruiser based at the Upper Town Landing in Southwest Harbor.

Bass Harbor Cruise (244-5356). Two daily cruises in summer season, Monday to Saturday, observing lobstering, seals, osprey.

Seal Harbor Deep Sea Fishing Charter (276-5063). Two trips daily in season, Seal Harbor town pier.

Blackjack, a thirty-three-foot Friendship sloop (288-3056 or 276-5043), offers one-and-one-half-hour cruises, six days a week, in season.

Golden Anchor (288-5033), a sloop based at the Golden Anchor Inn in Bar Harbor, offers daily sails from West Street in Bar Harbor.

Swan's Island Ferry *Everett Libby* (244-3254) offers daily year-round service from Bass Harbor to Swan's Island. It's a forty-minute ride each way, and you should bring a bike or rent one at **The Captain's Galley,** a restaurant (sandwiches and ice cream) near the dock on Swan's Island— roughly 6000 acres, flat, and ringed with paved roads which take you to the village of Minturn (where the **Sea Breeze** restaurant is open year-round). There is a public beach, but no overnight lodging.

LAND EXCURSIONS   **Downeast Transportation** (667-5796), based in Ellsworth, is an enterprising new public transit system which takes an extremely scenic run to Winter Harbor on Mondays and Thursdays. It's possible to spend a number of pleasant hours in Winter Harbor eating lobster and taking a scenic walk, or renting a moped with which to explore Schoodic Point (part of Acadia National Park). On Tuesdays and Thursdays the bus runs from Ellsworth to Stonington, where it's possible to connect with the mail boat to Isle au Haut, yet another part of the National Park, blessed with hiking paths. Both rides are picturesque and cost $2.80 round trip.

SWIMMING   **The Bar at Bar Harbor.** This is a sand bar, accessible from Bridge Street, and safe to walk for two hours each day at ebb tide. Bring a picnic and explore the paths.

Within the park there is supervised swimming at Sand Beach, four miles south of Bar Harbor; and at Echo Lake, eleven miles west. At Seal Harbor there is a small, free town beach, with parking in a small lot across Route 3. At Lake Wood near Hull's Cove there is a pleasant, freshwater beach, ideal for children. The trick is finding it: turn off Route 3 at the Cove Motel and follow the unpromising road; take your first left up a dirt road, which leads to a parking area; there is a short walk down to the beach. No facilities or lifeguard, but warm water.

GOLF AND TENNIS   **Kebo Valley Golf Club** (288-3000). Open May through October, daily; eighteen holes on Route 233 in Bar Harbor, "eighth oldest golf course in America." **The Northeast Harbor Club** (nine holes), and the **Causeway Club** in Southwest Harbor (nine holes) also welcome guests. For a fee you can use the tennis courts at **Atlantic Oaks by the Sea** (288-5218).

SAILING   In addition to the day sails listed above, you can rent sailboats and take sailing lessons from **Manset Boat Company** (244-5626) in Manset, near Southwest Harbor.

THEATER   **Acadia Repertory Theatre** is based at the Masonic Hall, Route 102 in Somesville (244-7260); it is a resident theatre group which performs a half dozen plays during July and August, some at the Bar Harbor Club.

LODGING   According to the Bar Harbor Chamber of Commerce there are approximately 3000 beds in town; the chamber's booklet lists double rooms from $7 per person. We cannot claim to have inspected every room, but we offer this partial listing to places we have actually checked out.

The Ledgelawn (288-4596), year-round, 66 Mount Desert Street. The seventeen rooms with baths range in price from $30 to $80, depending on their size, bath, and view, also if they happen to have a fireplace. The inn is furnished with oriental rugs and antiques. It offers a pool of its own, a sauna, also privileges at the Bar Harbor Club with tennis and an Olympic-sized pool. Breakfast served, complimentary wine and cheese in the evening, free pickup at airport and ferry.

Manor House Inn (288-3759), 106 West Street. Open May through October. Central to everything, a homey feeling in an 1887 house. There are eleven guest rooms, all with private baths, some with fireplaces ($48 to $80), also one-bedroom cottages at $300 per week, breakfast included. Guest privileges with the Bar Harbor Club, which means use of the pool and tennis courts.

Thornhedge (288-5398). Open mid-March to mid-December. A yellow shingle turn-of-the-century mansion with nine guest rooms, five with baths, some with fireplaces. Very clean, coffee and muffins served each morning in the ornate diningroom; $34-52 for double room with breakfast.

Hearthside Inn (288-4533), open late June-October, 7 High Street. A small inn with nine rooms, some fireplaces in the rooms, some balconies, private and shared baths; $26 to $60 (for a suite of two rooms, fireplace) including breakfast and after-dinner coffee.

Mira Monte Inn (288-4263). May to mid-October; nine rooms with shared baths in an 1865 house on Desert Street. A few rooms have fireplaces; $26-30 for rooms with shared baths, $38-50 for those with private, $6 extra for every child under twelve.

The Central House (288-4242). Year-round, 60 Cottage Street. Built in 1887 by the owners of the Hope diamond. There are twelve guest rooms furnished with a flare ($30-$45, $5 extra for each additional person), some with fireplaces, balconies. Not as private as the other inns because of the popularity of its restaurant, which is open for lunch and dinner, serving lunch on the porch in summer.

Cleftstone Manor (288-4951). Open May through October, Eden Street. Another 1890s mansion with nineteen guest rooms, twelve with private baths, many fireplaces but none working during our stay. Wine and cheese served in the evening, tea and biscuits at four, not geared to children.

Bar Harbor Motor Inn (288-3351), mid-May to late October. The core building was The Reading Room, a private club for wealthy cottagers. It is now an attractive dining room and lobby. All fifty-four rooms have private baths, many overlook the water. There is a pool, and the inn is set in manicured green grounds at the bottom of Bar Harbor's Main Street, next to the municipal pier. $68-94 double, high season.

Atlantic Oakes (288-5218), year-round. Eden Street, next to the *Bluenose* ferry terminal. This is a modern facility on the site of the Sir Harry Oakes estate: sixty-nine units, many with balconies, twelve with kitchens. There are tennis courts on the grounds, and both sailboats and rowboats at the dock. $62-75 double, cheaper off season.

Hinckley's Dreamwood Motor Court (288-3510). May 15-October 15,

Bass Harbor Head Lighthouse

Route 3 north of town; twenty-four units including three two-bedroom ($36-50) (fireplaces and full kitchen $336 per week). A three-day minimum for housekeeping units in season. The rate for two people is $32-46 in season; most rentals are by the week and booked by March. It has a heated pool, adjacent to the High Seas Restaurant.

Mount Desert Island Motel and Cottages (288-4670). Motel units are set well back from Route 3, all with picture windows facing on a rear meadow, all with decks large enough to accommodate a family of five. The cottages are just one bedroom but charming, with fireplaces and screened porches. The coffee shop serves a breakfast.

Emery's Cottages on the Shore (288-3432), May to mid-October, Sand Point Road. Twenty-one cottages, twelve with kitchenettes, electric heat, tv, showers; a fine, out-of-the-way site; $32-40 per day, $295-325 per week.

Golden Anchor Inn (288-5033), one of the few hostelries in the area open year-round; off Route 3 on West Street. 75 units, swimming pool, docking facilities, restaurant overlooking harbor. Summer rates $60-$65 double, lower rest of the year.

The following establishments in Bar Harbor offer reasonably-priced beds: **McKay Cottages** (288-3531), 243 Main Street, offers thirty rooms year-round; $7 to $12 per person; family rooms are $7 to $9 per person. **Dow Cottage Inn** (288-3112), also open year round, charges $7 to $14 (with private bath) per night. **Elmhurst Inn** (288-3044), 40 Holland Avenue, is a fine old antiques-furnished home on the fringe of Bar Harbor offering ten rooms plus efficiency units for $25-50 double. Inquire from the Chamber of Commerce about other cottages in the $14-per-night range.

YWCA, 36 Mount Desert Street (288-5008) offers twenty-six rooms, singles and doubles, and dorm room for eight women, open all year, also has a gym and tennis courts. Cheapest place in town and very pleasant, central.

LODGING BEYOND BAR HARBOR   **The Moorings** (244-5523). April through mid-October. A delightful inn in Manset. There are nine rooms in the inn, also a five-unit motel and two cottages. The Moorings is geared to yachtsmen, also to children and pets. Every kind of boat (including canoes) can be rented next door and sailing lessons are given. The dining room is next door (see food). Rates go from $20 for a small single, to $50 for Eagle Watch Cottage, complete with a fireplace, two bedrooms.

The Claremont (244-5036), in Southwest Harbor. June 19-September 14 for the main inn; May 15-October 15 in the cottages; a guest house is open year-round. This is the oldest hotel on Mount Desert, built in 1883 and recently renovated. All twenty-two rooms in the main house have private baths; there are eight cottages—most of them two-bedroom with fireplaces—and two guesthouses, each with its own livingroom. Rates are $94 to $114, two meals included; less off season, European plan.

Asticou and Cranberry Inns, Northeast Harbor (276-3344 or 276-3702). The Asticou is open April to November, the Cranberry Inn year-round.

An elegant inn built in 1902: sixty rooms—forty in the main building, twenty in smaller lodges which include the former Cranberry Inn across the road (six rooms with fireplaces). There are also six octagonal, glass-sided cottages with cooking facilities. The dining room is formal. There is also a cocktail lounge, tennis, and a swimming pool; $54-68 single, $86-96 double, $92-106 for suites and cottages, two meals included. Cheaper off season, no meals included.

Harbourside Inn, Northeast Harbor (276-3272), June through September. Built in 1888, a handsome mansion with eighteen guest rooms, each with private bath, four with kitchenette, two suites with fireplaces, $48-75 including complimentary breakfast.

Grey Rock Inn (276-9360), Northeast Harbor. May to early October. A 1911 mansion nicely furnished, many fireplaces, nine rooms, $48 to $55 double, breakfast included.

Harbor Light Tourist Home in Southwest Harbor (244-3835). A big Victorian house in a central location, an old-style guest home; $25 with private bath, $20 with shared bath.

Appalachian Mountain Club Echo Lake Camp (244-2747). Late June through August. Accommodations are platform tents. Meals are served in a central dining hall. There is also a rustic library-reading room and an indoor game room. The focus, however, is the outdoors; there are boats for use on the lake, daily hikes, and evening old-style fun. Reservations should be made on April 1. Rates are slightly higher for non-AMC members, but are still very reasonable and include all meals, served family style. A minimum of one-week stay (Saturday to Saturday), and two weeks are suggested. Write for a brochure to: Echo Lake Camp, AMC, 5 Joy Street, Boston, Massachusetts 02108.

Crocker House Country Inn, Hancock Point (422-6806). Memorial Day through Labor Day. Just twenty minutes north of Bar Harbor, Hancock Point has a different feel entirely. The attractive inn offers fourteen rooms, one with a private bath; $18 single to $90 for the entire third floor, including four bedrooms, a sitting room and bath. Across the road sits the smallest post office I have ever seen, and there is the Hancock Village Improvement Society next door with two tennis courts, a dock, and sailing lessons. Dinner is open to the public and has a good local reputation.

RESTAURANTS **Bar Harbor Motor Inn** (288-3351). The formal dining room is open 6-10; meals are $10 to $20, elegant, overlooking the water.

La Domaine, "Restaurant Francais" in Hancock (422-3395). Generally rated as one of the best restaurants in the state, and we must confess to not having tested it. We have heard mixed reviews. Very French; entrees from $7.75 to $14, dinner reservations advised.

Testa's (288-3327), 53 Main Street. Open June 15 to September 23, when the family moves to Palm Beach where they run a second restaurant. There are seventeen rooms upstairs here, but Testa's is primarily a dining landmark, serving three daily meals in a polished wood atmosphere; prices are moderately expensive, but not if you order the specials.

Moorings Restaurant (244-7070), beside The Moorings inn (see Lodging) in Manset. Seasonal dining, both lunch and dinner, a varied seafood menu in a pleasant atmosphere, children's menu.

Beal's Lobster Pier, Clark Point Road in Southwest Harbor, seasonal. A no-frills lobster pound with rock bottom prices; eat lobster and steamers on picnic tables by the water; they stop boiling at 5:30.

Fisherman's Landing on the pier at West Street (288-4632). Good for lobster and a fine view.

Jordan Pond House. See Acadia National Park, open for tea and dinner.

Town Farm Restaurant (288-3359) in Bar Harbor. Seasonal. Delicious natural foods, specializing in soups and salads and reasonable prices. A bit tricky to find; Kennebec Place behind a park by the fire station.

Bubba's (288-5871), 30 Cottage Street. Gourmet burgers, sandwiches, and drinks all day and evening.

Acadian Restaurant (288-4493) in Hulls Cove on Route 3. A cozy little restaurant that is good value, fine baking. Open for breakfast: 7-11:30, for dinner from 5.

Brick Oven Restaurant (288-3708), open May through mid-October, 21 Cottage Street, specializes in seafood, lots of atmosphere, also good food and reasonable prices.

Jordan's (288-3586), a restaurant and "variety store," 80 Cottage Street, open all year, good for blueberry muffin breakfasts and light lunches.

Harbor View Restaurant, Main Street in Bar Harbor, with a real view of the harbor in the background, a park in the fore, good for breakfast and lunch, open 7 AM to 2 PM daily in season, specializing in imaginative, reasonably priced breakfasts.

Long's Downeast Clambakes (244-5255) on Route 102 offers old-style clambakes by reservation only, May through October daily, 5:30-7:30.

Sea View Restaurant (288-3726), open mid-June to mid-October, 7-11 for breakfast, then again 5-11 for dinner. One mile north of Bar Harbor on Route 3, friendly atmosphere and good value; dinners in the $10 range.

SPECIAL EVENTS   Summerlong: **Band concerts,** Mondays and Thursdays at 8 PM on the Village Green.

June: **Antique Car Rally** on the third weekend.

July 4: **Parade,** lobster festival, dancing, fireworks.

Mid-July: **Acadian Scottish Festival** in Trenton. **Southwest Harbor Days** (also third weekend in August); boat races, walking tours, parade, art exhibit on the green in Bar Harbor.

Early August: **Bar Harbor Festival;** a series of concerts and recitals at various sites throughout the area.

September: **Half-Marathon Race** (13.1 miles), beginning at the Bar Harbor athletic field, fourth weekend.

Boston Globe

INLAND

In and Around Bridgton

From the summit of Pleasant Mountain you are said to see fifty lakes, ten of them right in the town of Bridgton.

Before the Civil War, Bridgton's pioneer tourists could actually come by boat all the way from Boston. From Portland they would ride twenty miles—throught 28 locks—on the Cumberland and Oxford Canal, thence across Sebago Lake, up the Songo River, Brandy Pond, and Long Lake to Bridgton. In the 1870s Maine's "big ditch" (as the canal was known) was abandoned, but by then travelers could come by train to Sebago Lake and the remaining fifteen miles by narrow gauge railroad, riding in the same cars which now circle a cranberry bog as the Edaville Railroad in Carver, Massachusetts.

By the 1870s a number of summer hotels had opened in Bridgton, and dozens of farms took in summer boarders. Current accommodations are 1980s equivalents of these pleasant, reasonably priced places.

One exceptional summer hotel—the Tarry-A-While—survives. There are also a few motels, but what there are hundreds of are cottages —classic Maine lake-side cottages, with screened porches and knotty pine interiors. Many come with boats, since the lakes are well-stocked with fish. Nearby Sebago Lake is famed for salmon.

Golf and tennis are readily available in town, and both sailboats and canoes can be rented. At the Causeway in Naples, just down Long Lake, you can go parasailing. You can also board the *Songo River Queen II*—a paddle-wheel-powered excursion boat—for a ride across Brandy Pond and through the one lock surviving from the 1830 canal. It's a very pleasant ride to the mouth of Sebago Lake down the Songo River, which is about as windy as a river can be (it's one-and-one-half miles as the crow flies, six miles as the Songo twists and turns).

Information sheets distributed by Bridgton's Chamber of Commerce outline a number of driving tours through surrounding lake and hill towns. They inform you that you are just a thirty-minute drive from the Sabbathday Lake Shaker Museum in one direction, forty-five minutes from Willowbrook at Newfield (a reconstructed late eighteenth-century village) in another. The White Mountains of New Hampshire are also less than a half hour's drive, and Portland is just twenty-eight miles away.

But the fact is that most visitors to Bridgton don't go anywhere. They swim and fish, fish and swim. On rainy days they browse through the

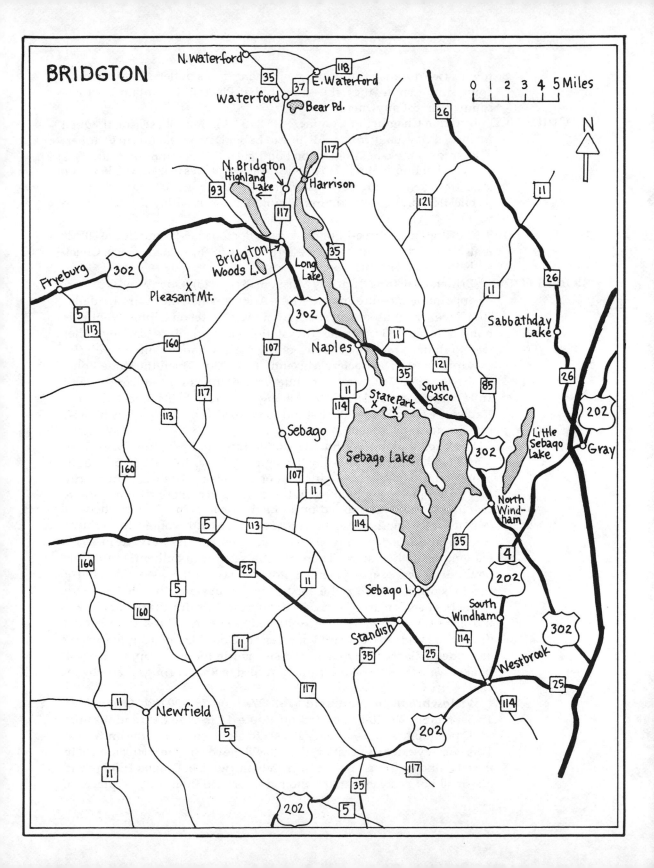

town's two dozen antique shops and many crafts outlets. If it is winter, come sun or snow, they ski—downhill at Pleasant Mountain or cross-country almost anywhere.

GUIDANCE   **Bridgton Chamber of Commerce** (647-3472). Box 236, seasonal. Open Memorial Day, daily from mid-June to Labor Day, weekends in October; a downtown walk-in information booth near the junctions of Routes 302 and 117. For information also phone the town offices (647-2331/2365). For local dining and events see *The Bridgton News* and the *302 Traveler*, a free publication printed weekly in the summer and monthly the rest of the year.

GETTING THERE   Bridgton is a three-hour drive from Boston via I-95 and Route 302. It is also one of the few towns in western Maine to enjoy bus service. Check with **Vermont Transit.**

SIGHTS TO SEE   **Bridgton Historical Society Museum** (647-5145). Open May-October; by appointment before and after July-August, when the hours are daily: 10-5. Free. The museum, set back from Main Street on Gibbs Avenue, is housed in an 1890s former fire station, and displays, among other memorabilia, slides and movies of the narrow gauge railroad.

Naples Historical Society Museum (693-6220). Open the same hours as the Bridgton Museum, has slide presentations on the Cumberland and Oxford Canal and the Sebago-Long Lake steamboats. Located on the Naples green on Route 302, behind the information center, it is housed in a former brick schoolhouse.

The Sabbathday Lake Shaker Community and Museum (926-4596). May 30 to Labor Day, Tuesday through Saturday: 10-4:30. $2 per adult, $1 per child, $3.50 for a walking tour of the village, Route 26. There are a half dozen practicing Shakers in the community, more than anywhere else in the country. Founded by an Englishwoman in 1775, by the Civil War the sect numbered 6000 American men and women in eighteen communities. Today, only six of these communities survive in shape enough to tell their story. There are still seventeen authentic buildings on the 1900-acre property, and visitors can see the 1794 Meeting House, the 1839 Ministry Shop, the 1850s Boys' Shops and the Shaker Store. There has been a marked increase in interest in the furniture, music, and life of these Yankee monks who followed Mother Ann Lee's injunction to "put your hands to work and your heart to God." Trained students serve as guides at Sabbathday Lake, and sisters run the gift shop, which sells Shaker wares and the extraordinary record of Shaker songs made by the sisters here.

Willowbrook at Newfield (793-2784 or 793-2210). Open May 15-September 30: 10-5. Located off Route 11 in Newfield, admission: $3.50 per adult, $2 per student aged six to eighteen years, free under six. This is a very extensive restoration of a village core to the way it looked in the late nineteenth century. It is entirely the work of Donald F. King and his small but dedicated staff, who have restored thousands of pieces of furniture, machinery, and vehicles to mint condition. Devastated by a fire in 1947, the village was almost a ghost town when Mr. King began buying buildings in the sixties. The complex now includes twenty-seven buildings with more than 10,000 items on display. There is a restaurant for light lunches and a Christmas etcetera gift shop open most of the year.

Spratt-Mead Museum in Bridgton Academy, North Bridgton (647-2330). Open by appointment, and Saturdays: 10-2 in July and August. A local historical collection including Indian artifacts, stuffed birds, and red clay pottery.

Hopalong Cassidy in Fryeburg. The Fryeburg Public Library, 98 Main Street, open year-round, Tuesday-Thursday and Saturday: 11-5, Friday: 5-8. The library has a special room full of memorabilia belonging to Clarence Mulford, creator of Hopalong, including his gun collection and many interesting mementoes.

Nathaniel Hawthorne's Boyhood Home, Hawthorne Road off Route 302, open in July and August, Sunday: 2-4. If you happen to be passing by, it's worth a stop to see the setting and exterior of this unexceptional house, but not worth a detour.

Parson Smith Homestead in South Windham (892-5315). By appointment; $1 adults, 50c children. A Georgian farmhouse with an exceptional stairway and hall, some original furnishings.

Marrett House and Garden in Standish, Maine. May through October 15, Tuesday, Thursday, Saturday, Sunday: 2-5; $1, under twelve 50c. Famous because money from Portland's banks was stored here for safekeeping during the War of 1812. A Georgian mansion, it remained in the same family from 1789 until 1944; architecture and furnishings reflect the changing styles over 150 years.

Sebago Lake State Park (693-6612) offers 1337 acres; 287 campsites (May-October 15), as well as picnicking facilities and fine swimming. There are also scheduled summer programs in the amphitheater. The entrance is on Route 302 between Naples and South Casco. $1.50 day use fee; $6 camping for out-of-staters.

ADULT SUMMER COURSES **Bridgton Arts and Crafts Society.** Open weekends in June, September, and October. Monday-Saturday: 10-4 in July and August. Instruction is available in a variety of arts and crafts.

Maine Folk Dance Camp (647-3424), Wood Pond. For more than thirty years, a center for learning and performing folk dances from many countries.

SWIMMING Most camps, cottages, and lodges have their own waterfront beaches or docks, and there are also fine little sand beaches maintained by the town on Long Lake (a short walk from Main Street), on Woods Lake (Route 117) and on Highland Lake. There is also a fine beach at Sebago Lake Park, long enough to comfortably accommodate the heavy traffic it gets.

SKIING   Pleasant Mountain Ski Area (647-2022). A 2007-foot-high isolated hump, one mile west of the center of town. Maine's oldest ski area (opened in 1936), it offers twenty miles of terrain, a 1250-foot vertical drop and snow-making. There are three chairlifts, three T-bars, a summit warming hut, two base lodges, a nursery, cafeterias, and pretty much everything else you expect of a first-rate ski area. Cross-country trails are planned for the winter of '82-'83. The nearest real ski mountain to Portland (just twenty-five miles away), it gets a heavy weekend crowd but is peaceful midweek. Lifts and lodging packages are reasonably priced: $70 for five nights at the Punkin Valley Inn, to $160 at the Pleasant Mountain Inn including two daily meals. It has the reputation of being a truly pleasant mountain to ski.

OTHER SPORTS   Golf and tennis are both available at Bridgton Highlands Country Club (647-3491).

Canoes can be rented from **North Country Outfitters** in North Bridgton (647-3953), and from **Mainstream Canoe** (647-5218). Besides canoeing on the lakes there is outstanding canoeing on the Saco River; introductory daytrips for novices are offered by **Saco Bound,** just over the New Hampshire border in Center Conway (603-447-2177), and by **Saco River Canoe and Kayak** in Fryeburg (935-2369); both firms also offer rentals.

Power boats can be rented from Sebago Lake Camp in North Sebago.

Scenic plane rides begin at **Naples Flying Service,** Naples Causeway (693-6591).

Parasailing is offered from the Naples Causeway (693-6861).

BOAT EXCURSION   *Songo River Queen II* (693-6861). A 90-foot-long sternwheeler built in 1982 which runs daily in July and August, frequently in June and September, offering one-hour cruises on Long Lake and two-and-one-half-hour sails down through the Songo River Lock to Sebago Lake. There is a snackbar and restrooms aboard—two luxuries which you don't get on the small mailboat which also makes the run to Sebago Lake. The ride costs $5 per adult, $3 per child on the Queen, $4 per adult, $2 per child on the mailboat. Either way it is a ride not to be missed, if you have never been through a canal lock or emerged from a narrow backwater into an immense lake (Sebago is the second largest lake in Maine).

ENTERTAINMENT   At the **Thomas Playhouse** (655-7728) in South Casco on Route 302, a resident company presents dinner theatre performances late June through early September.

At the **Ward House** in Waterford Village (583-4106), "The Genial Showman," a presentation of *The Life and Adventures of Artemus Ward,* Sunday evenings, late June through early September.

Movies: The Magic Lantern, Main Street, Bridgton presents film classics, first-run cartoons. Weekly **band concerts** are every Wednesday evening in July and August.

Sebago Long Lake Musical Festival (627-4939) is a series of concerts and recitals during July and August at Bridgton Academy Chapel.

INNS   **Tarry-A-While** (647-2522), June 20 to Labor Day, is a delightful old summer resort: its sixty rooms are scattered between the main lodge and other buildings on its thirty-acre grounds. Daily rates include breakfast and dinner ($30 to $45 per person per day; $187 to $205 per week) as well as tennis, use of boats, and two fine beaches on Highland Lake.

The Artemus Ward House (583-4106) in Waterford. May 25-October 15, November 15-Easter. A handsome home built in 1805 on Keoka Lake. The setting is still much as Charles Farrar Browne (better known as Artemus Ward) described it: "The village . . . is small. It does not contain over forty houses, all told; but they are milk white, with the greenest of blinds . . . To the right of us is a mountain—to the left a lake." Ms. Baker has furnished the house with a sure sense of style, and her reputation for tea (served 3-6) has spread throughout the state. Bed and breakfast is $32 single, $35 double.

Migis Lodge (655-4524), June 12 through October 12, is a fine old resort right on Sebago Lake which offers a few rooms in the main lodge and twenty-five in twenty-three cottages scattered in the pines on ninety acres. Rates are $30 to $53 per person per day, American Plan (three meals); children under three are not permitted in high season. All cottages have fireplaces, and guests enjoy use of the private beach, lawn games, water-skiing, sailboats, canoes, and boat excursions.

Aimhi Lodge (892-6538), sixty years in the same family and accommodating just seventy-five guests, a wonderfully old-fashioned resort in North Windham on Little Sebago Lake; rates average $39 per person per day for one-, two- and three-room cottages, all with Franklin stoves and screened porches, including three meals served in the rustic dining room. There are game rooms, lawn games, a beach, and rental boats.

Pleasant Mountain Inn and Cottages (647-2431). Year-round except April. There are seven units in the inn, eight more in duplex cabins, all with fireplaces. Handy to the ski area in winter; during summer, a sand beach, tennis, motor boats, canoes, and a sailfish are available. Modified American Plan (two meals) applies only in high summer and winter seasons; $160 per person for a five-night ski package, lifts included (MAP), or $37 double (MAP) per day.

Waterford Inne (583-4073). East Waterford, year-round. An 1825 house, now a small beautifully decorated inn off by itself; meals are served family style by reservation.

Kedarburn Inn Valley Road in Waterford (583-6182) An 1858 mansion in the historic village and within walking distance of Keoka Lake. Open year-round for bed (five newly refurbished rooms) and breakfast, and for weekend brunch. $40 for the biggest room with private bath, $35 double, $32 single; breakfast included.

Olde Rowley Inn, North Waterford (583-4143), year-round. The core of this old stagestop dates back to 1790 and gives a wonderful sense of age. It sits right on the road in the middle of a picturesque old hill town in which the fire department sponsors a dance every Saturday during the summer, and there is a World's Fair in August. The five guest rooms in the inn are all nicely furnished, and meals (open to the public) are painstakingly prepared. Rates are $32 per room including a full breakfast, $28 single, $10 for children under ten.

COTTAGES   "Maine Vacations Housekeeping Cottages," an association leaflet listing best cottage colony and single rental cottages in the Bridgton area, is helpful in locating what you want, and is available from the Chamber of Commerce. A dozen places are detailed, giving specifics such as fireplaces, docks, boats, wood stoves, and grills. Weekly rates were $150 to $250 in 1981, and while the better-known cottage colonies such as Brookline and Taylor Town fill for the summer by May, the smaller clusters still have weeks available well into the summer and offer exceptional value. The Chamber of Commerce Information Bureau (647-3472) has a long list of what's vacant.

Chute Homestead Cottages on Long Lake in Naples (693-6435), open mid-June to Labor Day, is a complex of eleven housekeeping cottages (weekly rentals) plus some smaller cottages and eight chalet rooms available for shorter stays. Most cottages have fireplaces, and there is maid service, use of canoes, tennis, a sauna, a small beach and snack bar, plus weekly clambakes and chicken barbeques; cottages are $448 to $644 weekly in high season, rooms are $46 to $59 per night, cheaper off season.

For a listing of other cottages in the Naples area write the Naples Business Association, P.O. Box 412, Naples, Maine 04055, or phone (693-3285 or 693-6751). For similar listings about cottages in the Sebago Lake area contact the Windham Chamber of Commerce, P.O. Box 1015, North Windham, Maine 05062, or (892-8265).

RESTAURANTS   Switzer Stubli (647-2522). June 14 through Labor Day for breakfast, lunch, and dinner. "The only Swiss Restaurant in Maine" is the proud and true boast of this dining room, since its chef is imported specially every summer from the Alps to prepare dishes like "Kaninchen Bundnerart" (rabbit in wine sauce). Prices are for a complete dinner, including soup, salad, and pastry. The dining room is set above lawns sloping down to Highland Lake, in the fine Tarry-a-While Resort (see Lodging). There is a children's menu and a liquor license.

Mountain View Farm (583-4820), Maple Ridge Road in Harrison, offers special Saturday night buffets for $7.95 ($3.95 for children), plus Friday night lobster dinners at $6.95. These are 1981 prices. Reasonably priced Sunday dinners are served at 1:30.

Punkin Valley Inn Restaurant (657-2652), west of Pleasant Mountain on Route 302, specializes in fixed price meals that offer plenty for your money: Friday night fish fries, night buffets, and "Soup-to-Nuts Dinners."

The Cracked Platter (583-4708), middle of Main Street in Harrison, is open 6 AM to 1 AM every day but Sunday (7 AM-1 AM) and offers good dining value, plus live entertainment on Friday and Saturday nights.

Albert's House of Fine Foods in Naples (693-3256) is another family restaurant with moderate prices and live entertainment on Saturday nights in summer.

The Bellringer, Main Street, Harrison (583-4576), open for breakfast, lunch, and dinner daily except Mondays in summer, offers some atmosphere with its meals, also good ice cream.

ANTIQUES   Bridgton offers some two dozen antiques shops, all listed in a brochure available from the Chamber of Commerce.

SPECIAL EVENTS   **Fourth of July** is big both in Bridgton and Naples. Bridgton events include a major lobster/clam bake at the Town Hall, as well as a roadrace, concert and fireworks. In Naples the fireworks over the lake are spectacular.

In late July a major **crafts fair** at the Town Hall is sponsored by the Bridgton Arts and Crafts Society and on the third weekend of the month antiques dealers gather from throughout New England for a three-day **Lake Region Antique Show** at the high school (Rte. 302).

Check the local summer calendar for performances by the **Maine Folk Dance Camp** (an adult camp on Woods Pond) and concerts by **Camp Encore-Koda** (music camps for boys and girls respectively).

First weekend in October the **Fryeburg Fair** is held at the fairgrounds in Fryeburg. It is an old-fashioned agricultural fair, and one of the most colorful in the country.

Bethel and Maine's White Mountains

An obvious farming and trading site, Bethel flanks the Androscoggin River, and its town common is the junction for routes west to the White Mountains, north to the Mahoosucs, east to the Oxford Hills, and south to Maine's lake country.

When the trail from Portland to Montreal began stopping here in 1851, Bethel also became an obvious summer retreat for city people. Nothing fancy. Families stayed the season in the big white farmhouses which still abound. They feasted on home-grown and home-cooked food, then walked it off on nearby mountain trails.

Hiking remains the big lure for many visitors to the area. The White Mountain National Forest comes within a few miles of town, and trails radiate from nearby Evans Notch. Just twelve miles to the northwest there is also Grafton Notch State Park, offering some short hikes to spectacles like Screw Auger Falls, and a wealth of well-equipped picnic sites. Blueberrying and rockhounding are local pastimes and the hills are also good pickings for history buffs. They were once far more peopled than they are today, and entire villages have vanished.

Hastings, for instance, is now just the name of a National Forest campground, but once it was a thriving community complete with post office, stores, and a wood alcohol mill which shipped its product by rail direct to Portland, thence to England. Pictures of Hastings' story—along with hundreds of other vintage photos—can be seen at Ed Quinn's Steam Era Railroadiana Museum in Gilead.

The Bethel Inn, born of the railroad era, is still going strong. Opened in 1913 by millionaire William Bingham II and dedicated to a prominent Boston neurologist (who had himself come to Bethel to recoup from a breakdown), it originally featured a program of strenuous exercise, one admired by the locals (wealthy clients actually paid the doctor to chop down his trees) as well as by the medical profession. It is still recognized as a pioneering concept in physical therapy. The inn's current exercise program is limited to golf, tennis, swimming, boating, and cross-country skiing. In the past few decades Bethel has become a genuine skiing center, the nearest resort town to three ski areas: Sunday River, just a few miles north up Route 2; Mount Abram in nearby Locke Mills to the east; and Evergreen Valley to the southwest in East Stoneham.

Whatever the season and direction I explore around Bethel, I am struck

NORWAY 14 MI.
PARIS 15 MI.
DENMARK 23 MI.
NAPLES 23 MI.
SWEDEN 25 MI.
POLAND 27 MI.
MEXICO 37 MI.
PERU 46 MI.
CHINA 94 MI.

Fredrik D. Bodin

Signpost on Route 35 in Lynchville

not only with the beauty and peace of the landscape, but with its variety. Evans Notch, for instance, is a narrow, wilderness kind of defile, with nothing like the alpine openness of the slopes around Kezar Lake, in turn nothing like Bethel, and still very different from the work-a-day towns to the east.

GUIDANCE   The **Greater Bethel Chamber of Commerce,** Box 527 (824-2346), publishes an excellent area guide and maintains a walk-in summer season information center in the Gem Shop, Route 2 north of the village.

Mid-October through April, Sunday River maintains a reservation service for all area lodging (824-2187).

GETTING THERE   By car it is a convenient waystop between New Hampshire's White Mountains (via Route 2) and the Maine coast. From Boston take the Maine Turnpike to the Gray Exit, then Route 26. There is no longer any scheduled bus service to Bethel, but charters and limo service are available from Portland and Boston.

SIGHTS TO SEE   **Moses Mason House** (824-2908), open July and August, Tuesday-Sunday: 1-4, and year-round by appointment. $1 per adult, 50c per child under twelve. This exquisite Federal-style mansion is proof of the town's early prosperity. Maintained by the Bethel Historical Society, it has Rufus Porter murals in the front hall, and fine woodwork, furnishings; also a research facility for the region.

Steam Era Railroadiana Museum in Gilead (836-2673), late June to early October, Thursday to Sunday: 9:30-4:30, and by appointment. $1 per adult, 50c per child. The small museum, behind Ed Quinn's home on Bog Road (off Route 2), is crammed with relics from the Grand Trunk Line in its days of steam. There is a wealth of nineteenth-century equipment and printed matter, and early twentieth-century relics, ranging from a window from the 1902 Portland station to precisely detailed models of locomotives.

Artist's Covered Bridge across the Sunday River, four miles northwest of North Bethel in the town of Newry. Extremely picturesque—a weathered brown bridge built in 1872 and painted by numerous nineteenth-century landscape artists, notably John Enneking. A great spot to sun and swim. Other swimming holes can be found at intervals along the road above the bridge.

HIKING   The **White Mountain National Forest,** although primarily in New Hampshire, includes 41,943 Maine acres. For details about the five campgrounds in Maine, also for hiking advice, contact the Evans Notch Ranger District, Bridge Street, Bethel (824-2134). Leaflets available from the Greater Bethel Chamber of Commerce suggest a number of trails in Evans Notch, ranging from a half-mile trek to the top of the Roost, to the seven-mile hike to the top of the Caribou trail.

National Forest campgrounds in this area include Hastings, Basin Pond, Cold River, and Crocker Pond. There is also Cold River Camp, a facility maintained by the **Appalachian Mountain Club,** offering no-frills lodging in cabins, three daily meals in a central lodge, and a

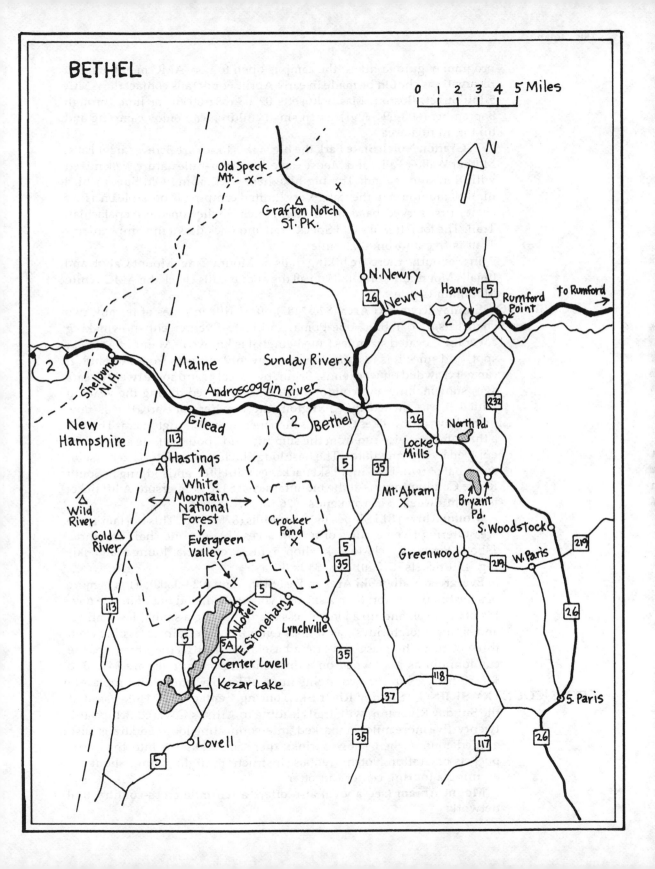

BETHEL

0 1 2 3 4 5 Miles

N

Old Speck Mt. x

x

△ Grafton Notch St. Pk.

○ N. Newry

26 Newry

Hanover 5 Rumford Point

2 to Rumford

Maine

Sunday River x

Androscoggin River

2

Gilead

2 Bethel

26

232

North Pd.

Locke Mills

Shelburne N.H.

New Hampshire

113

Hastings
△

White Mountain National Forest

Evergreen Valley

Crocker Pond x

5

35

5

35

Mt. Abram x

Bryant Pd.

S. Woodstock

Greenwood

219 W. Paris

219

△ Wild River

Cold △ River

113

5

x

5

N. Lovell

5A E. Stoneham

Lynchville

Center Lovell

Kezar Lake

35

118

37

35

117

26

26

S. Paris

Lovell

5

program of guided hikes; the camp is open to non-AMC members, but reservations should be made in early April. For details contact the AMC, 5 Joy Street, Boston, Massachusetts 02108 (532-0636), or June through September (603-694-3291). Even small children can enjoy camping and hiking in this area.

In **Grafton Notch State Park** the big sights to see are Screw Auger Falls, Mother Walker Falls, and Moose Cave, a quarter-mile nature walk mixed with flora and legend. The big hike here is climbing Old Speck, third highest mountain in the state. Very limited camping is possible on a first come, first served basis at Grafton Notch Shelter on the Appalachian Trail. The loop trek up Old Speck Trail and back down the Firewarden's Trail is five-and-one-half miles.

In Shelburne there are hiking trails on Mount Crag, Mount Cabot, and Ingalls Mountain; for details on all the above trails check the AMC White Mountain Guide.

SKIING   **Sunday River Ski Area** (824-2187) offers fifteen miles of terrain, two chair lifts, two T-bars, one Poma, and forty-five percent snowmaking coverage. Located six miles from Bethel, it is known in Maine as a top ski spot, and since it is just one hour and twenty minutes from Portland, it can get crowded on weekends. Begun by a local group some twenty years ago, snowmaking and condominiums were added during the years in which it was owned by Killington (the big Vermont area); it is now owned by youthful Les Otten, its manager in the Killington era. There is a three-mile novice run from the summit, and about half the area can be enjoyed by intermediates. The base lodge includes a cafeteria, a nursery, and a bar or two. Five-night ski packages with lifts, and lodging in South Ridge Condominiums at the mountain cost $120 per person. A lift ticket is $10 midweek, $15 weekends, $26 for two days.

Mount Abram Ski Slopes in Locke Mills (875-2601). This is a family ski area offering twelve miles of terrain accessible via one chair and three T-bars. Services include a ski shop, rentals, cafeteria, lounge, and skiing. Lift tickets: $12 all day, $8 half day.

Evergreen Valley Ski Area in East Stoneham (923-3300). This is more of a destination resort than a ski area you drive in and out of in one day. It's off by itself and up a long access road, offering a sauna, ice skating, and riding (sleigh rides), as well as ten miles of terrain accessible from three chairs. The glass-and-stone baselodge is attractive; many of the condominiums are owned on a time-sharing basis; rates are $41.50 to $46.50 per person for two nights in an efficiency unit with fireplace.

CROSS-COUNTRY SKIING   **Sunday River Ski Touring Center** (824-2410), based at the Sunday River Inn, with trails leading to Artist's Covered Bridge and twenty-five more miles of marked, interconnecting loops and trails; also guided tours (when snow shrinks there are treks up into the snow pockets of Grafton Notch), rentals, instruction, night skiing, about everything a touring center can offer.

Mount Abram (see above) also offers a ten-mile cross-country trail network.

The Bethel Inn (824-2175) maintains its own twenty-five kilometer trail network, and a five-mile competition course; also offers rentals and instruction.

Evergreen Valley Ski Touring Center (928-3300) in East Stoneham offers twenty-five miles of marked, groomed trails on the verge of the White Mountain National Forest.

ROCKHOUNDING   This area is particularly rich in minerals. Rockhounds should stop at the **Gem Shop** on Rte. 2 north of Bethel. Also be sure to visit **Perham's Maine Mineral Store** in West Paris, a landmark in its own right, claiming 90,000 visitors per year. It displays samples of all the minerals to be found in Maine, dispenses maps to its own five quarries, and sells stones polished and set in jewelry, also in the rough. Above a heap of glistening rocks by the door a sign says: "10c for 10 pounds." **Bumpus Mine** on Routes 5 and 35 is another commercial rockhounding spot, noted for gem beryl, rose and smoky quartz, and felspar. Other defunct mines can be found along hiking paths.

FISHING   "A Guide to Local Fishing" leaflet, available from the Greater Bethel Chamber of Commerce, gives tips on the best spots to catch brook and rainbow trout. It suggests that you try Lake Christopher for land-locked salmon, and North Pond and Songo Lake for bass, pickerel and perch.

OTHER ACTIVITIES   **Monorail Rides** at Mount Abram (875-2601) operate July 1-Labor Day, noon to 4 PM; during this time the base lodge cafeteria is also open. Route 26 in Locke Mills.

For golf, **The Bethel Inn and Country Club** (824-2175) offers nine holes.

Long Horn Stables (928-3300 or 583-4805); trail rides, cookouts. Sleigh rides at **Evergreen Valley** Resort in East Stoneham.

LODGING   **The Bethel Inn and Country Club** (824-2175). This rambling yellow structure and its mansion-like cottages dominate the town's common. There are sixty-five guest rooms, all with phones and private baths; the common rooms downstairs are extensive and formal, but there is nothing starchy about the Downstairs Bar (food is served there as well as in the main dining room), and there is an indoor game room for children, also a sauna. In addition to the golf course and cross-country trails, there is a handy beach and boathouse (canoes and sailfish) on Songo Lake. Rates run $33 per person with two daily meals, cheaper if you take advantage of such packages as the $300 per couple, six-day special, two daily meals included. Check toll-free reservation lines for your area.

Sunday River Inn (824-2410). Winter season only. A friendly, informal atmosphere in which children are welcome; see ski touring, which is what it is about; rates: $27 per person per night (double), MAP.

The Norseman Inn (824-2002). January to March, and June through August. This 200-year-old farm-turned-mansion-turned-inn has acquired a strong following during its past twenty years' ownership by Claus and Jakki Wiese. It's a homey place with massive fireplaces in its public rooms, and thirteen guest rooms ranging from $28 to $36 MAP. Homegrown food and Scandinavian dishes are the specialty.

L'Auberge (824-2774), Mill Hill Road in Bethel, open most of the year; a former barn, now a pleasant inn with eight guest rooms (two with shared baths) and two dormitory rooms; breakfast and lunch are served, breakfast included in $21 per couple, special rates for groups renting the entire space.

Philbrook Farm Inn (466-3831). Open May 1-October 31 and December 26-March 31. The last local survivor among the dozens of farms which began taking guests in the 1860s. The fifth generation of Philbrooks is now managing this grand old inn, secure in its own 1000-acre preserve. Sited above the floodplain of the Androscoggin, it's on the opposite side of the river from Route 2, accessible only via an antique bridge from tiny Shelbourne, New Hampshire, or by dirt road from Bethel. It faces the Carter-Moriah range and backs against trail-webbed Mount Cabot. Rates for the nineteen rooms are $25 per person per day with two meals; there are also four charming and reasonably priced rental cottages. During winter cross-country ski trails meander off in all directions from the door.

Center Lovell Inn in Center Lovell (925-1575). May through mid-October, and mid-December through early March. A striking old house with a widow's walk and gables in its mansard roof, set high on a knoll overlooking Kezar Lake, just four rooms, sharing two baths. Open to the public for dinner. Chef-owner Bill Mosca specializes in northern Italian dishes carefully prepared; he also offers suckling pig on Memorial Day, New Year's, and for a Harvest Dinner; rates average $35-50 per person, MAP.

Westways in Center Lovell (928-2663). Open most of the year. Built as an executive retreat for the Diamond Match Company, this is a mansion overlooking Kezar Lake, designed to accommodate fourteen guests. It has its own bowling alley, stable, and dock; $50 for bed and breakfast for two, $70 in a suite. The dining room is open to the public for dinner by reservation.

Farrington's on Lake Kezar, Center Lovell (925-2500). Twenty-three cottages with one-to-three bedrooms, fireplace, and screened porch; plus twenty-one rooms in the main house. Three daily meals in the cheerful dining room; all resort facilities; $58 per day MAP.

Hewnoaks (925-6051) in Center Lovell, overlooking Lake Kezar, six very attractive cottages.

Conrad's Tourist Home (824-2505), Main Street house, spotless, three rooms, $15 double.

South Ridge Condominiums (824-2187) at Sunday River Ski area offer one- two- and three-bedroom efficiency units, available year-round, very reasonable off season.

FOOD   **Mother's,** Main Street in Bethel (824-2589), year-round, daily for dinner: sandwiches, quiches, homemade soups, desserts, reasonable prices, bar.

Boiler Room in Bryant Pond, Route 26. Open daily, year-round, 11:30

AM to 1 AM. One of Maine's more unusual restaurants, housed in the brick powerhouse of a former clothespin factory. A huge 1880s steam engine (once the power source for the plant) sits in the middle of the lounge, and the tables are big wooden spools. Down in the Wine Cellar patrons tap their own wine from the spigots in their individual booths. On top of this the food is good, and genuinely German.

Maurice's (743-2532), 113 Main Street (Route 26) in South Paris, open year-round daily except Monday: 5-10 and for Sunday brunch. Amid the lineup of fast food places is this widely respected French restaurant; moderately expensive.

Bull Dog Diner (824-2295). Railroad Street in Bethel, daily 5 AM to 1 PM. The place in town for breakfast, also good for reasonably priced luncheon specials.

SPECIAL EVENTS   Mid-February: **Winter Carnival** with church suppers, a play, other special programs.

Late March: **Pole, Paddle and Paw Race** is a combination ski and canoe event closing the ski season.

Mid-July: **Mollyockett Day,** variety of colorful happenings, commemorates the Indian princess who befriended early settlers.

Mid-December: **Christmas parade** and tree-lighting ceremony on Main Street.

Maine's Western Mountains

THE RANGELEY LAKES REGION

The Rangeley Lakes include six large lakes and some three dozen ponds within a ten-mile radius of the village of Rangeley. The big lure here is fishing: landlocked salmon, and brook trout. There is also a sense of splendid isolation—thanks to 450 square miles of commercially forested land, and genuine beauty—thanks to the mountains which hump up in every direction, inviting you to climb.

Rangeley has been a resort area since the steamboat days, as you can see from the vintage of the dozens of log "lodges" and "camps" which describe themselves as "rustic." All hidden in the pines, they have brick fireplaces with solid stone hearths, well-worn wooden furniture, rocking chairs, and hearty meals. A surprising number of places remain open year-round, thanks to the fishermen who begin arriving in early Spring, followed by folk who enjoy swimming, sailing, golfing, horseback riding and such—as well as fishing. Then there are foliage buffs in September, hunters in October through November, skiers and snowmobilers through March. A sign outside Doc Grant's Restaurant proclaims that Rangeley is 3107 miles from the North Pole, and the same distance from the Equator. Rangeley actually feels like it is a million miles from everywhere, but with all the amenities.

GUIDANCE **Rangeley Lakes Region Chamber of Commerce** (864-5571) is open all year, Monday-Friday: 9-6, Saturday: 9-5, and in summer months Sunday: 10-2. The chamber keeps tabs on all vacancies and will make reservations.

GETTING THERE There is no public transport to Rangeley. **Steve's Air Service** (864-3347) will pick you up at Portland Jetport.

SIGHTS TO SEE **Wilhelm Reich Museum** (864-3443). Open July and August, Tuesday and Friday: 10-4 and by appointment. $2.50, under twelve free. A pioneer psychiatrist and general scientist concerned with "objectifying the presence of a ubiquitous life force." The 200-acre property, "Orgonon," should be visited for the view of mountain and water which you can enjoy from the promontory on which Reich is buried next to one of his many inventions, a "cloudbuster." The museum occupies a stone observatory which Reich helped design; it contains biographical exhibits, scientific equipment, paintings, and the library and study which remains as it did during Reich's life.

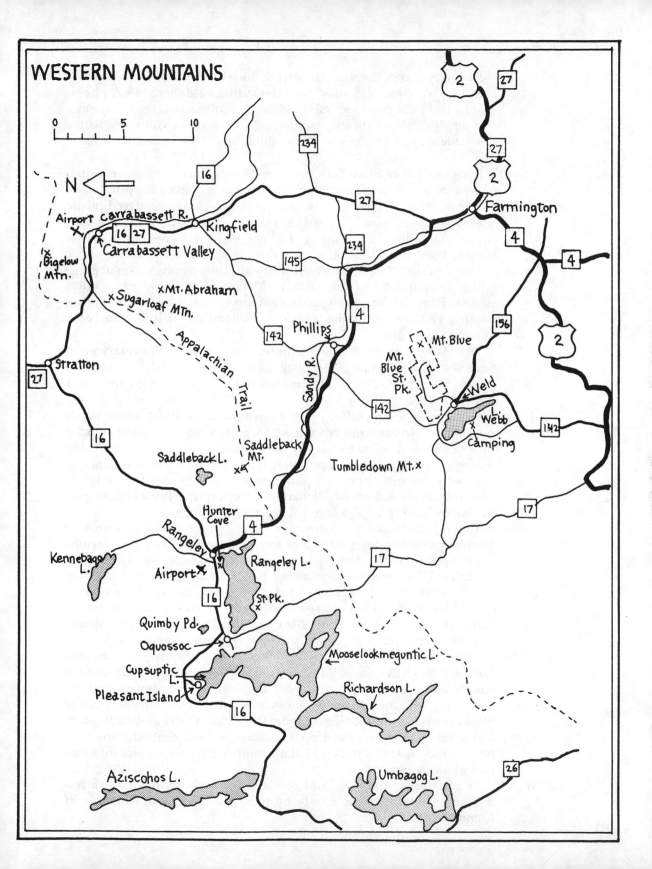

Rangeley Lakes Region Historical Society, open July-September, Monday, Wednesday, Friday, Saturdays: 10-2, middle of town, photographs and local memorabilia—including Squire Rangeley's spitoon.

Rangeley Public Library. An unusually pleasant town library with a fine collection of local mementoes, children's books; good for a rainy day.

Rangeley Lakes State Park covers 691 acres, including more than a mile of shoreline on the southern rim of Rangeley Lake between Routes 17 and 4. There is a pleasant swimming area and forty scattered picnic sites, also a boat launch, a children's play area, and fifty camping sites suitable for trailers. Camping is $4.50 per resident, $6 per out-of-stater; the day use fee is $1.50; off-season rates in spring and fall.

Small's Falls   The Sandy River drops abruptly through a small gorge which you can climb behind railings. Marked off Route 4, twelve miles south of Rangeley, a popular picnic spot and a swimming hole for daring youths. You can follow the trail to the **Chandlers Mill Stream Falls,** equally spectacular.

The Maine Audubon Society **Hunter Cove Wildlife Sanctuary** is off Route 14/16 west of Rangeley Village, across from the Edelweiss cross-country ski center. Color-coded trails wind in and out of the trees and along the cove.

FISHING   Brook trout are plentiful in local streams. Black bass, white perch, pickerel, brown trout and brook trout are also found in the lakes, and the big catch is landlocked salmon for which the big season is early spring through the end of September. There are a number of fishing camps in the area which supply boats, equipment, and even guides. See Lodging. The six lakes are **Aziscohos, Richardson, Cupsuptic, Mooselookmeguntic, Kennebago, Umbagog,** and **Rangeley.**

HIKING   The regional map published by the Rangeley Lakes Chamber of Commerce outlines more than a dozen well-used hiking paths, including the portion of the **Appalachian Trail** which passes over Saddleback Mountain. The longest hike is up **Spotter Mountain** (four-and-one-half miles to the top), and the most popular is the mile trail up to the summit of **Bald Mountain;** both yield sweeping views of lakes, woods, and more mountains. Other favorites are **Bemis Stream Trail** up Elephant Mountain (six hours round trip), and the mile walk into **Angels Falls.**

BOATING   **Davis Marine** (864-3451) in Rangeley rents motor boats, sailboats, and canoes. Cobb's Rosebuck Mt. Camps, Birchwood, Mooselookmeguntic House, and Town Lake Motel all offer boats. Rangeley is departure point for an eight-mile paddle to Oquossoc. On Lake Mooselookmeguntic there is a twelve-mile paddle to Upper Dam, then a carry around the dam and another eight miles of Upper Richardson Lake through "the Narrows" to South Arm. Check with the Chamber of Commerce for information about campsites.

CAMPING   In addition to the state and private campgrounds there are a few wilderness sites accessible only by boat; inquire at the Chamber of Commerce.

SKIING   **Saddleback Mountain** (864-3380), ninety percent snowmaking coverage, an 1800-foot vertical drop, two chairlifts, two T-bars serving twenty-six trails ranging from a half mile to five miles long. There is a restaurant, ski shop, and nursery in the base lodge, and a warming hut on the summit. Lift tickets are $17 per day. Weekend packages, including lodging and lifts, go for $109 to $133 per person, five-day packages are $165 to $203.

For cross-country skiing: **Edelweiss Touring Center** (864-3891) offers thirty miles of trails of varying width and terrain, all marked and groomed.

SNOWMOBILING   In Rangeley Lake State Park there are three miles of marked trails with access to the lake. In Mount Blue there are twenty more miles of marked and groomed trails with access to Webb Lake and a connection trail (maintained by the state) with Rangeley Lake State Park. In addition

Winter view from Saddleback Mountain   J. Norton/M. D. C. I.

there are over 100 miles of groomed eight-foot-wide trails throughout the region.

OTHER SPORTS   **Tennis** can be played at the Rangeley Town Courts. **Bike rentals** are available from Sundown Lodge in Oquossoc (864-3650). **Mingo Springs Golf Course** (864-5021), offers eighteen holes, rental clubs, and carts. Trail rides are available at **The Farmhouse,** Route 4 south of Rangeley (864-3346), and the **Double S Bar Stable** in Oquossoc (864-3663).

MUSIC AND DRAMA   **Rangeley Friends of the Performing Arts** sponsor a weekly program of top entertainers during July and August in churches, lodges, and the local school auditorium. Art and craft instruction is available from the **Rangeley Summer Craft School** (864-5261).

INNS   **The Rangeley Inn and Motor Lodge** (864-3341), year-round except spring, a classic old middle-of-town New England inn. A three-story wooden landmark, it offers forty-five guest rooms, ten in the motel out back. Most of the old rooms have been tastefully renovated; the claw-foot bathtubs have been kept but spiffed up, and the dining room is attractive. The whole building is warmed by an efficient wood-burning furnace. Rates are $23 single to $49 for six people, or $39 to $59 for the one- and two-bedroom units in the motel; special golf and skiing packages are available, as well as modified American plan.

Saddleback Lake Lodge (864-5501), mid-June to October. The Lodge House contains a dining room, pub, game room, and carpeted common room complete with books and hearth. The nineteen lake-side cottages accommodate from two to six persons, each with a living room, most with fireplaces and screened porches; there are also canoes, motor boats, two tennis courts, a putting green, and swim area: $39 to $45 per person including three meals, half price under age twelve, free under age two.

Country Club Inn (864-3831). Open mid-June to mid-October. Surrounded by an 18-hole golf course and overlooking the lake, handy to the village. This is definitely a golfer's dream and has the ambiance of a country club, but with unbeatable views; rates are $35 per person (double) to $48 (single) with two meals; three-day golf packages are $89 per person, week-long packages are $246 per person. The dining room is open to the public for dinner.

Davis Lodge (864-5569) year-round. Built as a home in 1910, this log building has a great deal of charm—a dozen rooms upstairs and a welcoming common room where dinner and inn guests gather around the hearth. Better known as a dining than a lodging spot; $15 per person per day including breakfast.

FISHING CAMPS   The following establishments are American Plan (three daily meals):

Bald Mountain Camps (864-3671), open May 15-Labor Day. The surviving part of a complex which dates from 1897, nicely old-fashioned with fireplaces in fifteen cabins and a log-style dining room, a safe sand beach, tennis courts, and lawn games: $43 per adult, $23 ages eleven and twelve, $16 ages six-ten, $8 below five years. For a brochure write Rose and Ronald Turmenne, PO Box 332, Bald Mountain, Maine 04964.

Quimby Pond Camps (864-3675). Open year-round. One mile off Route 4 on Quimby Pond. The cottages all have fireplaces and the special here is American Plan for $33 per person; but you can also rent the camps as efficiency units which accommodate from two to fourteen—$179 to $239 per week, geared to fishermen, hunters (registered guides are available at $45 per day), and snowmobilers.

Cobb's Bosebuck Mt. Camps (243-2945). At the north end of Aziscohos Lake. May through September. The lodge houses a dining room and a sitting room filled with books; the main building and cabins are heated with wood stoves; the cabins have kerosene lamps; a boat with motor and gas is $45 for three days; rates including three daily meals are $37, less during off-fishing weeks.

Pleasant Island Lodge and Cottages (864-3722). May to September. Thirteen log cabins on Cupsuptic Lake, two and three bedrooms with fireplaces, also tennis, swimming, and boats. For a folder write Don and Pam Young, Oquossoc, Maine 04964.

HOUSEKEEPING COTTAGES   Mooselookmeguntic House (864-3627). An unbeatable site on the grounds of an old summer hotel—a number of log camps with fireplaces go for $30 to $50 (sleeps five) per day, or $175 to $300 per week; canoe rentals are $10 per day.

Sundown Lodge and Cottages (864-3650), open June through September, three delightful cottages with fireplaces, weekly rentals: $150 for the smaller cottage, $210 for each of the larger ones. Lawn games, rental bikes, a splendid sense of isolation overlooking Mooselookmeguntic Lake.

Rangeley Manor (864-3340), open year-round. Sixteen efficiency cottages, some with fireplaces, plus eight motel rooms, lawn games, free rowboat, other boats available. One week minimum in high season: $31-43 double, $210-294 weekly. Higher in winter.

Russell's Motor Camps (864-2204). May to October 6. Waterfront location but handy to the village, rustic cottages for two to eight people, $26-33 per day, $163-205 per week. There are lawn games and a cookout pit.

SKIING ACCOMMODATIONS   Cabin-Condo Care (864-5241) manages complete condominiums at the base of Saddleback Mountain, along with a number of other condos in the area.

The Farmhouse (864-3446), two miles from the Saddleback access road, offers efficiency suites and a ski dorm. $45 per night per apartment, $7.50 for a bunk.

RESTAURANTS   Rangeley Inn (864-3341). Closed during Mud Season (mid-April to mid-May), also Thanksgiving to Christmas. Serving breakfast, lunch, and dinner with a degree of style.

Doc Grant's Restaurant and Cocktail Lounge, Main Street, 7 AM-9 PM, light lunches in the lounge until 1 AM, breakfast during deer season from 5 AM. Dependable quality and moderate prices.

Davis Lodge (864-5569). Dinner and Sunday brunch are served in this attractive dining room.

Sportsmen Table at Quimby Pond Camps (864-3675). Year-round, dining by reservation.

Oquossoc House (864-3881). Open May to November 1. A pubby atmosphere; dinner specials, food at reasonable prices, a gathering spot for the area.

The Gingerbread Country Store. Open seasonally from 8 AM to 10 PM, except Sunday 10-9. The marble soda fountain is the big attraction—you are challenged to consume a $3.95 Bald Mountain Special (ice cream, nuts, cream etc. etc.). Don't miss the gingerbread with ice cream and sauce.

Viola's Guest House (864-5989) offers ten upstairs rooms—but the time, we feel, to come is for breakfast, served from 7 to 12 on Viola's sunny porch.

Red Onion Restaurant Bar (864-5022), year-round. Downtown pizza and basics.

SPECIAL EVENTS   Late February: Winter Carnival.

Early March: **Sled Dog Races:** teams from throughout the East compete in sixteen-mile race.

July 3: **Fireworks display.**

Mid-July: "A Wild Mountain Time" water and logging festival.

Mid-August: **Sidewalk art show.**

Late August: **Rangeley Lakes Gun Show.**

Late September: **Fall Foliage Festival.**

MOUNT BLUE AREA

The two towns of Phillips and Weld offer some fine inns along with fishing, hiking, and a satisfying sense of being off the beaten path. Time your visit to take a run on the Sandy River-Rangeley Lake Railroad (a very special narrow gauge railroad which runs as much on volunteer enthusiasm as on steam).

SIGHTS TO SEE   Phillips Historical Society. Open August, Friday and Saturday afternoons and by appointment (639-2011/2881). The library and historical society are both housed in an 1820 house in the middle of town. The collection includes many pictures about the railroad (see below), and an attic full of clothes for children to try on.

Sandy River-Rangeley Lakes Railroad (639-3001 or 353-8382). Open May-November, first and third Sunday, also on July 4 and Labor Day: 10-6. From 1873 until 1935 this narrow gauge line spawned resort and lumbering communities along its 115-mile length. Begun as seven distinct lines, it was eventually acquired by the Maine Central, which built shops and a big roundhouse in Phillips. Over the past decade volunteer Wesley Speer has produced a replica of the old steam locomotive, and others have helped to lay a mile of track, so you can now rattle along in an 1884 car just far enough to get a sense of getting around Franklin County back when. A depot houses railroad memorabilia. $1. Children under 12 free.

Mount Blue State Park in Weld (585-2261). The 6000-acre park includes Mount Blue itself, towering 3187 feet above the valley floor, and a beachside tenting area (136 sites) on Lake Webb which is three miles wide and six miles long, good for catching black bass, white perch, pickerel, trout, and salmon. Boats may be rented from the ranger in charge, and there is a recreation hall complete with fireplace. Despite its beauty, this is one of the few state camping facilities that rarely fills up.

HIKING   The tried and true trails are **Bald Mountain** (three miles round trip), **Mount Blue** itself (three-and-a-quarter miles) and **Tumbledown Mountain,** a particularly varied climb with a high altitude, good for fishing. The AMC *Mountain Guide* and *Fifty Hikes in Maine* by John Gibson (Backcountry Publications) gives details about these and other local trails.

SPECIAL EVENT   Third weekend in August: **Phillips Old Home Days;** public suppers, dancing, special exhibits.

LODGING   **The Weld Inn** (585-2429). Open year-round. The core of this rambling white classic was built as a doctor's home in 1899, later converted to the town's first inn, and enlarged in 1903. It now has thirteen bedrooms, two with private bath ($18 per person with breakfast), four housekeeping cottages, and two family lodges. There is a sandy beach on the lake just across the road.

The old-fashioned dining room seats forty-nine and is open for breakfast and dinner; during summer months light lunches are served on the porch, where there is an ice cream stand with the creamiest cones we know. Bed and breakfast is $17.50 for a single, $14.35 per person double, $12.75 per person for three, $11.50 per person for four. The two-bedroom housekeeping cottages are $198 a week, and the motel units (one-bedroom efficiencies) are $28 per night, $185 per week. There is no off season here. In winter months this is a popular spot for snowmobilers and cross-country skiers, since a groomed trail runs all the way from Mount Blue to Rangeley State Park. It is maintained by the state, well groomed with the help of local snowmobile clubs.

Kawanhee Inn (585-2243). July to mid-August. Owned by Camp Kawanhee for Boys (the oldest private camp for boys in the state under the same ownership and management), this splendid inn is run primarily for the convenience of visiting parents. It is a wonderfully "rustic" log building with fireplace and furniture to go with its exterior. There are a few rooms upstairs in the main building, and ten housekeeping cabins accommodate from three to five guests (each has a living room with a large stone fireplace). The dining room is open to the public for dinner, Tuesday through Sunday, 6-9 PM. Cabins rent for $40-45 per day, $185-250 per week.

SUGARLOAF AREA

Sugarloaf USA is Maine's largest ski mountain. Actually the second-highest mountain in the state after Katahdin, it faces another 4000-footer across a narrow valley, which makes for superb scenery, but has hampered the growth of a four-season resort community at its base.

Sugarloaf sits above the narrow Carrabassett Valley, up a seven-mile access road, a full sixteen miles north of Kingfield (the nearest real town), and nine miles south of the lumbering village of Stratton. Over the past thirty years inns and restaurants have opened along the wooded wayside in the valley. They have always been packed with skiers all winter, but are pressed to make a go of it during the remainder of the year. In the past few years condominiums have mushroomed on the mountain itself.

We can't think of a ski area where we would rather be in February. The skiing is as varied and challenging as any in New England—and it is the only area that offers snowfields for spring skiing. There is also extensive cross-country skiing and a zany, friendly atmosphere that's hard to beat. But when we came through last August, the valley was dead—as dead as Bar Harbor in February.

GUIDANCE   The **Sugarloaf Area Association** maintains a year-round service for lodging places, ranging from condominiums through motels and inns: 237-2861 or 237-2000.

GETTING THERE   This can be a problem, since Sugarloaf is closer to Quebec City (three-and-one-half-hours' drive) than to Boston (theoretically four-and-one-half hours). The closest airports are Waterville and Augusta, both one-and-one-quarter hours away, both served by **Bar Harbor Airlines** connecting with New York, Boston, and most New England cities. Shuttle service from the airports is available from **Sugarwheels Shuttle Service** (237-2861), and there are rental car concessions at both airports. **WEB Air** (237-2701), based at the Sugarloaf Inn, and **Carrabassett Valley Aviation** (235-2288) both offer charter service. From Boston the best route by car is up the Maine Turnpike to the Augusta exit, then ME 27 right on up.

GETTING AROUND   **Sugarwheels Shuttle Service** (237-2861) ferries skiers from inn to inn within the valley.

SKIING   **Sugarloaf USA** (237-2000 for information and snow conditions, mid-November to mid-April) offers thirty-six miles of trails geared more to the expert than to the novice, but with ample intermediate skiing. In all there are forty-five trails and slopes, and above-timberline snowfield skiing in the spring. There is a four-passenger gondola to the summit, also five double chairlifts, five T-bars. This area has the best vertical drop in all New England (rivaled only by Stowe and Killington). Snowmaking covers 110 acres, including the expert Narrow Gauge and a gentle three-mile-long tote road down from the top, the nearest thing Sugarloaf has to a beginner's trail. The Ski School employs thirty full-time certified instructors using the American Teaching method, and there are ski shops, rentals, and restaurants, pubs, and a nursery that in 1982, at least, is *free*. Lift tickets are $17 adult, $10 junior; $98 adult per week, $59 junior per week.

CROSS-COUNTRY SKIING   **Carrabassett Valley Recreation Center** (237-2205). Route 27, fourteen miles north of Kingfield, 8 AM-9 PM in season. This modern resort area's version of a meetinghouse is a town-owned, year-round social center which offers cross-country equipment, rentals, and maps for an eighty-mile system of trails, varying from the abandoned roadbed of the Sandy River Railroad (see Phillips) to real wilderness skiing near the Bigelow Preserve. Much of the system is groomed, and a hut system is planned.

HIKING   There are a number of 4000-footers in the vicinity, and rewarding trails up **Mount Abraham** and **Bigelow Mountains.** Pick up detailed hiking maps locally or check the AMC *Mountain Guide, Fifty Hikes in Maine* by John Gibson, or *The Maine Atlas* (DeLorme Publishing).

OTHER ACTIVITIES   **Canoe Rentals**   Cathedral Pines Campground (246-3491), and Chip Carey (265-2273). **Tennis**   Town of Stratton courts, Left Bank Pool and Racquet Club at the Valley Crossing, also see the Sugarloaf Inn and Winter's Inn under Lodging. **Scenic Airplane Rides**   Carrabassett Airport, Route 17 (235-2288).

MUSEUM   **Kingfield Historical Society.** Besides the usual memorabilia there is much here to see about the Stanley Steamer, an early steam-run auto invented by twin brothers from Kingfield.

MOUNTAIN LODGING   Peter Webber's **Sugarloaf Inn** (237-2701). Year-round, on the mountain. A beginner slope from the Sugarloaf base lodge ends at this four-story inn, and the convenient Sawduster Chair carries inn guests as well as novices up to the main complex. In all, there are forty-eight rooms in the inn—nicely decorated, as are the public rooms. This is the most elegant place to stay in the valley; in summer it offers tennis courts and a swimming pool ($36 double, $26 single in summer, $106 per person with two meals for two nights in winter). Attached to the Sugarloaf Inn is a small forest of adjacent condominiums, including the former Blue Ox Inn: $40-60 per couple for two nights in winter.

Village South, Gondola Village, and **Mountainside Condominiums** (237-2000), all right at the ski lifts, sleep a total of 575 people. Rates are from $120 for two people for two nights to $311 for a unit sleeping ten; cheaper by the week.

VALLEY LODGING   **Hotel Carrabassett/Left Bank Condominiums** (235-2115). Modern rooms and river-side condominiums similar to those on the mountain.

Judson's Sugarloaf Motel (235-2641). Year-round. Of all the valley's 1950s motels, this is the most likeable: bright, pleasant dining room, pine walls and red-checked tablecloths, good food from 7:30 AM to 8 PM. Rooms come with two meals a day ($24 to $35 per day, or $110 to $163 per person per week) and children are $3 per day with meals extra.

Luce's Mountain View Motel (246-2033). Year-round. A small, very clean motel with housekeeping and two-bedroom apartments, $25-30 per person for two nights; homey and family-run by Ralph and Mildred Luce.

Capricorn Lodge (237-2801). A standard motel with some newly renovated efficiency units with lofts. $50-63.

Red Stallion Inn (235-2791). Standard motel rooms with private baths, and skiers' quarters with shared baths, barnboard furniture, double beds; $54-76 per person for two days, MAP.

The Widow's Walk (246-6901) in Stratton. A Victorian guesthouse with six guest rooms, each with twin beds and semi-private bath, and a game room. $32 per person for two nights, or $44 with two meals.

Winter's Inn (265-5421) in Kingfield. An 1898 yellow mansion designed by the Stanley brothers (better known for their "steamers") for their friend Amos Winter. It has been restored to offer fifteen luxurious rooms. The dining room has a French menu, truly elegant. $84 to $110 per person for two days, MAP.

Longfellow (265-4394). Primarily a restaurant, but with nine rooms upstairs in the middle of town; $20 per person for two nights.

Sugarloafer's Ski Dorm (265-2041). For groups and tough young skiers, dorms accommodating 200: $34 for two days with two daily meals, $30 without linens.

Chalet and condo rentals throughout the area are available through **Sullivan Agency Vacation Rentals** (235-2400).

RESTAURANTS   **The Papillon** (265-5421) at the Winter's Inn is good for a splurge. Dinner is served from 5 PM until 9 weekdays, 10 on Friday and Saturday, reservations requested. A sample menu: crevette Nicoise, escalope de veau Amandine and crepe Normande. Under $20 per person.

One Stanley Avenue (265-5541). Closed Mondays, open for dinner: 6-9:30. Chef-owned with everything proudly made on the premises; a sample menu might be scallops mornay or roast duck with cherry glaze, preceded by hearts of palm, topped off with raspberry cheesecake—$20 with wine.

Red Stallion Inn (235-2791). Since Sugarloaf's beginnings this has been the hottest apres ski spot, one in which a crowd stays for dinner (this always includes a special, as well as steak and lobster). The loud bands continue late into the night on weekends.

Judson's Sugarloaf (see Lodging) is always good for a dependable meal in a pleasant dining room at reasonable prices.

Country Mile in Stratton (246-2131). Good for dinner; an extensive menu including shrimp and duckling, children's menu. $10-for-dinner bracket.

Stratton Diner (246-3111). Open year-round, daily, 6 AM to 8:30 PM on weekdays, 7-7 on Sunday. Booths and good food, reasonable prices.

Gepetto's Restaurant and Deli up at the mountain offers breakfast, lunch, dinner, apres ski entertainment.

Jake Cassidy's Restaurant Bar. Also at the mountain, a pub-style apres ski and dining spot. **Maxwell's** and **The Trufflehound** are two other mountain eateries.

SPECIAL EVENTS   Late January: **White White World Winter Carnival;** a week-long event with theme parties, national body sliding championships, barrel stave ski races, the whole affair culminating the first weekend in February.

March: **Canoeski;** giant slalom in canoes. **Heavyweight ski championships** (contestants must weigh more than 250 pounds).

April: **Sugarloaf Pentathlon** and **Whitewater Canoe Race.**

Late June through late August: **Summer Theater** in Skowhegan.

August 1: Stratton-Eustis-Flagstaff **Old Home Days.**

Late September: **Sugarloaf Art Show** at Sugarloaf Base Lodge; gondola runs daily during show.

Columbus Day Weekend: **Sugarloaf Skiers Homecoming.**

December: **Yellow Nose Vole Day;** snow dance, bonfire, torchlight parade.

Maine's North Woods

The green, mountain-and-water-spotted carpet over almost half of Maine's interior is privately owned. The state's official highway maps show no public roads through the six-and-one-half-million acres bordered on the north and west by Canada. The ownership of this sector, technically known as the "Unorganized Townships," dates from the 1820s when Maine was securing her independence from Massachusetts. The mother state, her coffers at their usual low, stipulated that an even division of all previously undeeded wilderness be part of the separation agreement. The woodlands were quickly sold by the legislature for 12½c to 38c an acre, bought cooperatively by groups in order to cut individual losses from what were deemed high risks at the time.

The vast inland tracts, mostly softwood, became valuable only in 1844 when the process of making paper from wood fibers was rediscovered. It seems that the method, first used in 105 AD, had been forgotten for centuries. New England paper mills were using rags at the time.

But by the turn of the century, pulp and paper mills had moved to their softwood source, and assumed management responsibility and taxes for most of the unorganized townships. Mergers have since increased the size, and decreased the number, of these companies. A dozen major landowners now pay the lion's share of the area's land tax and the cost of maintaining thousands of miles of private gravel roads, the ones not shown on the state highway maps but open to visitors.

Map/Guides to this area are available from two principal sources: North Maine Woods, Box 382, Ashland, Maine 04732 (435-6213), and the Paper Industries Information Office, 133 State Street, Augusta, Maine 04330.

The North Maine Woods is a compact two-and-one-half-million acre forest bounded on two sides by Canada and including the Allagash and St. John Rivers. You enter this kingdom through a dozen manned checkpoints, pay the fee, and promise to abide by the rules.

The Paper Industries Information Office furnishes maps to Scott Paper Company lands (870,000 acres around Moosehead Lake, Wyman Lake, and Bingham), Georgia Pacific holdings (along the extreme eastern coast of Maine and the New Brunswick border), and Great Northern land (between Scott and North Maine Woods territories, including the heavily traveled road from Greenville to Baxter State Park).

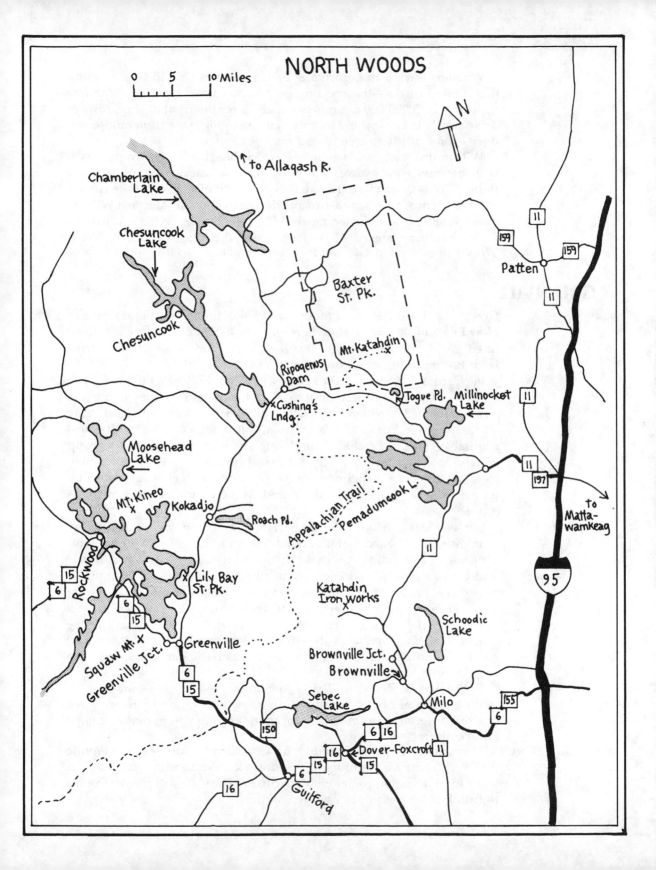

Whenever using these private roads motorists should bear in mind that lumber trucks—transporting pulpwood in tree lengths which frequently weigh 200,000 pounds per load—have the right of way. Always drive slowly because these mighty vehicles—not to mention moose and deer—come hurtling around corners unexpectedly.

Within this vast, commercially forested North Woods two preserves have been set aside expressly to provide a wilderness experience for the public: 200,000-acre Baxter State Park, and the ninety-two-mile ribbon of lakes, ponds, rivers, and streams designated as the Allagash Wilderness Waterway (see Canoeing the Allagash under "What's Where"). There are other routes into Baxter State Park, the Allagash, and the North Woods in general at Greenville, "New England's Last Frontier."

GREENVILLE

Greenville sits at the toe of Moosehead Lake, the largest natural lake in New England. If it were anywhere else, its 400 miles of shore would be lined with summer cottages. But it is a five-and-one-half-hour drive from Boston, a full day's drive from most other cities.

Back around the turn of the century you could board a Pullman car in New York City and ride straight through to Greenville, there to board a steamer for the Mt. Kineo, a palatial summer hotel on a cliffy island in the lake. Greenville began as a farm town, but it soon discovered its most profitable crops to be winter lumbering and summer tourists—a group which, now that train service and grand hotels have vanished, today consists largely of fishermen, canoeists, and hunters, augmented by winter skiers at Squaw Mountain, and an increasing number of cross-country skiers.

But you don't have to be a sportsman to enjoy Moosehead Lake. Immense, and backed by mountains (Big and Little Squaw in the foreground, the Katahdin range in the distance), it possesses unusual beauty and offers a family a wide choice of rustic, old-fashioned "camps" at reasonable prices. Greenville's string of old lakefront buildings resembles a stage set for a Western. The town remains a lumbermen's depot and jump-off point for excursions into the wooded wilderness to the north. Sanders Store, with its extensive stock of topographical maps, canoes, camping and fishing gear, as well as basic hardware, has been the center of town since 1857.

Registered guides specializing in hunting, fishing, or canoeing expeditions can easily be found within a few miles, and there are three charter air services in town, all geared to ferrying you to remote camps and campsites.

GUIDANCE Moosehead Region Chamber of Commerce, Box 581, Greenville (695-2702). Late May through the first week in September, daily: 9-5. A walk-in information center on Main Street. The staff will phone around to find lodging for you. In winter, write.

GETTING THERE   By air: **Delta** and **Bar Harbor Airlines** to Bangor. Local air services will meet you.

By car: Maine Turnpike to Newport, Rte. 7 to Dexter, Rte. 23 to Guilford, Rte. 15 to Greenville.

GETTING AROUND   **Folsom's Air Service** (695-2821). Dick Folsom, the dean of backwoods aviators, has been in business since 1946 and is now the largest seaplane operator in the Northeast. He also operates two fishing camps. For a number of other camps, Folsom's provides phone (two-way radio) as well as taxi service.

Jack's Flying Service (695-3020) caters to Allagash canoe trips; as does **Moosehead Flying Service, Inc.**, (695-2950); operated by "Maine's only Lady Bush Pilot," and specializing in canoe, fishing, and backpacking packages.

SIGHTS TO SEE   **Moosehead Marine Museum** (695-2716). Open in summer daily 10-4; otherwise write: PO Box 1151. *The Katahdin*, last of the lake steamers, is moored at the old Scott Ship Yard in Greenville Jct., and is still undergoing restoration. Eventually she will be a floating museum; meanwhile, there is a fine storefront museum downtown displaying photos of steamboat days on Moosehead.

Eveleth-Crafts Sheridan Historical Home. Open June through mid-October, weekdays 10-4, free, Pritham Ave. An 1880s home, housing Moosehead Historical Society exhibits, including local lumbering tools and memorabilia. There are also special exhibits and seasonal Thursday evening lectures, concerts, films.

Squaw Mountain (695-2272). One of Maine's major ski mountains, with sixteen trails served by one chairlift and three T-bars, thirty percent snowmaking coverage. The complex at the base of the lifts includes Squaw Mountain Inn (see Lodging) as well as a restaurant, bar, cafeteria, ski school, shop, and nursery. During summer months the chairlift operates, hoisting you up to the top of the mountain for a spectacular view.

Lumber Camp Tours (695-2241). Scott Paper Company offers summer season "Woodlands Tours" Wednesdays and Thursdays, 8-3:30. Instead of bearded men heaving axes you will see clean-shaven men in big machines: harvesters, skidders, loaders, and slashers, which scientifically reduce trees to "four foot sticks."

Katahdin Iron Works. Open May 30-Labor Day, daily 10-6. From Rte. 11, five miles North of Brownville Junction, take a gravel road six miles. This is the restored stone blast furnace and charcoal kiln marking the site of an iron works that annually produced some 2,000 tons of raw iron for nearly fifty years. Since you have come this far, you should proceed on down the road and across the gatehouse bridge to the Gulf Hagas Trail; your reward is a view of the 250-foot-deep canyon cut by the west branch of the Pleasant River.

Chesuncook. One of the few surviving examples of a 19th-century North Woods lumbermen's village, and now on the National Register of

Historic Places. In summer access is by charter aircraft from Greenville, or by boat from Chesuncook Dam. In winter you can come by snowmobile. Thoreau was here and wrote about it in its heyday, but noted, "Here immigration is a tide which may ebb when it has swept away the pines." Today a church, a graveyard (relocated from the shore to a hollow in the woods when Great Northern raised the level of the lake a few years ago), an inn (see Lodging), and a huddle of houses is all that remains of the village.

Lily Bay State Park. Open from ice-out to mid-October, eight miles north of Greenville, offering a grassy picnicking area, sandy beach, boat launch facilities, and eighty-nine campsites.

LODGING   "Camps" here refer to anything from a primitive cabin to an exquisite log building. The Chamber of Commerce has extensive listings.

The Birches in Rockwood (534-7305). Year-round. This is my idea of what a North Woods lodge should be: a central clapboard house, complete with stone hearth and windows on the lake, also a very wooden dining room and a game room. Seventeen hand-hewn cabins, each with a fireplace or Franklin stove, are hidden from each other along the lake; you can have them either as housekeeping units ($240 to $260 per week) or with three daily meals and maid service ($38 per person per day, or $255 per person per week, half price under age ten). If you opt for the housekeeping you can still drop into the dining room for a meal. During warm weather months there are boat rentals from the marina. From December through April this is a ski touring center offering guided tours, boasting 150 to 180 inches of snow in an average winter.

Wilsons (695-2549). Greenville Junction. Open year-round since 1865. Unfortunately, the centerpiece hotel, floated up the lake in 1860, is closed; the fourteen cottages rent from $180 to $300 (sleeping six) per week; all cottages are equipped with wood stoves, heated with gas.

Squaw Mountain Inn (695-2272). Open late June through ski season. The modern complex at the base of the ski area's lifts includes fifty-five hotel-style rooms which rent for $25 double in summer, $20 per person or $36 double in winter. Facilities include an indoor pool and sauna, and there are a variety of packages for all seasons: a five-night lifts and lodging including two daily meals is $215 per person, double occupancy. Squaw Mountain offers extensive ski touring as well as downhill skiing.

Little Lyford Pond Lodge (695-2821: contact through Folsom's Air Service) or write for a brochure: Joel and Lucy Frantzman, Box 688, Brownville, Maine 04414. Year-round. Since the 1870s these log cabins (heated with wood stoves) have been offering hideaways in the woods less than three miles from Gulf Hagas. In summer there is fishing, hiking, and canoeing; in winter some forty miles of ski touring. Access is Folsom's from Greenville—or you can ski in from Rte. 11 north of Brownville, roughly six and-one-half miles.

Guests are limited to ten at a time; dining is in the main lodge which also has an eclectic library, and there is a sauna.

Chesuncook Lake House (695-2821: Folsom's Air Service). Open year-round. An unpretentious 1864 farmhouse built on the site of the older log cabin which served as center for the lumbering camp (see Sights). There are twelve gas-lit guest rooms, also three cabins. Maggie McBurnie serves three meals a day and her husband meets guests at Cushing's Landing at the south end of the lake and ferries them in. Otherwise you can fly in from Greenville with Folsom's. The rate is $36 per person per day with three meals; or $11 per day, $135 per week (double occupancy) in a housekeeping cottage. Registered guides and rental boats also available.

RESTAURANTS   **The Birches** at Rockwood (see Lodging).

The Cabbage Patch (695-2252). Year-round, near the railroad depot, open for dinner only, 4-9:30, a pub atmosphere, specializing in steak but offering a full menu, moderate prices.

Boom Chain. Year-round, open for breakfast and lunch and dinner, downtown across from the A & P. Pleasant.

Stambaugh's Coffee House (695-3385). Year-round, 9 AM to 3 PM; outstanding baking, soups and salads, counter and table service on Main Street just up from Sanders Store, reasonably priced.

Flatlander's Pub (695-3592). Good for sandwiches and pizzas, open for lunch and dinner. Downtown across from the Exxon Station.

Lakeview Manor (695-3810). Year-round, dinner only, closed Mondays and Tuesdays; by reservation only, the area's elegant dining spot.

Greenville to Baxter Park

Since this is the classic drive which everyone makes, we would like to pass on a few tips as of '82.

(1) **Lily Bay State Park** (see Sights) is a good spot to picnic and swim.

(2) **Kokadjo's store** (695-2593), open daily, 7 AM-10 PM, serves hot drinks and light meals, also rents out a few camps.

(3) **Cushing's Landing** is worth a stop: a haunting, beautiful place. The woodsman's memorial here was created from a post in the doorway of a Bangor tavern; it's decorated with tools of the trade and an iron beanpot.

(4) **Ripogenus Dam.** This is departure point for a number of white water rafting expeditions. You can get a view of the river plunging down through gorges by driving across the dam. Pray's Store (723-8880) sells most things, and there are rental cottages.

(5) **Abol Bridge.** There is a store here, but don't stop for microwave hot dogs the way we did. There is better fare and picnic tables at Togue Pond, just outside the Baxter State Park gatehouses.

Baxter State Park (723-5140). For reservations and information write: Reservation Clerk, Baxter State Park, 64 Balsam Drive, Millinocket 04462. Campgrounds are open May 15-October 15 and through a special use permit. During summer months the gates are open, 6 AM-10 PM.

Boston Globe/Joseph Dennehy

Exploring the Maine wilderness near Baxter State Park

This is a 200,000 acre park surrounding mile-high Katahdin, highest (5267 feet) peak in the state. There are forty-six mountain peaks in all, and 150 miles of well-marked hiking trails.

This largest of Maine's state parks was the 1931 gift of Percival Baxter—who had unsuccessfully urged creation of such a preserve during his two terms as governor.

It takes two-and-one-half hours to drive around the park's perimeter and, given the vastness of the area, the widely scattered campgrounds vary in popularity. Everyone wants to be at Russell or Chimney Pond near the base of Katahdin. A total of 1000 people per night can be accommodated in the nine major campgrounds; rates vary from $1 (for a group area) to $20 (for a cabin at Daicey Pond). Available spots include shelters and tent sites. Reservations should be made by mail with the correct fee enclosed beginning January 1 of the year you are coming. Canoe rentals are available at Russell Pond, South Branch Pond, and Daicey Pond.

Patten Lumberman's Museum (528-2650), on Rte 159 in Patten. Open Memorial Day to Labor Day, Tuesday through Saturday 9-4; Sunday 12-4. Weekends until Columbus Day, and by appointment. $1 per adult, 50c under age twelve. The museum, which encompasses more than 2000 displays housed in nine buildings, was founded in 1962 by bacteriologist Caleb Scribner and log driver Lore Rogers. Exhibits range from giant log haulers to "gum books," the lumberman's scrimshaw: intricately carved boxes in which to put spruce gum, a popular gift for a sweetheart. There are replicas of logging camps from varying periods, dioramas, machinery, and photos, all adding up to a fascinating picture of a vanished way of life.

Mattawamkeag Wilderness Park (947-4585), off Rte. 2 at Mattawamkeag, a half hour's drive off I-95: fifty campsites ($5), ten Adirondack shelters ($6), a small store, recreation building, picnic facilities ($1), fifteen miles of hiking trails, sixty miles of canoeing on the Mattawamkeag River with patches of white water. An eight-mile gravel road leads into the park. For reservations and details write to: Reservation Clerk, Mattawamkeag Wilderness Park, PO Box 104, Mattawamkeag, Maine 04459.

INDEX

ZIP CODES

Bar Harbor	04609	Greenville	04441	Rangeley	04970
Bath	04530	Kennebunk	04043	Rockland	04841
Belfast	04915	Kennebunkport	04046	Rockport	04856
Bethel	04217	Kingfield	04947	Searsport	04974
Blue Hill	04614	Lincolnville	04849	Sebago Lake	04075
Boothbay	04537	Matinicus	04851	Southwest Harbor	04679
Boothbay Harbor	04538	Monhegan Island	04852	Stonington	04681
Bridgton	04009	Naples	04055	Tenants Harbor	04860
Bristol	04554	New Harbor	04554	Thomaston	04861
Brunswick	04011	Newcastle	04553	Vinalhaven Island	04863
Bucksport	04416	Newfield	04056	Waldoboro	04572
Camden	04843	Ogunquit	03907	Weld	04285
Cape Neddick	03902	Owl's Head	04270	Wells	04090
Carrabasset Valley	04947	Pemaquid	04554	Wiscasset	04578
Castine	04421	Phillips	04966	York Beach	03910
Damariscotta	04543	Port Clyde	04855	York Harbor	03911
Deer Isle	04627	Portland	04101-2-3-11-12	York Village	03909

Books on Maine and New England